ACCOUNTS FOR SOLICITORS

AUSTRALIA
The Law Book Company
Brisbane ● Sydney ● Melbourne ● Perth

CANADA
Carswell
Ottawa ● Toronto ● Calgary ● Montreal ● Vancouver

AGENTS
Steimatzky's Agency Ltd, Tel Aviv;
N.M. Tripathi (Private) Ltd, Bombay;
Eastern Law House (Private) Ltd, Calcutta;
M.P.P. House, Bangalore;
Universal Book Traders, Delhi;
Aditya Books, Delhi;
MacMillan Shuppan KK, Tokyo;
Pakistan Law House, Karachi, Lahore

ACCOUNTS FOR SOLICITORS

Richard Halberstadt, LL.B.(LOND.)

Solicitor

Fifth Edition

LONDON ● SWEET & MAXWELL ● 1995

First Edition 1979
Second Edition 1982
Third Edition 1985
Fourth Edition 1989

Published in 1995 by
Sweet & Maxwell Ltd of
South Quay Plaza, 183 Marsh Wall,
London E14 9FT.
Phototypeset by LBJ Enterprises Ltd.
of Aldermaston and Chilcompton.
Printed by The Alden Press Ltd., Oxford.

A CIP catalogue record for this book
is available from the British Library

ISBN 0 421 52970 9

No natural forests were destroyed to make this product,
only farmed timber was used and re-planted.

PREFACE

This book is only concerned with the double-entries to record the dealings which take place in a solicitor's office.

All the illustrations, examples and exercises are fictional. The characters chosen and the sums of money involved have merely been selected so as to provide meat for the accounts. I am well aware, for instance, that in many of the conveyancing examples, although the example involves payment of stamp duty, no stamp duty would normally have been payable or, if in an exceptional case it had been payable, it would not have been of the amount stated in the example. This, I hope, will not detract from the object of the exercise (and of this book) which is not to teach the details of conveyancing but rather how to make the basic double-entries in a solicitor's books of accounts.

I should like to thank all my colleagues who have helped me with the book and particularly Ray Dean, Dai Jones, Lesley King and Malcolm Maddock, for the comments and suggestions they made. I would also like to express my appreciation to the publishers for their assistance and patience. Nevertheless, my greatest thanks must go to my former students. Theirs was the inspiration for the book and they, albeit unknowingly, provided much of the material. However, they will be pleased to note that this time the mistakes, of which there are bound to be some if not many, are all mine.

I also wish to acknowledge the permission given by The Law Society to use past examination questions. I have, however, had to adapt these questions slightly in order to take account of changes in conveyancing procedure, VAT rates and the examination syllabus. I must point out that the answers to these questions are my own and so, again, any mistakes are mine.

London
May 1995

RICHARD HALBERSTADT

CONTENTS

Preface   v

Introduction: How to Pass an Accounts Examination   1

Chapter 1: Bookkeeping   7
Chapter 2: Double-Entry   13
Chapter 3: Double-Entry—Further Steps   21
   A: Balancing   21
   B. Layout   22
   C: Types of Account   24
   D: Trial Balance   27

Chapter 4: The Books Kept by a Solicitor   31
   A: The Books   31
   B: The Books of Double-Entry   31
   C: Other Books   34

Chapter 5: Office and Client Account   39
   A: The Two Sets of Accounts   39
   B: The Books of Double-Entry   41

Chapter 6: Modern Methods of Keeping Accounts   43

Chapter 7: Basic Postings   51
   A: Receipts   51
   B: Payments   52
   C: Balances—Client Account   55
   D: Balances—Office Account   56
   E: Delivery of a Bill   59

Chapter 8: Transfers   61
   A: Bank Transfers—Client Account to Office Account   61
   B: Bank Transfers—Office Account to Client Account   63
   C: Ledger Transfers   65

Chapter 9: Value Added Tax   69
   A: The General Law   69
   B: Basic Entries   75
   C: Payments on Behalf of a Client—Methods of Treatment   78
   D: Payments—Double-Entries—Inputs   81
   E: Output Entries   84
   F: The Timing of the Tax Point—Output   86

Chapter 10: Miscellaneous Postings   89
   A: Abatements   89
   B: Bad Debts   90
   C: Splitting   92
   D: Cheques Payable to a Third Person   93
   E: Indorsed Cheques, etc.   93
   F: Returned Cheques   94

Chapter 11: Revision Exercises   97

Contents

Chapter 12: Costs   99

Chapter 13: Interest on Clients' Money   103
  A: Accounting to the Client for Interest   103
  B: General Deposit   111

Chapter 14: Miscellaneous Items   115
  A: Miscellaneous Sundry Disbursements   115
  B: One Party Paying Another's Legal Costs   117
  C: Agency   120
  D: Insurance Commissions   124

Chapter 15: Conveyancing   129
  A: Deposits   129
  B: Mortgages   130
  C: Client Buying and Selling Houses Simultaneously   134
  D: Statements   135
  E: Exercises on Conveyancing   140

Chapter 16: Trusts   147

Chapter 17: Revision Exercises   149

Appendix: Answers   167

Index   259

HOW TO PASS AN ACCOUNTS EXAMINATION

Much of what is going to follow may seem obvious. The danger is that it will seem so obvious, and not relevant to you, that you will ignore it. Bear in mind that each year a certain number of candidates in accounts examinations fail, and they probably fail because they have not followed these rules.

A. PREPARING FOR THE EXAMINATION

1. This will probably be the first examination that you have taken in bookkeeping/accounts. It is a practical subject and in the examination you will be asked to draw up accounts. As such, it will be very different from an academic university examination. You will not be asked, as at university, to "explain" or "discuss"; instead, the examination will be concerned with your practical ability, *i.e.* can you do the accounts? In preparing for the examination, therefore, it will not be enough merely to understand the subject. Much of the subject may, in fact, seem very straightforward and obvious merely from reading a textbook and/or watching a tutor explaining (and maybe even doing) the accounts. The crucial point is that you will have to do them yourself. This requires practice.

2. The only way to get sufficient practice is to do exercises. These take time. As a basic rule, it is better to spread out exercises as much as possible rather than cramming them together. "Little and Often" is probably the best advice. Thus, rather than spending three hours one day doing six accounts exercises (each individual exercise lasting about 30 minutes), it is probably better to do one exercise a day, *i.e.* 30 minutes each day, over six days.

3. **How to use this book**
    This is not a book for reading and contemplation; instead, it is more of an exercise book. A good method of study would be:

    (a) read a section through quickly;
    (b) turn to the relevant exercises and do the first one, copying from the example in the text;
    (c) check the answer and, if correct, continue to the second exercise, etc.;
    (d) after a few exercises, try the next one without copying from the text;
    (e) when you have done all the exercises in that section, and not before, proceed to the next section.

4. **Do all the exercises in numerical order**
    Do not leave any out. The exercises are graded throughout the book. It is very tempting to try to do the hardest one first but this must be resisted. Master each exercise or group of exercises before proceeding to the next one.

5. **Speed**

One certain fact about the examination is that you will have a lot to do in the time. This means that you will have to be able to do the accounts quickly. One of the main purposes of the exercises is to build up speed. It is one thing to be able to say: "Oh I can do that—in about 25 minutes"; it is quite another thing to be able to do it in five minutes. A lot of the exercises in this book may seem repetitious. This is deliberate, the idea being that with repetition you will get faster. When doing the exercises, to begin with, concentrate on getting the answers right. However, as you progress, become aware of how long each exercise is taking you. As you get nearer to the examination, it is essential to time yourself. As a guide, some of the later questions have time limits suggested.

6. **Tidiness**

This is often an emotional subject. However, the fact is that it is the students who are tidy that pass accounts examinations. You should work neatly from the very start. If you are naturally a tidy person, you will do this anyway. If, however, you are not naturally tidy, don't put it off. It is a great temptation to do all the preparation work "in rough" and say: "When it comes to the examination, I will do it neatly." You will find this impossible. If you are not by nature tidy, you will be unable suddenly to "switch on" neat work. On the contrary, the strain of an examination can cause even a tidy person to work untidily. The only way that anyone, whether naturally tidy or not, can ensure that they can produce neat work in an examination is to develop the habit beforehand.

Do not crush your written answer to a question into a space the size of a postage stamp; spread it out. From time to time, you are bound to make a mistake and wish to alter your answer. If your accounts are all crushed together, it will be impossible to make corrections. Furthermore, well spaced out work is more pleasing to the eye and will be easier for your examiner to follow. When setting out a column of figures for addition, make sure that the figures are set out with the vertical columns in straight lines. As well as making the work look tidy, it will also help to eliminate maths errors.

7. **Presentation**

Alongside the topic of tidiness is that of presentation. Accounts is the art of presenting financial information. This means that not only is it essential to present the right information (*i.e.* the figures must be correct) but also there is a skill in the way in which the information is presented. This means paying attention to the way the accounts are laid out: which items go on the left and which on the right, the order in which items appear, and, very importantly, "headings". It is very easy for a beginner to assume that so long as the figures are correct, the answer is right and will get full marks. This is not so. If you fail to put the proper headings to the accounts, you will lose marks. Again, it is a question of practice. If, all the way through the exercises, you put in the proper headings, by the time you get to the examination it will have become a habit. You will not want to spend time and energy in an examination worrying over what heading to put in; there will be other much more pressing matters to which you will need to devote your mind.

Therefore, when checking your answers, first check that your figures are correct, but secondly (and this is just as important) look critically at your work for tidiness and presentation; if this had been presented to you by an examination candidate, by your articled clerk, or even by an accountant or bookkeeper employed by you, would you be satisfied with the way in which it was presented?

8. **A special word for non-mathematicians**

Up to now the advice has all been fairly stern stuff and concerned with "do's" and "don'ts". What about those people who are a little apprehensive about the subject? "But I was never any good at maths" is a cry I hear often. Don't be frightened. You are doing an accounts examination, *NOT* a maths examination, and you do not need to be good at adding up to do accounts. Of course, if you do make mathematical errors your answers will not be right, but generally you will not lose very many marks if your only errors are those of addition and/or subtraction. Tidiness will help here. So often untidiness and mathematical errors go hand in hand. In any event, you are allowed to use a calculator and, if you are at all nervous about your ability to add up and/or subtract swiftly, you should use one.

So often, students who have had bad experiences with maths at a younger age approach accounts with fear and trepidation. If you were not good at maths at school, don't assume you won't be able to do accounts. They are not the same, and you might be in for a pleasant surprise. I know a number of students who hated maths, who assumed they were going to hate accounts as well, but who actually finished up enjoying the subject—even preferring it to such things as the Perpetuity Rule, Capital Gains Tax, and the Rule in *Howe v. Lord Dartmouth*!

B. THE EXAMINATION ITSELF

1. Get to the examination in good time. This may seem very obvious and not worth saying, but in every single examination there are some late arrivals. Then, too, there are those who have only just made it and arrive panting, flushed and totally in the wrong frame of mind to cope instantly with an examination. Therefore, plan in advance how to get there, and allow plenty of time for emergencies.

2. **Plan your time in the examination**

This is probably the most common mistake made by candidates in examinations. As soon as you are given the examination paper, allocate your time between the questions. Allow yourself some time at the beginning to familiarise yourself with the paper and a little time at the end, say five or 10 minutes, to read through your answers. Then, divide the rest of the time rateably between the questions according to the way in which the marks are allocated. When answering a question, *on no account go over the allocated time*. If you do run out of time, stop, and start the next question. You can always come back to the first question at the end.

Don't waste time if, for example, an account will not balance. It is not uncommon for an examination candidate to be faced with the problem that, having done a long, complex, question, the account does not balance. What should you do now—give up and do the next question, or go back and try to find the reason? The answer is always to go on to the next question. The next one may carry 50 per cent of the marks. You may find your error quickly, it may take you all the rest of the exam, or you may still be looking when the exam ends! It could be that the only thing wrong is a maths error which, at the most, would have cost you only one mark. However, if you give up the other question, you give up the 50 marks that go with it—all to save one mark! It is not worth it. Finish the whole paper first. Then come back, if there is time, to see what you have done wrong.

3. **Read the examination paper carefully**

The second most common fault in examinations involves misreading some part of the examination paper.

Read the general instructions about the paper (usually at the top) and, if there is an answer book, read any instructions on it. Do this BEFORE reading any of the individual questions. It is a good idea, before the examination, to have obtained past copies of exam papers and to familiarise yourself with the instructions given before. In such a case, all you need to do is check that they are the same and make a note of any changes, and then you can begin to look at the questions.

The next stage is probably to have a quick read-through of all the questions and then to plan your time (see paragraph 2). You now face the problem of "which question to do first?" Some people just take the questions in their chronological order. Some like to do the most difficult questions first, on the basis that they can tackle it when they are fresh. What I have noticed is that, very often, students who have failed an examination say to me that the first question they did was a bad one. This demoralised them and they then went from bad to worse. My own preference is to do the easy question first. There is of course the danger of spending too much time on it, because "I know something about this". If that danger is resisted, then it can be a good policy because it may build up confidence.

Once you have decided on a question, read it through very carefully indeed; read every word. Do not start to draw up any accounts until you have finished reading it through. When you have read it through, check and see precisely which accounts the examiner has asked you to show. These must be presented correctly. All too often, students draw up accounts that they have not been asked to show and omit those that they have been asked to show. If the question involves recording dealings with clients and says "Prepare the entries in the Client Ledger", it is not necessary to show a Cash Account, but all necessary Client Ledger Accounts should be shown (e.g. the stakeholder account—being a Client Ledger Account—will have to be shown). If VAT is involved, check what rate of VAT is to be used. For convenience, in this book the standard rate of VAT has been taken as 10 per cent throughout. Most exams specify the rate you are to use; if your paper does not specify, use the rate in force at the time of sitting the exam.

4. **Show all workings**

Throughout the examination you will have to make calculations, *e.g.* you have to charge a client with VAT. In your answer, you should not only show what you think the relevant figure is, but also how you reached it, *i.e.* your calculation. If you do not show any workings and your final figure is wrong, the examiner will probably not know what you have done wrong and will have to make a guess. If your error is a trivial one, a maths error or a transposition of figures (you calculated VAT at 10 per cent of £340 instead of £430), you will lose very few marks indeed. If, however, you made a serious error involving a lack of understanding of basic principles, you will lose a large number of marks. The danger of showing no workings is if you make a minor slip, with no workings shown, the examiner assumes you have made a major error and you lose many more marks than you would have done had you shown your workings.

5. In addition to showing workings or calculations, many candidates are tempted to write essays explaining their answers. In general, this should be unnecessary; the accounts that you produce should speak for themselves. Very occasionally, a short

note can be helpful. If the question involves a transaction and you decide that it does not need recording, a short note to this effect can help an examiner; he will now know that you knew that no entry was needed, rather than that you did not know what to do and left it out. The two rules to follow are:

(a) try to avoid writing notes;
(b) if you have to write one, keep it short.

6. There are a number of errors that should be avoided at all costs. These include:

(a) debiting a CLIENT ACCOUNT and crediting an OFFICE ACCOUNT or vice versa (see page 39);
(b) receiving clients' money and putting it into OFFICE ACCOUNT (see pages 56–58);
(c) over-drawing CLIENT ACCOUNT (see page 55).

These are all very serious errors, involving the breach of a major accounting principle.

7. **Don't throw away the easy marks**

So often students seem to be devoting all their energy towards some relatively minor point at the expense of basic principles. In order to pass the examination, you must get "the basics" right. Bear in mind that in all examinations some marks are easier to get than others. Probably the easiest marks to get in an accounts examination are those for drawing up the right accounts, in the proper form, and with the right headings; getting the right figures is more difficult. Remember too that it is relatively easy to get the first 40–45 per cent of the marks. The next 10–15 per cent are a little more difficult to get, the next 15–20 per cent very difficult to get, and the last 20–25 per cent impossible for all but the most gifted of persons to get. You do not have to get everything correct in order to pass. You won't fail just because your account doesn't balance. If a safe pass is what you are after, do not waste time on all the little intricacies; concentrate on the basic principles.

8. **Don't panic**

This is where the value of good preparation should show. If you have done sufficient exercises in preparation (including those with a time limit), they should give you confidence. You will have spent many hours doing your practice work. If you have done this properly, you should pass. You will have met all the basic principles and practised them many times. Just occasionally, an examiner thinks up a transaction which is slightly different from all the others usually encountered in that exam. On no account give up, saying: "We haven't been taught this—I can't do it." You ought, provided you have mastered them well enough, to be able to work the relevant entries out from basic principles. In any event, remember that the examiner knows that it is different and therefore likely to cause difficulties. This new, or different, item will only be one of several transactions and, on its own, probably will not carry that many marks. It will certainly be in that category where the marks are "very difficult to get." Do not neglect the other items carrying more marks and marks which are easier to get.

The best advice, then, is to prevent panic from starting. You need to plan in advance so that you will not panic on the day. Perhaps what this means is that you should make up your mind that, whatever happens, you will not panic. However, what if the worst happens and you become aware that you are getting into a panic? The thing to do is to stop, shut your eyes for a minute or two, and rest. Then begin again. Now I realise that this is difficult to do; it is more than likely that what is inducing the panic is the lack of time left in which to complete the paper. The idea of stopping and "wasting some more time" seems abhorrent, but you must. It is far better to do 15 minutes of good work than 20 minutes of muddled work. When you are under pressure and not concentrating well, you are liable to make any number of silly, but disastrous, errors that you would never have made if calm. The most important thing, in this context, is that through your practice work on exercises you should have built up a routine so that, when it comes to this examination, you should plod through your routine methodically and calmly.

9. **Approach the exam questions in a positive way**

Far too many students approach exams in a negative way; they look through the exam paper seeking points which they do not know how to answer. It is true that if the examinations are demanding, it will be a very rare event to be able to go into an examination and answer every single question correctly. However, if you have prepared conscientiously, and the examination is a fair one, the reverse will be true, namely that there should be plenty of material which you can answer. It is better to go into an examination with a positive approach (looking for what you can do) rather than the negative approach. Thus, when reading a question, look out for what you *can* do, and concentrate on the basic principles of the subject.

10. Finally, remember that good exam technique can never be a substitute for inadequate preparation. The fact of the matter is that, although a few students fail because of poor technique, the majority who fail do so because of inadequate preparation.

Chapter 1

BOOKKEEPING

1. The object of bookkeeping is to record information. A bookkeeper's task consists of keeping records (accounts) of all transactions which affect a business, so that the information contained in the accounts can be communicated to persons interested in the business. These persons include:

(a) the owners and/or managers of the business;
(b) a prospective purchaser of the business;
(c) creditors;
(d) employees;
(e) the Inland Revenue and the Commissioners of Customs and Excise.

2. So far as concerns the owners and/or the managers of the business, the two chief questions to which they will want answers are:

(a) is the business making a profit?, and
(b) is the business solvent?

The first question is answered by looking at a record called a *Profit and Loss Account* and the second by looking at a document called a *Balance Sheet*.

3. Whether the business has made a profit (and if so how much) is discovered by deducting the expenses of the business from the income. Basically, therefore, the Profit and Loss Account consists of a list of all the income of the business and a list of all the expenses. The latter are then deducted from the former.

Profit and Loss Account

	£
Income	3,000
Expenses	2,000
Profit	1,000

4. Basically a business is insolvent if it is unable to pay its debts (or liabilities). The Balance Sheet lists all the liabilities of the business and all the assets.

Balance Sheet

	£
Assets	XXX
	XXX
	5,000
Liabilities	XXX
	XXX
	5,000

5. **Capital**

(a) One of the conventions of bookkeeping is that, although the proprietors may own the business, for the purposes of bookkeeping they are regarded as an entity separate from the business. They are merely regarded as persons with whom the business deals. The investment made by the proprietors is called "capital" and is a liability of the business. It represents the amount which the business owes to the proprietors and which would be paid to them if the business were wound up.

(b) The first transaction which takes place with most businesses is that the proprietor introduces cash or other assets into the business.

(c) *Example*

The proprietor introduces £1,000 cash in order to start the business. In such a case, from the point of view of bookkeeping, the proprietor is regarded as a creditor of the business (*i.e.* someone to whom the business owes money). Thus at this stage the business owns £1,000 in cash but owes £1,000 to the proprietor. The Balance Sheet would at this stage look as follows:

Balance Sheet

	£
Assets	
Cash	1,000
Liabilities	
Capital	1,000

6. **Assets**

There are two major kinds of assets: fixed and current assets. Fixed assets are those bought for permanent use in the business and are not bought for the purpose of being resold. They are held for the purpose of earning profits and will vary from business to business. Thus the business of a motor trader would have garage premises as fixed assets, whereas the motor cars which are bought for the purpose of re-sale would not be fixed assets. On the other hand, a firm of solicitors who bought a motor car, say for use by one of the partners, would regard the motor car as a fixed asset. The chief current assets of a business are stock, debtors and cash.

These are often known as circulating assets because a trader will use cash to buy stock which he will sell to customers. These customers will then become debtors who in due course will pay the business in cash. These assets are thus constantly circulating. Those assets which are cash or which can be swiftly converted into cash are known as liquid assets; the most common items are cash and debtors. The trading stock of a business will vary from business to business depending on the trade carried on. What would be a fixed asset for one business will be trading stock for another. Thus a desk would be a fixed asset for a solicitor whereas it would be a current asset for a business dealing in office furniture.

Example (continued)
The business buys a car for £700 cash as a fixed asset. The business still owes the proprietor £1,000 but now owns a car worth £700 and cash of £300.

Balance Sheet

	£
Assets	
Motor car	700
Cash	300
	1,000
Liabilities	
Capital	1,000

7. Liabilities

Liabilities owing to persons other than the proprietor fall into two categories—long-term liabilities and current liabilities. The basic difference between the two is the length of time within which the liability has to be satisfied. The relevant test is whether the liability has to be satisfied in the next accounting period. Thus if the accounts cover a period of 12 months and the liability is payable within the next 12 months, it is a current liability, whereas if it is payable in more than a year's time, it is a long-term liability. A bank overdraft which is repayable on demand is a current liability, whereas a special bank loan repayable in five years would be a long-term liability.

Example (continued)
A friend of the proprietor lends the business £500 cash, to be repaid in two years. The business now owes £1,500 (£1,000 to the proprietor, £500 to the friend) and owns a car worth £700 and cash of £800.

Balance Sheet

	£
Assets	
Motor car	700
Cash	800
	1,500
Liabilities	
Capital	1,000
Loan	500
	1,500

The business then buys stock of £300 from A Supplier, payment to be made in one month's time. This will mean an additional asset will be held (stock worth £300) but there will be an additional liability to A Supplier for £300.

Balance Sheet

	£
Assets	
Motor car	700
Stock	300
Cash	800
	1,800
Liabilities	
Capital	1,000
Loan	500
A Supplier	300
	1,800

8. The basic formula for the Balance sheet is:

$$\text{LIABILITIES} = \text{ASSETS}$$

The two parts of the balance sheet should always be equal, however many transactions have taken place. The assets may change, but this will not alter the total of the assets. For example, the business may own £1,000 in cash and later purchase some furniture for £400—the total of the assets still equals £1,000 but, instead of a single item of cash, the business owns furniture worth £400 and cash of £600. On the other hand, the total of the assets may increase (or decrease) but the liabilities of the business will always increase (or decrease) proportionately. Thus the business may borrow £5,000 from the bank. The result will be that the assets will increase by this figure but the liabilities will also increase by the same amount owed to the bank.

9. Accounting principles or conventions

  (a) When determining what entries to make in a set of accounts, accountants observe various principles or "concepts".

  (b) *The going concern concept*
It is assumed that the business is continuing its activities in the foreseeable future. This may be relevant when valuing the assets of a business. If the assets are valued on the basis that the business is a going concern, a very different figure may be reached from the one which would have been reached if the assets had been valued on the basis that the business was being discontinued.

  (c) *The consistency concept*
This means that similar accounting policies should be applied from one year to the next. Thus if one method of valuation is followed in the first year of business, a similar method should be followed in the second and subsequent years. This could be relevant when it comes to valuing stock in hand or work in progress at the end of a financial period. If a different method of valuation

is used from year to year, then the accounts produced over a series of years will be misleading.

(d) *The prudence concept*

This means that only profits which have been realised should be included in the accounts. On the other hand, liabilities and losses likely to arise but not yet realised should be taken into account. Thus, if there is doubt, a loss should be included and a profit should be omitted. This is particularly relevant when considering the depreciation or appreciation of fixed assets after they have been purchased.

(e) *The accruals concept*

All income and expenses in the accounting period to which the accounts relate should be taken into account, without regard to the date of receipt or payment.

Chapter 2

DOUBLE-ENTRY

1. **Account**

An account is a record, *i.e.* a written report of events or transactions that have occurred. A business will need to keep a whole set of accounts to record all the dealings in which the business engages. There will need to be a separate account (or record)

(a) for each person with whom the business deals, to record the dealings with that person;
(b) for each type of asset (or thing) owned by the business, to record dealings with that asset;
(c) for each type of transaction which determines the size of the profit (or loss) eventually made by the business. These transactions can be sub-divided into transactions which produce *income* (or a profit) for the business, and those which produce an *expense* (or a loss).

2. **Transaction**

A business transaction involves a transfer of values. The value may be money, goods or services. Money may be paid to a creditor or received from a debtor, a shop may sell goods to a customer or buy goods from a wholesaler, a hairdresser may cut a customer's hair, or a solicitor may give legal advice to a client. The transactions are always recorded in terms of money. Thus, if a shop sells a pair of shoes to a customer for £10, the accounts will record that the sale was worth £10 (and not that it was a sale of two shoes).

3. **The two aspects of a transaction**

Every business transaction has two aspects or two sides to it. If the proprietor introduces £1,000 cash into the business, the business will hold assets of £1,000 but will also owe the proprietor the same amount. In this case, the assets have increased by £1,000 but the liabilities have also increased by the same amount. If the business then buys fixed assets for £600, cash will decrease but the fixed assets will increase.

4. **Ledger**

Originally the accounts of a business were kept in a book which was called a *ledger* and each page in the ledger was called a *folio*. Nowadays the accounts are too many to be kept in a single book but the name of the ledger still remains.

5. An account, or folio, is divided into two halves: a left-hand side and a right-hand side. The left-hand side of the page is called the *debit* side and the right-hand side is called the *credit* side.

6. Whenever a transaction takes place, two entries are made (hence the "double-entry" system). One entry is made on the left-hand side of an account (*i.e.* an account is debited) and another entry is made on the right-hand side of an account (*i.e.* an account is credited). Usually the two entries are made on different accounts, although sometimes they are made on the same account.

7. Thus the accounting equation is realised, namely that THE SUM TOTAL OF ALL THE LEFT-HAND ENTRIES (*i.e.* DEBITS) ALWAYS EQUALS THE SUM TOTAL OF ALL THE RIGHT-HAND ENTRIES (*i.e.* CREDITS). At first, it may be useful to avoid thinking in terms of debits and credits and merely to think in terms of left-hand entries and right-hand entries. It is important to realise that these words debit and credit are being used in a technical sense to mean the left-hand side of an account and the right-hand side of an account. They must not be confused with the normal use of such words in everyday language. A common error is to think of a debit as "a bad thing" and a credit as "a good thing." Thus, if money is received, one might think of only crediting an account. What has to be realised is that when "a good thing" happens (*e.g.* money is received) two entries have to be made, *i.e.* a debit AND a credit.

8. AT ALL TIMES THE BASIC RULE OF BOOKKEEPING MUST BE BORNE IN MIND, NAMELY **FOR EVERY DEBIT ENTRY THERE MUST BE A CORRES-PONDING CREDIT ENTRY** (and vice versa).

9. **Cash**

The account to record dealings with cash is called the *cash account*. This account is common to all businesses. It will record all the receipts of cash and all the payments of cash. As stated above, the account is divided into two halves. All the receipts are traditionally recorded on the left-hand side of the page (*i.e.* debits) and all the payments are recorded on the right-hand side of the page (*i.e.* credits).

Thus, *so far as the Cash Account is concerned*:

DEBIT RECEIPTS
CREDIT PAYMENTS

Example 1
Cash of £800 is received from Alice.

(a) *The first entry*

DEBIT (*i.e.* left-hand side) the Cash Account

Cash
| **800** | |

(b) *The second entry*
This can be worked out from the first entry. Since that was a DEBIT (*i.e.* a left-hand entry), it follows that the other entry must be a CREDIT (or right-hand entry). The money was received from Alice and therefore an account must be kept to record all the dealings with her. The entry is therefore made on that account as follows:

CREDIT the account of Alice

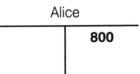

Example 2
Cash of £70 is paid to Bill.

(a) *The first entry*

CREDIT (*i.e.* right-hand side) the Cash Account

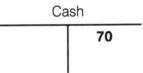

(b) *The second entry*
This can be worked out from the first entry. Since that was a CREDIT (right-hand entry), it follows that the other entry must be a DEBIT (left-hand entry). The money was paid to Bill and therefore an account must be kept to record all the dealings with him. The entry is therefore made on that account as follows:

DEBIT the account of Bill

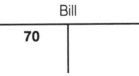

10. **Purchases and sales of trading stock**
   (a) All businesses which deal in goods will need to record their dealings with their trading stock. What their trading stock is will vary from business to business (*e.g.* a motor dealer would have motor cars as his trading stock, whereas a furniture shop would have furniture). Solicitors do not deal in goods but these transactions are useful as an illustration of basic bookkeeping principles.

(b) By convention, instead of having a single account to record dealings with trading stock, traders have two separate accounts, one to record all the purchases (the *Purchases Account*) and another to record all the sales (the *Sales Account*).

(c) The purchases are all entered on the left-hand side of the Purchases Account (*i.e.* DEBIT) and the sales are all entered on the right-hand side of the Sales Account (*i.e.* CREDIT).

(d) *Example 1*

The business buys goods worth £30 from Charles.

(i) *The first entry*

DEBIT (*i.e.* left-hand side) the Purchases Account

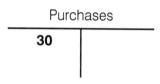

(ii) *The second entry*

As the first entry was on the DEBIT (or left-hand side) of the Purchases Account, it follows that there must be another entry on the CREDIT (or right-hand side) of another account. The goods were bought from Charles and it follows that the relevant account will be the account of Charles. The entry therefore is:

CREDIT the account of Charles

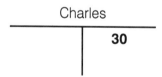

(e) *Example 2*

The business sells goods worth £80 to Diana.

(i) *The first entry*

CREDIT (*i.e.* right-hand side) the Sales Account

Sales
| | 80 |

(ii) *The second entry*

As the first entry was on the CREDIT (or right-hand side) of the Sales Account, it follows that there must be another entry on the DEBIT (or left-hand side) of another account. The relevant account will be an account in the name of Diana. The entry is therefore:

DEBIT the account of Diana

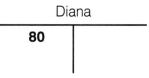

11. **Purchases, sales and cash—examples**

(a) May 1. The business buys goods worth £50 from Edward, payment to be made on June 1. This is known as a purchase on credit terms. In this sense, the word "credit" is not being used in its technical bookkeeping sense but in its everyday language sense. It means that the goods do not have to be paid for until a later date. The double-entry is:

DEBIT the Purchases Account
CREDIT the account of Edward

If one looks at the account of Edward, this shows that the business has bought goods worth £50 from him and thus the business owes £50 to Edward.

(b) June 1. The business pays Edward the £50. The double-entry is:

CREDIT the Cash Account
DEBIT the account of Edward

If one looks now at the account of Edward, it will be seen that the two sides of his account are equal. The technical phrase for this is that the account "balances." This must be correct, because the business previously owed £50 to Edward, it has now paid Edward the amount due, and so there is no money owing to him.

(c) July 1. The business sells goods worth £60 to Fred, payment to be made on August 1. This is known as a sale on credit, *i.e.* the goods do not have to be paid for until a later date. The entries are:

CREDIT the Sales Account
DEBIT the account of Fred

If one looks at the account of Fred, this shows that the business sold goods worth £60 to him and thus Fred owes £60 to the business.

(d) August 1. The business receives the £60 in cash from Fred. The entries are:

DEBIT the Cash Account
CREDIT the account of Fred

If one looks now at the account of Fred, it will be seen that the two sides balance. The business was previously owed £60 by Fred, he has now paid the amount due, and so there is nothing owed by him to the business.

12. **Summary**

(a) *Receipt of cash*

DEBIT the Cash Account
CREDIT the account of the person from whom the money was received

(b) *Payment of cash*

DEBIT the Cash Account
CREDIT the account of the person to whom the money was paid

(c) *Purchase of trading stock*

DEBIT the Purchases Account
CREDIT the account of the person from whom the goods were bought

(d) *Sales of trading stock*

CREDIT the Sales Account
DEBIT the account of the person to whom the goods were sold

13. **Exercises**
Assume that all purchases and sales are on credit.

(1) Record the following dealings with Alice:
Receive cash £1, £2, £3. Pay cash £6, £7, £8. Receive £10, £11, £12.
Pay £13, £14, £15. Receive £16, £17. Pay £18, £19, £20.

(2) Record the following dealings with Bill and Carol:
  (a) Buy goods from Bill £21, £22, £23. Sell goods to Bill £26, £27, £28. Buy
      goods from Bill £31, £32, £33. Sell goods to Bill £34, £35, £36.
  (b) Buy and sell goods from and to Carol as follows:
      Buy £41. Sell £42. Buy £43. Sell £44. Buy £45.

(3) (a) Record dealings with Dick:
         Buy goods £51. Pay Dick £51 cash. Buy goods £52. Pay £52. Buy goods
         £53. Pay £53.
     (b) Record dealings with Ellen:
         Sell goods £56. Receive cash from Ellen £56. Sell goods £57.
         Receive £57. Sell goods £58. Receive £58.

(4) Record the following dealings:
Buy goods £61 from Fred. Sell goods £62 to George. Pay cash £63 to Fred.
Receive £64 from George. Buy goods £65 from Fred. Sell goods £66 to
George. Pay £67 to Fred. Receive £68 from George. Buy £69 from Fred. Sell
£70 to George.

Chapter 3

DOUBLE-ENTRY—FURTHER STEPS

A. BALANCING

1. This accounting technique is used on two occasions:

    (a) at the foot of each page of an account;
    (b) at the end of each accounting period.

2. When one reaches the bottom of a page, one does not merely turn over and start a fresh page. Instead, the entries are stopped a line or two before the end of the page so that the account can be balanced and then only the balance is carried forward to start off the new page.

3. At the end of each accounting period, a trial balance has to be prepared (see p. 27). Before the trial balance is drawn up, each account has to be balanced.

4. **Procedure**

    (a) The entries on the account of Alice are as follows:

Alice

Cash	15	Purchases	25
Cash	30	Purchases	40

(b) There are three steps.

Step 1
Add to the lighter side the amount needed to make both sides equal.

Alice

Cash	15	Purchases	25
Cash	30	Purchases	40
Balance	**20**		

N.B. This is one part of a double-entry. It is often known as the "balance *carried* down". It is most important to realise that there therefore needs to be a corresponding entry somewhere in the system (see Step 3).

Step 2
Insert the totals of both sides which should now be equal. This is not a double-entry.

Step 3
The corresponding entry for Step 1 above is now made below the total.

Alice

Cash	15	Purchases	25
Cash	30	Purchases	40
Balance	20		
	65		65
		Balance	**20**

This entry is known as the "balance *brought* down".

(c) The balance is called a debit or credit balance according to the side on which it is brought down (*i.e.* the entry made in Step 3, above). Thus, in the example above there is a credit balance (*i.e.* it has been brought down on the right-hand—credit side).

B. LAYOUT

5. **Presentation of an account**

DR[b]   Cash Account No. 10[a]   CR[b]

Date[c]	Details[d]	Fo[e]	Amount[f] £	Date[c]	Details[d]	Fo[e]	Amount[f] £
May 1	Margaret	2	300				

(a) The account is headed with the name of the account and the number.
(b) The account is divided into two halves. The left-hand side is the debit side and this can be shown by the letters DR in the top left-hand corner. The right-hand side is the credit side and this can be shown by the letters CR in the top right-hand corner.[1]
(c) The first column on each of the two sides is for the date of the transaction.
(d) The second column on either side is for details of the transaction. Note that this is the broadest of the columns. Here, one enters sufficient information about the transaction to communicate to the reader what is involved. One of the items of information which should normally be given is the name of the account where the other entry appears. Thus, if some money is received from Margaret, the name of Margaret appears in the details, so suggesting that the other entry is on the account for Margaret.

---

[1] These letters "DR" and "CR" are not normally shown.

(e) The narrowest of the columns is that headed "Fo." This is an abbreviation for folio number. It is used to provide a cross-reference primarily for the purposes of an audit. Thus this could show the number of the account where the corresponding entry appears, *e.g.* the number of Margaret's account might be 2.

(f) The last of the columns is that for the amount of money involved in the transaction. Note that one does not need to write the pound sign each time. It is sufficient to enter the pound sign once only on each side at the top of the columns.

6. **Alternative presentation of an account**

Date	Details	Fo	Debit £	Credit £	Balance £

(a) Instead of dividing the account into two sides with four columns either side for the date, the details, the folio reference and the amount, this layout uses six columns. There is only one date column, one details column, and one folio reference column. Then there is a column for the debits and a column for the credits. One of the interesting features of the alternative layout is that the final column is for the balance.

(b) *Example 1*
Cash of £100 is received from Charles. The entry in the cash account using this layout is as follows:

Cash Account No. 10

Date	Details	Fo	Debit £	Credit £	Balance £
Feb. 1	Charles	3	100	—	100

(c) *Example 2*
Cash of £60 is paid to Diana. The Cash Account would now look as follows:

Cash Account No. 10

Date	Details	Fo	Debit £	Credit £	Balance £
Feb. 1	Charles	3	100	—	100
Feb. 2	Diana	4	—	60	40

(d) The advantage of this is that the account will always show the current balance. It may happen from time to time that an account shows an unusual balance. For instance, one would hope that normally the cash account would have a debit balance (*i.e.* showing cash in hand). On occasions, however, there may be an overdraft at the bank and there would therefore be a credit balance on the cash account (see *post*, page 32).

(e) *Example 3*
Pay Edward £150 cash.

Cash Account No. 10

Date	Details	Fo	Debit £	Credit £	Balance £
Feb. 1	Charles	3	100	—	100
Feb. 2	Diana	4	—	60	40
Feb. 3	Edward	5	—	150	110CR

(f) If an account which should normally have a credit balance happens at some time to have a debit balance (*e.g.* of £40), then the figure is shown as follows: 40DR

C. Types of Account

7. Accounts can be grouped into three different types:

(a) Personal;
(b) Real;
(c) Nominal.

8. Personal accounts

(a) These accounts record dealings with persons. There will be a separate personal account for each person with whom the business deals. An example of a personal account is the Capital Account. This is the personal account of the proprietor of the business and should show, at any time, the amount owing to him or her.

Example
Proprietor introduces £5,000 cash. The double-entry is:

DEBIT the Cash Account
CREDIT the Capital Account

Cash	Capital
5,000			5,000

(b) A person who owes money to the business is known as a debtor and his account should show a debit balance.

Example
Goods are sold to Alice for £100 and thus Alice owes the business this amount. The double-entry is:

CREDIT the Sales Account
DEBIT the account of Alice

(c) A creditor is someone to whom the business owes money and his account should show a credit balance.

Example
Goods are bought from Brian for £5,000 and thus the business owes this amount to Brian. The double-entry is:

DEBIT the Purchases Account
CREDIT the account of Brian

9. **Real accounts**

Real accounts record dealings with assets or things owned by the business. There will be a separate account for each type of asset held. Most real accounts record dealings with fixed assets, *e.g.* premises, machinery, fixtures and fittings, and motor vehicles.

Example
Buy machinery for £8,000 cash. The double-entry is:

CREDIT the Cash Account
DEBIT the Machinery Account

Real accounts should show a debit balance.

10. **Nominal accounts**

Nominal accounts record dealings with intangibles: expenses and income. An example of an income account for a trader would be the Sales Account. This is a nominal account because its purpose is to record the income derived from the sales of the trading stock. The chief income account of a solicitor is called the

Costs Account, which records the earnings of a solicitor from charging clients with costs for acting on their behalf. (See *post*, pp. 34–35.) Examples of expense accounts include wages, rent and rates, lighting and heating, postage and telephones.

Example 1—Expenses
Pay wages £340. The double-entry is:

CREDIT the Cash Account
DEBIT the Wages Account

Example 2—Income
Sell goods to Charles for £200. The double-entry is:

CREDIT the Sales Account
DEBIT the account of Charles

Expense accounts should usually have a debit balance. Income accounts should usually have a credit balance.

11. Summary of balances

(a) *Personal accounts*

   Debtors: should have a DEBIT balance
   Creditors: should have a CREDIT balance

(b) *Real accounts*

   Assets: should have a DEBIT balance

(c) *Nominal accounts*

   Expenses: should have a DEBIT balance
   Income: should have a CREDIT balance

D. TRIAL BALANCE

12. The trial balance is a list of all the accounts together with the balance appearing on each account, the debit balances being listed in one column and the credit balances in another. The totals of the two columns should be equal, or "balance."

13. A trial balance is drawn up at regular intervals. How often this is done depends on the choice of the manager of each business. It can be done monthly, weekly, or even daily, if this is what the manager requires.

14. A major purpose of preparing a trial balance is to check the accuracy of the accounts. Another purpose is as a preliminary step for the preparation of final accounts.

15. Provided the system has been maintained accurately, the sum total of all the debits should always equal the sum total of all the credits. Further, if each account is balanced properly, the total of all the debit balances should still agree with the total of all the credit balances. It is, however, important to realise that not all bookkeeping errors are revealed by a trial balance. The following will not be revealed:

(a) *Errors of omission*
Obviously, if the bookkeeper omits to enter a transaction altogether, the total of all the debits and the credits will be equal but the accounts will be inaccurate because they fail to record the particular transaction.

(b) *Errors of commission*
Such an error occurs where the correct amount is posted to the wrong account, *e.g.* £100 of goods were bought from A and the Purchases Account is debited with £100 but the corresponding credit of £100 is entered on the account of B (instead of A). The debits will still equal the credits but the accounts will incorrectly show that the firm owes B £100.

(c) *Errors of principle*
Such an error occurs where a transaction is dealt with in a fundamentally incorrect manner, *e.g.* money spent on an expense is incorrectly posted to an account recording the purchase of fixed assets. This error is similar to an error of commission in that an entry is made on an incorrect account. The difference is that if an error of principle is not corrected, the final accounts will be inaccurate, *e.g.* expenses will be stated incorrectly and so will the fixed assets. On the other hand, with an error of commission, if the error is not corrected the Profit and Loss Account and Balance Sheet will still be correct (*e.g.* in the previous paragraph the total creditors figure will be accurate—it is only the details of the creditors which will be wrong).

(d) *Errors of original entry*
This type of error occurs where the entries are made on the correct accounts but the wrong figure is inserted. Thus if £50 is received from C and is entered on the Cash Account and on the account of C as £500.

(e) *Compensating errors*
This type of error occurs where two or more errors are made which cancel each other out. Thus the Cash Account shows that £80 was paid to F and £30 was paid to G but these were incorrectly entered as £60 paid to F and

£50 to G on the accounts of F and G. The two errors would thus cancel each other out and the Cash Account would come out correctly but the accounts of F and G would be inaccurate.

16. Method of preparing a trial balance

There are two steps:

(a) Balance each individual account;

(b) Prepare the trial balance. This is done by heading a piece of paper with the date at which the trial balance is drawn up. Each account is then listed and the appropriate balance put in the appropriate column. It is important to realise that the trial balance is not an account, *i.e.* no double-entries are involved. It is merely a list of existing balances.

17. *Example*

At the end of December the balances on the accounts of a trader are as follows:

Capital (credit) £20,000, Debtors (debit) £500, Creditors (credit) £4,000, Premises (debit) £15,000, Machinery (debit) £8,000, Cash (debit) £20, Wages (debit) £600, Rates (debit) £30, Income (credit) £150.

The Trial Balance would look as follows:

Trial Balance as at December 31

		DR £	CR £
Capital			20,000
Debtors		500	
Creditors			4,000
Premises		15,000	
Machinery		8,000	
Cash		20	
Wages		600	
Rates		30	
Income			150
		24,150	24,150

18. Exercises

(1) The following events occur:

February 1. D decides to start a business and puts in capital of £5,000.
February 2. D buys stock from S Ltd on credit for £10,000 and for cash £4,000.
February 3. D sells goods to A for cash £13,000 and on credit for £1,000, and to B on credit for £2,000.
February 10. D pays S Ltd.
February 11. A pays D the amount due.
February 12. B pays D £1,500.

Prepare the accounts of D to record the above, including a trial balance.

(2) Sally starts a business. On March 1 she puts in capital of £1,500 and borrows £3,000 from X.

March 1. Sally pays one year's rent for premises £500.
March 1. She buys fixtures and fittings for cash £750.
March 1. She buys stock for cash £1,500.
March 8. She sells stock for cash £2,000.
March 8. She pays electricity bill £25.
March 8. She pays wages £150.
March 8. She buys stock on credit from Tom £2,000.
March 9. She sells stock for cash £4,000.
March 9. She sells stock to Rachel on credit £500.
March 10. She pays Tom £1,500.
March 10. She sells stock to Rachel on credit £250.
March 20. Rachel pays £750.

Prepare the accounts to record the above, including a trial balance.

(3) Prepare a trial balance from the following figures:

Capital £2,200. Rent £620. Furniture £250. Rates £35. Sundry Expenses £12. Purchases £3,100. Sales £2,800. Debtors £915. Creditors £840. Cash £908.

(4) Prepare a trial balance as at December 31 from the following details:

Capital £40,000. Loan £10,000. Rates £3,000. Premises £28,000. Motor Vehicles £13,000. Fixtures £1,800. Wages £14,000. Purchases £30,000. Sales £50,000. Postage and Telephones £900. Lighting and Heating £2,800. Creditors £4,500. Debtors £8,600. Cash £2,400.

Chapter 4

THE BOOKS KEPT BY A SOLICITOR

A. THE BOOKS

Books of Double-Entry

Cash Book
Petty Cash Book
Clients' Ledger
Private Ledger
Nominal Ledger

Other Books

Bills Delivered Book
Journal

B. THE BOOKS OF DOUBLE-ENTRY

Obviously even with a medium-sized business there would be too many accounts to keep them all in the same book (or ledger). The accounts therefore are kept in a series of books which amount in effect to sub-divisions of the Ledger.

1. **Cash book (CB)**
   (a) One needs to distinguish between money passed through the bank account and money kept in cash on the premises. In order to do this, there will need to be two cash accounts, one to deal with the cash in the bank and the other to deal with the petty cash kept on the premises: the first Cash Account (Cash in Bank) is kept on its own in the *Cash Book* and the second (Cash in Hand) in another separate book—the *Petty Cash Book*.
   (b) *Money paid directly into the bank account*
   All business receipts should be banked promptly. Money received should be handed immediately to the Cashier. Each day he should pay all the money received into the bank and have in his possession a copy of the paying-in slip. From this slip, the double-entries can be made up, *i.e.*:

   DEBIT the Cash Book
   CREDIT the account of the person from whom the money is received (see *post*, page 40).
   (c) *Money paid out by cheque*
   The Cashier will also be responsible for all payments by cheque. He would therefore write out all the cheques (and the counterfoils). From the counterfoils, the double-entries can be made up, *i.e.*:

   CREDIT the Cash Book
   DEBIT either the account of the person to whom the money was paid (see *post*, page 40) or the relevant account in the Nominal Ledger in respect of expenses or fixed assets.

(d) *Overdraft*

The balance in the Cash Book should normally be a debit balance representing cash in the bank. If, however, the solicitor has an overdraft at the bank, the balance on the Cash Book would be a credit balance.

Example
March 1. There is a nil balance in the solicitor's bank account.
March 2. The solicitor receives £10 from Albert, as a loan.
March 3. The solicitor pays £30 on rent, thus overdrawing the bank account.

Cash Book

March 2	Albert	10	March 3	Rent		30
	Balance c/d	**20**				
		30				30
			March 3	Balance b/d		**20**

Albert

		Cash	10

Rent

Cash	30		

(e) *Dishonour of cheque*

When a solicitor receives notification that a cheque received and paid into the bank has been dishonoured the entries are as follows:

CREDIT the Cash Book
DEBIT the account of the person from whom the money was received

Example
May 1. A cheque for £400 is received from Charles and paid into the bank.
May 10. The bank notifies you that the cheque has been dishonoured.

Cash Book

May 1	Charles	400	May 10	Charles Cheque dishonoured	**400**

Charles

May 10	Cash. Cheque dishonoured	**400**	May 1	Cash	400

2. **Petty Cash Book (PCB)**

Whoever handles the small items of petty cash expenditure, whether the Cashier or some other person, will keep a separate book—the Petty Cash Book. The system most commonly adopted for the handling of the petty cash is known as the *imprest* system. At the start of each week, the person handling the petty cash is given a float (the imprest amount). Whenever a petty cash payment is made, a petty cash voucher has to be completed and, if necessary, signed by a person in authority. Petty cash is only handed out in exchange for a completed voucher. The virtue of such a system is that at any time the petty cash in hand plus completed vouchers should equal the imprest amount. At the start of each week, the float is restored to the imprest amount by reference to the completed petty cash vouchers in the possession of the person handling the petty cash.

Withdrawing the float (the imprest amount) from the bank

CREDIT the cash book
DEBIT the petty cash book

Example
£20 is withdrawn out of the bank for petty cash.

During the week, the person handling the petty cash hands out money in exchange for completed petty cash vouchers. These petty cash vouchers constitute the authority for the payments and from them the appropriate double-entries can be made:

CREDIT the Petty Cash Book
DEBIT the appropriate ledger account

Example
Pay £5 in respect of Postages out of Petty Cash.

3. **Clients' Ledger (CL)**

A solicitor will need at least one ledger account for each client to record the dealings with that client. This will be a personal account. All these accounts will be kept in the *Clients' Ledger* (for entries see *post*, Chapter 5).

4. **Private Ledger (PL)**

This contains any account that a solicitor wishes to keep private. This will probably include:

(a) Capital Account;
(b) Drawings Account;
(c) Costs Account.

5. **Nominal Ledger (NL)**

(a) This ledger contains all the remaining accounts. It is sometimes known as the *General Ledger*. The accounts most commonly kept in this ledger will be accounts recording expenses and perhaps fixed assets.

(b) *Expenses*
Examples of such accounts will be Wages and Salaries, Rent and Rates, Lighting and Heating. Entries will normally be made on these accounts when the particular expense is paid.

Example
The solicitor pays wages of £550.

Cash			Wages & Salaries	
	550		550	

These accounts should show a debit balance.

(c) *Fixed Assets*
Examples of such accounts will include premises, fixtures and fittings, machinery and equipment. Entries will normally be made on these accounts when the asset is paid for.

Example
The solicitor buys and pays £670 for fixtures and fittings

Cash			Fixtures & Fittings	
	670		670	

Real accounts will normally show a debit balance. (If a fixed asset is bought but not paid for until later see *post*, page 37).

C. OTHER BOOKS

6. **Bills and the Bills Delivered Book**

(a) When a solicitor sends a bill to a client charging the client with costs, a copy of the bill should be kept. From this document, an entry can be made in a formal Bills Delivered Book. However, the Solicitors' Accounts Rules 1991 (SAR), Rule 11(3) provides that it is sufficient to maintain a file containing copies of all the bills which have been sent out. This is the most simple method to adopt. Whether a formal book is maintained or simply a file of copy bills sent out, Rule 11 provides that the record must distinguish between profit costs and disbursements.

(b) From the copy of each bill (or the Bills Delivered Book), the bookkeeper can make up the appropriate double-entries in the ledgers, *i.e.*:

CREDIT the Costs Account (in the Private Ledger)
DEBIT the account of the appropriate client (in the Clients' Ledger)

(c) The Costs Account is the main income account of a solicitor. It may be helpful to think of this account as the solicitors' equivalent of a Sales Account. Thus the entries are all on the credit side.

(d) *Example*
June 1. Send a bill to Alice for £800 costs.

CREDIT the Costs Account
DEBIT the ledger account of Alice

July 1. Receive the amount due from Alice.

DEBIT the Cash Book
CREDIT the ledger account of Alice

7. Journal

(a) This is sometimes used as a preliminary step (called an original entry or a prime entry) before making the double-entries.

(b) If used at all, it can be used for the following transactions:

   (i) Correction of errors;
   (ii) Bad Debts;
   (iii) Depreciation of assets and other closing adjustments;
   (iv) Transfers when preparing final accounts;
   (v) Transfers of clients' money (see *post*, Chapter 8);
   (vi) Purchase of fixed asset on credit.

(c) *Correction of errors*

Example
(i) £50 received from Alice was incorrectly posted to Bill.

(ii) The error is corrected as follows:

DEBIT the account of Bill (*i.e.* the account on which the incorrect entry was made).
CREDIT the account of Alice (*i.e.* the one on which the entry should have been made).

The entry of the debit on the account of Bill is the correct way of eliminating an error. The same result could have been achieved by crossing out the incorrect entry but the method used above is the proper one to adopt.

(d) *Bad debts*

The writing-off of bad debts is a common experience of all businesses. Thus every business needs to keep an account to record this—the account usually being called "the *Bad Debts Account*". It is a nominal account and records the expense to the business of having to write off various debts as bad.
The events will begin with a customer or client owing the business a sum of money, *e.g.* AB Client owes the business £50 (*i.e.* he is a debtor).

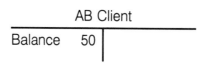

The customer or client then defaults in payment. Maybe he is made bankrupt (or where he is a company the company is wound-up) or maybe the proprietor of the business decides that it will not be worth the trouble and expense of attempting to enforce the payment. In any event, the decision is made to write this off as a bad debt. The entries are:
(i) *The first entry*
CREDIT the account of the customer or client. The result is that this account is now closed. The customer or client is no longer shown as owing the money.
(ii) *The second entry*
DEBIT the Bad Debts Account. This now records the writing-off of the bad debt as a business expense.

Example
The debt of £50 due from AB Client is written off.

AB Client		Bad Debts	
Balance 50	Bad Debts **50**	AB Client **50**	

(e) *Purchase of fixed asset on credit*

Example
A solicitor buys some machinery for £1,000 from A Supplier on credit. The entries are:

DEBIT the real account
CREDIT a ledger account in the name of the supplier. This will probably be kept in the Nominal Ledger (not the Clients' Ledger because the supplier is not a client as such)

Machinery		A Supplier	
1,000			**1,000**

(e) The layout of the Journal and the way entries in it are made depend entirely upon the accounting system in use in each particular office. Basically, however, the Journal is a list of the relevant events (*e.g.* writing-off of bad debts) and indications of which account to debit and which account to credit. It is not necessary to keep this book at all, subject to one very important qualification. When a solicitor has to transfer clients' money from the ledger account of one client to another client (see *post*, page 68), it is compulsory under Rule 11 SAR to make a preliminary entry (or prime entry). If the solicitor maintains a Journal, then this book is the convenient one to use. If, however, the solicitor does not maintain a Journal, then some other record needs to be kept. In such a case, the book is often known as a Transfer Book. Again there is no prescribed layout for the book. Basically all it contains is a list of the transfers which are made.

Chapter 5

OFFICE AND CLIENT ACCOUNT

A. The Two Sets of Accounts

1. Solicitors handle both their own business money (office money) and money belonging to clients (clients' money). The Solicitors Accounts Rules 1991 (SAR) require a solicitor not only to keep the two sets of money physically separate, but also to record the entries separately in the books of account.

2. To achieve this, the solicitor needs two sets of books:

    (a) one set to record all dealings with clients' money—*CLIENT ACCOUNT*;
    (b) another set to record all the ordinary dealings in the running of the business (*e.g.* receipt of office money, paying rates, buying stationery)—*OFFICE ACCOUNT*.

3. THESE TWO SETS OF BOOKS MUST BE KEPT COMPLETELY INDEPENDENT.

    (a) For every DEBIT in OFFICE ACCOUNT, there must be a corresponding CREDIT in OFFICE ACCOUNT and vice versa.
    (b) For every DEBIT in CLIENT ACCOUNT, there must be a corresponding CREDIT in CLIENT ACCOUNT and vice versa.

The classic error is to debit CLIENT ACCOUNT and to credit OFFICE ACCOUNT or vice versa.

4. There are four basic sets of entries:

    (a) receipt of clients' money;
    (b) receipt of office money;
    (c) payment of clients' money;
    (d) payment of office money.

5. To record these a solicitor needs:

    (a) Two Cash Accounts—one for OFFICE ACCOUNT and one for CLIENT ACCOUNT.
    (b) Two personal accounts in respect of each client—one for OFFICE ACCOUNT and one for CLIENT ACCOUNT.

6. Receipt of client's money

DEBIT Cash Account—CLIENT ACCOUNT
CREDIT ledger account of client—CLIENT ACCOUNT

Example
Receive £60 clients' money from A.B. Client.

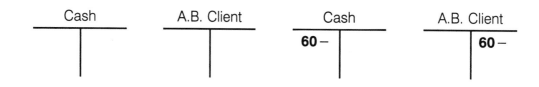

7. Receipt of office money

DEBIT Cash Account—OFFICE ACCOUNT
CREDIT ledger account of client—OFFICE ACCOUNT

Example
Receiver £30 office money from A.B. Client.

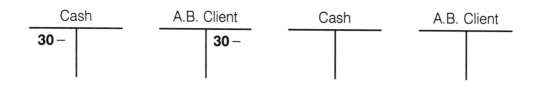

8. Payment of clients' money

CREDIT Cash Account—CLIENT ACCOUNT
DEBIT ledger account of client—CLIENT ACCOUNT

Example
Pay £50 clients' money to A.B. Client.

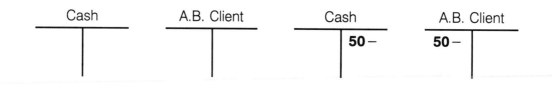

9. **Payment of office money**

CREDIT Cash Account—OFFICE ACCOUNT
DEBIT ledger account of client—OFFICE ACCOUNT

Example
Pay £40 office money to A.B. Client.

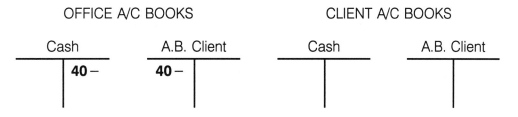

10. **Exercises**
Show all necessary entries.
 (1) (a) Receive £30 clients' money from Alice.
  (b) Pay £20 clients' money to Alice.
 (2) (a) Pay £1,000 office money to Brenda.
  (b) Receive £800 office money from Brenda.
 (3) (a) Receive £70 clients' money from Christine.
  (b) Pay £50 clients' money to Christine.
  (c) Pay £400 office money to Christine.
  (d) Receive £30 office money from Christine.

B. The Books of Double-Entry

11. **Cash Books (CB)**

 (a) The Clients' Cash Book—to record dealings with clients' money.
 (b) The Office Cash Book—to record dealings with business money.

12. **Petty Cash Book (PCB)**
 Only one petty cash book is needed, namely that to record dealings with office petty cash. Clients' money is not dealt with through the petty cash but, in general, immediately it is received it must be paid into the bank and consequently withdrawals of clients' money are made by cheque. There is no petty cash book in client account.

13. **Clients' Ledgers (CL)**

 (a) Clients' Ledger—CLIENT ACCOUNT
 (b) Clients' Ledger—OFFICE ACCOUNT

14. **Nominal Ledger (NL)**
 This contains all the other accounts other than those the solicitor wishes to keep private. However, none of these accounts will involve a dealing with clients' money and therefore only one nominal ledger is needed, namely that in OFFICE ACCOUNT. THERE IS NO NOMINAL LEDGER IN CLIENT ACCOUNT.

15. **Private Ledger (PL)**

This contains any account that a solicitor wishes to keep private, *e.g.* Capital Account and Drawings Account. These will not involve any dealings with clients' money and therefore only one Private Ledger is needed, namely that in OFFICE ACCOUNT. THERE IS NO PRIVATE LEDGER IN CLIENT ACCOUNT.

16. Instead of having two Cash Books, one for CLIENT ACCOUNT and one for OFFICE ACCOUNT, it is possible to have a single Cash Book with two sets of columns, one set for CLIENT ACCOUNT and the other set for OFFICE ACCOUNT.

17. It is possible to do the same for the Clients' Ledger.

18. The sets of accounts—OFFICE and CLIENT—are still entirely independent. They are only presented in the same book for convenience. Thus, still, for EVERY DEBIT IN OFFICE ACCOUNT THERE MUST BE A CREDIT IN OFFICE ACCOUNT, etc.

19. The other books (Petty Cash Book, Nominal and Private Ledgers) remain unchanged.

Chapter 6

MODERN METHODS OF KEEPING ACCOUNTS

1. The double-entry system of debit and credit outlined so far is based on the assumption that the double-entries are made by hand and are entered by clerks into books. Today some solicitors keep their accounts this way but most use more modern techniques of recording the information.

2. **Manual card system**

    (a) Instead of keeping books, with an account on each page of the book, a solicitor may keep the accounts in a series of loose-leaf cards. Each account is on a separate card and the cards are kept in special drawers or cabinets. The layout of these cards is the same as the alternative layout in the traditional ledger as follows:

Date	Details	Fo	Debit £	Credit £	Balance £

(See *ante*, page 23.)

    (b) A specimen double-entry would look as follows:

£100 is received from Alice.

Cash					
Date	Details	Fo	Debit £	Credit £	Balance £
	Alice		**100**		

Alice					
Date	Details	Fo	Debit £	Credit £	Balance £
	Cash			**100**	

3. **Carbon system**

Instead of writing the two entries separately on the two cards (Cash and Alice), the entries are made simultaneously by using a piece of carbon paper. One card is placed on top of the other, with the carbon paper in the middle. The entry is therefore written by hand on the top card and is simultaneously reproduced by means of the carbon on the card underneath.

Example
(a) £100 is received from Alice.
(b) The card of Alice is placed on top of the carbon paper and would therefore look the same as above (paragraph 2(b)), *i.e.*:

Alice				
Date	Details	Debit £	Credit £	Balance £
	Cash from Alice		**100**	

(c) The cash card (or sheet) is placed underneath the carbon and therefore the debit and credit columns of the cash sheet have to be reversed, *i.e.*

Example

Cash				
Date	Details	Credit £	Debit £	Balance £
	Cash from Alice		**100**	

4. **Computer accounts**

The precise layout of the accounts varies from system to system according to the type of computer used (this is particularly true in respect of the entries which need to be made to record VAT) but the principles of double entry are the same. Basically most computers use a layout similar to the manual card system illustrated above in paragraph 2.

5. From now on, the book will proceed on the basis that the accounts are kept on a computer. However, it is important to realise that the other two systems are fundamentally the same. With a manual card system, the accounts will look the same, the only real difference being that each entry has to be made separately and by hand. With a carbon system, the cash sheet will be different. Because the entries appear on it via the carbon, the entries have to be the other way round, *i.e.* Credits (Payments) on the left and Debits (Receipts) on the right. The ledger cards, however (*i.e.* the ledger cards of clients) will look exactly the same as those in the other two systems.

6. **Cash in bank—receipts and payments**

(a) There will be a Cash Account on which will be recorded all the items which formerly would have been recorded in the Cash Book. Whenever money is received and paid into the bank, or payments are made by cheque, the Cash Account is used.

(b) *Example*
   (i) Receive £100 from Paul.
   (ii) Receive £20 from James.
   (iii) Pay £30 to Paul by cheque.

Paul				
		DR	CR	Balance
(i)	Cash		100	100
(ii)	Cash	30		70

James				
		DR	CR	Balance
(ii)	Cash		20	20

Cash				
		DR	CR	Balance
(i)	Paul	100		100
(ii)	James	20		120
(iii)	Paul		30	90

7. Because a solicitor needs to keep separate records in respect of office money and clients' money, the Cash Account will need two sets of columns for credits, debits and balances—one set for OFFICE ACCOUNT, the other set for CLIENT ACCOUNT, as follows:

		OFFICE ACCOUNT			CLIENT ACCOUNT		
		DR	CR	Balance	DR	CR	Balance

8. **Petty Cash**

(a) When a payment is made out of petty cash, instead of using the Cash Account, a new Account, for petty cash, is used. The layout of this Account is the same as for the Cash Account, except that it contains only one set of columns, namely that for OFFICE ACCOUNT (see *post*, page 54).

Example
£5 is paid out of petty cash to Charles.

Charles							
		OFFICE ACCOUNT			CLIENT ACCOUNT		
		DR	CR	Balance	DR	CR	Balance
	Petty Cash	**5**		5			

Petty Cash				
		DR	CR	Balance
	Charles		**5**	5

(c) If money is withdrawn from the bank for the petty cash float, then the relevant entries are made on the Cash Account (payment) and the Petty Cash Account (receipt).

Example
£30 is withdrawn from the bank for petty cash. Office money is used.

Cash							
		OFFICE ACCOUNT			CLIENT ACCOUNT		
		DR	CR	Balance	DR	CR	Balance
	Petty Cash. Float	**30**					

Petty Cash				
		DR	CR	Balance
	Cash. Float	**30**		

9. **Clients' Ledger—entries**

(a) There will be a separate account or card for each client. There will need to be two sets of columns for debits, credits and balances, one set for OFFICE ACCOUNT, the other set for CLIENT ACCOUNT as follows:

		OFFICE ACCOUNT			CLIENT ACCOUNT		
		DR	CR	Balance	DR	CR	Balance

(b) *Payments by cheque*

Example
Pay £100 on behalf of Barnaby—office money.

Barnaby							
		OFFICE ACCOUNT			CLIENT ACCOUNT		
		DR	CR	Balance	DR	CR	Balance
	Cash	**100**		100			

The credit entry will appear on the Cash Account.

(c) *Payments out of petty cash*

Example
Pay £2 out of petty cash on behalf of Laurence, using office money.

Laurence							
		OFFICE ACCOUNT			CLIENT ACCOUNT		
		DR	CR	Balance	DR	CR	Balance
	Petty Cash	**2**		2			

The credit entry will appear on the Petty Cash Account.

(d) *Client Ledger Transfers*
For these transactions a new sheet can be used which may be called a "*Transfer Sheet*" or a "*Journal*" (see *post*, page 66).

10. **Nominal Ledger**
(a) The accounts contained in this Ledger will only require one set of columns, namely that for OFFICE ACCOUNT.
(b) *Payment of expenses*
There will be a separate account (or card) for each type of expense, *e.g.* wages.

Example
£400 is paid in respect of wages by cheque.

Wages		DR	CR	Balance
	Cash	400		400

The credit entry will appear on the Cash Account—OFFICE ACCOUNT.

If the expense is paid out of petty cash, then the credit entry will be on the Petty Cash Account and not the Cash Account.

(b) *Purchase of fixed asset*
There will be a separate account (or card) for each type of fixed asset, *e.g.* fixtures and fittings.

Example
£500 is paid by cheque in respect of fixtures and fittings.

Fixtures and Fittings		DR	CR	Balance
	Cash	500		500

The credit entry appears on the Cash Account—OFFICE ACCOUNT.

11. Private Ledger

(a) Only one set of columns is necessary, namely that for OFFICE ACCOUNT.

(b) *Capital*
When a partner introduces cash as capital, then the Capital Account (or card) of that partner is used.

Example
A sole practitioner introduces £10,000 capital.

Capital		DR	CR	Balance
	Cash		10,000	10,000

The debit entry will appear on the Cash Account.

(c) *Drawings*
   When the practitioner, or a partner, withdraws money from the business, a separate account or card for drawings is used.

Example
The practitioner withdraws £200.

Drawings				
		DR	CR	Balance
	Cash	200		200

The credit entry will appear on the Cash Account.

Chapter 7

BASIC POSTINGS

A. RECEIPTS

1. The first thing is to decide whether the money received is office or client's money (see *post*, page 57).

2. Pay the cheque into the appropriate Bank Account.

3. CREDIT the ledger account or card of the client in either the OFFICE ACCOUNT section or the CLIENT ACCOUNT section, as appropriate.

4. DEBIT the Cash Account, in the appropriate section.

Example 1—Receipt of clients' money
Receive £500 clients' money from Laurence.

Laurence (CL2)							
		OFFICE ACCOUNT			CLIENT ACCOUNT		
		DR	CR	Balance	DR	CR	Balance
	Cash					**500**	

Cash							
		OFFICE ACCOUNT			CLIENT ACCOUNT		
		DR	CR	Balance	DR	CR	Balance
	Laurence				**500**		

Example 2—receipt of office money
Receive £40 office money from Barnaby.

Barnaby (CL3)							
		OFFICE ACCOUNT			CLIENT ACCOUNT		
		DR	CR	Balance	DR	CR	Balance
	Cash		**40**				

Cash							
		OFFICE ACCOUNT			CLIENT ACCOUNT		
		DR	CR	Balance	DR	CR	Balance
	Barnaby	**40**					

5. If money is received for a client, not from the client himself but from a third person to hold on that client's behalf, the sum is credited direct to the ledger account of the client. DO NOT OPEN AN ACCOUNT FOR THE THIRD PERSON.

Example
Laurence is a plaintiff in an action, which he has just won against Violet. He was awarded £600 damages, which you now receive from Violet to hold on Laurence's behalf.

Laurence (CL2)							
		OFFICE ACCOUNT			CLIENT ACCOUNT		
		DR	CR	Balance	DR	CR	Balance
	Cash from Violet. Damages.					**600**	

The debit entry will appear on the Cash Account.

B. PAYMENTS

Payments by cheque

6. The first thing is to decide whether to make the payment out of office or clients' money:

(a) Consider whether the payment is authorised by Rule 7 SAR.
(b) Consider whether sufficient clients' money is held for that particular client (see *post*, page 55).

7. Draw a cheque on the appropriate bank account. If the cheque is drawn on the clients' bank account, remember Rule 11(7), SAR.

8. DEBIT the ledger account or card of the client in either the OFFICE ACCOUNT section or the CLIENT ACCOUNT section, as appropriate.

9. CREDIT the Cash Account, in the appropriate section.

Example 1—payments of clients' money
You hold £500 clients' money on behalf of Laurence. Pay £100 on his behalf; it is authorised by Rule 7 SAR.

Laurence (CL2)							
		OFFICE ACCOUNT			CLIENT ACCOUNT		
		DR	CR	Balance	DR	CR	Balance
	Cash					500	500
	Cash				**100**		400

Cash							
		OFFICE ACCOUNT			CLIENT ACCOUNT		
		DR	CR	Balance	DR	CR	Balance
	Laurence				500		
	Laurence					**100**	

Example 2—payment of office money
Pay £6 on behalf of Barnaby; you hold no clients' money.

Barnaby (CL3)							
		OFFICE ACCOUNT			CLIENT ACCOUNT		
		DR	CR	Balance	DR	CR	Balance
	Cash	**6**					

Cash							
		OFFICE ACCOUNT			CLIENT ACCOUNT		
		DR	CR	Balance	DR	CR	Balance
	Barnaby		**6**				

10. If the money is paid out not to the client himself but to a third person on the client's behalf, the sum is debited on the ledger account of the client. DO NOT OPEN AN ACCOUNT FOR THAT THIRD PERSON.

Example
Pay counsel £80, out of office money, on behalf of A.B. Client.

A.B. Client (CL1)							
		OFFICE ACCOUNT			CLIENT ACCOUNT		
		DR	CR	Balance	DR	CR	Balance
	Cash. Counsel	**80**		80			

The credit entry will appear on the Cash Account.

11. **Exercises**
Show Clients' Ledger only.

(1) You act for Alpha. Receive £800 clients' money. Pay £300. Pay £400. Pay £2. Use clients' money.

(2) You act for Beta. Pay £6. Pay £700. Pay £45. Use office money. Receive £300 office money.

(3) You act for Omega. Receive £38 clients' money. Pay £20 and £18 (use clients' money). Pay £16 office money. Receive £9 office money.

Payments out of petty cash

12. Office money is used (see *ante*, page 46).

13. Draw a petty cash voucher to obtain the money.

14. DEBIT the ledger or card of the client—OFFICE ACCOUNT.

15. CREDIT the Petty Cash Account.

Example
Pay £5 petty cash on behalf of A.B. Client.

A.B. Client (CL1)							
		OFFICE ACCOUNT			CLIENT ACCOUNT		
		DR	CR	Balance	DR	CR	Balance
	Petty Cash	**5**					

Petty Cash		DR	CR	Balance
	A.B. Client		5	

16. **Exercises**

Show all entries.

(1) Pay £4 petty cash on behalf of Alpha. Pay £3.20 petty cash on behalf of Beta. Pay £4.60 petty cash on behalf of Gamma.

(2) You act for Delta. Pay £6 petty cash. Receive £18, clients' money. Pay £1.70 petty cash.

C. BALANCES—CLIENT ACCOUNT

17. There is an important proviso to Rule 7 SAR, the effect of which is that a solicitor must not spend on a client's behalf more clients' money than is held at that time for that particular client.

Example
(a) Receive £50 from A.B. Client.

A.B. Client (CL1)		OFFICE ACCOUNT			CLIENT ACCOUNT		
		DR	CR	Balance	DR	CR	Balance
	Cash					50	50

The debit entry will appear on the Cash Account.

(b) If the solicitor wished to spend £40 out of clients' money, this would be possible.

Example

A.B. Client (CL1)		OFFICE ACCOUNT			CLIENT ACCOUNT		
		DR	CR	Balance	DR	CR	Balance
	Cash					50	50
	Cash				40		10

The credit entry will appear on the Cash Account.

(c) If, however, the solicitor wished to spend £70 out of clients' money, this could not be done without committing a breach of the Rules.

Example of a breach

		OFFICE ACCOUNT			CLIENT ACCOUNT		
		DR	CR	Balance	DR	CR	Balance
	Cash					50	50
	Cash				**70**		**20**DR

Table title: A.B. Client (CL1)

The credit entry will appear on the Cash Account.

19. Thus the account of a client (*e.g.* A.B. Client)—CLIENT ACCOUNT—should always have a CREDIT balance; a DEBIT balance means that Rule 7 SAR has been broken.

20. **Exercises**

If possible, make all the payments wholly out of clients' money; if this is not possible, make the whole payment out of office money. Do not make the payment partly out of clients' money and partly out of office money.

Show the Clients' Ledger only.

(1) You act for Alan. Receive £100 clients' money. Pay £60. Pay £70.

(2) You act for Brian. Receive £200 clients' money. Pay £30. Pay £400. Pay £50.

(3) You act for Charles. Receive £300 clients' money. Pay £200. Pay £150. Pay £75. Pay £30.

(4) You act for Donald. Receive £400. Pay £100. Pay £350. Pay £150. Pay £40.

D. Balances—Office Account

21. A similar problem arises when a solicitor receives money from or on behalf of a client: "Is it office or clients' money?" The money received will only be office money if it can be applied

(a) in reimbursement of sums already paid out by the solicitor on the clients' behalf out of office money; or
(b) in payment of the solicitor's fees or profit costs charged to the client for acting on his behalf, provided a bill has been sent to the client or the fee has been agreed with the client.

Thus the following receipts would be receipts of office money:

(a) The solicitor has paid £50 out of office money in respect of stamp duty on a conveyance and now receives the money back from the client.
(b) The solicitor has paid £30 out of office money in respect of a court fee and receives the money from the client.
(c) The solicitor sends a bill to a client charging £400 for profit costs and receives a cheque for that sum from the client.
(d) During an interview with a client a fee of £20 is agreed orally and the client immediately gives the solicitor a cheque for this amount.

The following receipts are receipts of clients' money:

(a) Money received from a client in respect of a payment which the solicitor has not yet made but which the solicitor will be making in future on the clients' behalf, *e.g.* money received from the client to pay counsel's fees, stamp duty, or purchase money on completion in a conveyancing transaction.
(b) Money received "generally on account of costs", where the solicitor has not yet paid out any money from OFFICE ACCOUNT in handling the matter on the client's behalf, and the solicitor has neither agreed a fee with the client nor sent a bill to the client.

Example 1
Receive £2,000 from A.B. Client generally on account of Costs. This is clients' money.

A.B. Client (CL1)							
		OFFICE ACCOUNT			CLIENT ACCOUNT		
		DR	CR	Balance	DR	CR	Balance
Jan 2	Cash					**2,000**	**2,000**

The debit entry will appear on the Cash Account.

Example 2
(a) Spend £50 on behalf of Laurence. No clients' money is held and so office money must be used.

Laurence (CL2)							
		OFFICE ACCOUNT			CLIENT ACCOUNT		
		DR	CR	Balance	DR	CR	Balance
Jan 2	Cash	**50**		**50**			

The credit entry will appear on the Cash Account.

(b) Now receive partial repayment from Laurence of £30. This is office money.

Laurence (CL2)							
		OFFICE ACCOUNT			CLIENT ACCOUNT		
		DR	CR	Balance	DR	CR	Balance
Jan 2	Cash	50		50			
Jan 3	Cash		**30**	**20**			

Cash							
		OFFICE ACCOUNT			CLIENT ACCOUNT		
		DR	CR	Balance	DR	CR	Balance
Jan 2	Laurence		50				
Jan 3	Laurence	**30**					

22. If, therefore, the client owes the solicitor £50 in respect of office money spent on his behalf and gives the solicitor £60, £50 of this will be office money and £10 clients' money. The Rules provide that clients' money must normally be paid into Clients' Bank Account and not Office Bank Account. If all the £60 were paid into Office Bank Account, a breach of the Rules would be committed (*i.e.* £10 clients' money has been paid into OFFICE ACCOUNT contrary to Rule 3 SAR).

Example of a breach

Laurence (CL2)							
		OFFICE ACCOUNT			CLIENT ACCOUNT		
		DR	CR	Balance	DR	CR	Balance
Jan 2	Cash	50		50			
Jan 3	Cash		**60**	**10**CR			

The debit entry will appear on the Cash Account.

23. Thus, the account of a client—OFFICE ACCOUNT—should always have a debit balance; a credit balance suggests a breach of Rule 3 SAR.

24. Exercises

Show Clients' Ledger only. If possible, receive all the money wholly into the OFFICE ACCOUNT. If this is not possible, make the receipt wholly into CLIENT ACCOUNT.

(1) You act for Ethel. Pay £100. Receive £70. Receive £40.

(2) You act for Fred. Pay £200. Receive £160. Receive £50. Receive £30.

(3) You act for George. Pay £300. Receive £400. Receive £50. Pay £580 out of office money. Receive £800.

25. **Summary**
You have probably broken the Rules if:

(a) You see the ledger account of a client—CLIENT ACCOUNT—with a DEBIT balance.
(b) You see the ledger account of a client—OFFICE ACCOUNT—with a CREDIT balance.

E. DELIVERY OF A BILL

26. The charging of costs involves OFFICE ACCOUNT alone.

27. File a copy of the bill in the "Bills Delivered Book" file.

28. DEBIT the ledger account of the client—OFFICE ACCOUNT—with the costs.

29. A new account, called a "Costs Account", is used. Thus the balancing entry is to CREDIT the Costs Account.

Example
March 5. Deliver a bill to Violet for £160 costs.

		Violet (CL4)					
		OFFICE ACCOUNT			CLIENT ACCOUNT		
		DR	CR	Balance	DR	CR	Balance
Mar 5	Costs	**160**		**160**			

		Costs		
		DR	CR	Balance
Mar 5	Violet		**160**	

30. Note that when a solicitor sends a bill to a client charging the client with the fee (or costs), he will probably also ask the client to reimburse him for payments made (or sometimes to be made) during the transaction on the client's behalf. When delivering the bill, DO NOT DEBIT THE LEDGER ACCOUNT OF THE CLIENT WITH THESE PAYMENTS. They are debited when paid out by the solicitor on the client's behalf.

Example
May 1. Pay £2 by cheque on behalf of Jacob.
May 2. Send Jacob a bill charging him £40 costs.
May 9. Receive amount due from Jacob.

		Jacob (CL5)					
		OFFICE ACCOUNT			CLIENT ACCOUNT		
		DR	CR	Balance	DR	CR	Balance
May 1	Cash	2		2			
May 2	Costs	40		42			
May 9	Cash		42	—			

31. **Exercises**
Show Clients' Ledger only.

(1) Deliver a bill to Harry for £60 costs. Receive payment.

(2) You act for Ian. Pay £50. Deliver a bill for £40 costs. Receive payment.

(3) You act for Joan. Pay £400. Deliver a bill for £650 costs. Receive payment.

(4) You act for Kate. Pay £80. Deliver a bill for £1,500 costs. Receive payment.

Chapter 8

TRANSFERS

A. BANK TRANSFERS—CLIENT ACCOUNT TO OFFICE ACCOUNT

1. It frequently becomes necessary to transfer a sum of money, which has been correctly paid into the Clients' Bank Account, into the Office Bank Account.

Example
(a) Receive £100 clients' money from A.B. Client.
(b) Send him a bill for £20 costs.

		A.B. Client (CL1)					
		OFFICE ACCOUNT			CLIENT ACCOUNT		
		DR	CR	Balance	DR	CR	Balance
(a)	Cash					100	100
(b)	Costs	20		20			

2. Rule 7 SAR. A solicitor is entitled to utilise the clients' money held on A.B. Client's behalf for the payment of this bill. This can be done by Bank Transfer.

3. The bank will transfer the £20 from the Client's Bank Account to the Office Bank Account, thus reducing the total balance of the former and increasing that of the latter.

Office Bank Account   *Clients' Bank Account*

4. **The double-entries**
   There are two steps:

   (1) Payment of clients' money;
   (2) Receipt of office money.

Step 1—Payment of clients' money

   DEBIT ledger account of client—CLIENT ACCOUNT
   CREDIT Cash Account—CLIENT ACCOUNT

Step 2—Receipt of office money

   CREDIT ledger account of client—OFFICE ACCOUNT
   DEBIT Cash Account—OFFICE ACCOUNT

Step 1: Payment of clients' money

		A.B. Client (CL1)					
		OFFICE ACCOUNT			CLIENT ACCOUNT		
		DR	CR	Balance	DR	CR	Balance
(a)	Cash					100	100
(b)	Costs	20		20			
(c)	Cash. Transfer				**20**		80

		Cash					
		OFFICE ACCOUNT			CLIENT ACCOUNT		
		DR	CR	Balance	DR	CR	Balance
(c)	A.B. Client. Transfer					**20**	

Step 2: Receipt of office money

		A.B. Client (CL1)					
		OFFICE ACCOUNT			CLIENT ACCOUNT		
		DR	CR	Balance	DR	CR	Balance
(a)	Cash					100	100
(b)	Costs	20		20			
(c)	Cash. Transfer		**20**	—	20		80

Cash							
		OFFICE ACCOUNT			CLIENT ACCOUNT		
		DR	CR	Balance	DR	CR	Balance
(c)	A.B. Client Transfer	**20**				20	

5. **Exercises**
Show Cash Account and Clients' Ledger.

(1) You act for Alice.
    (a) Receive £100.
    (b) Deliver a bill for £20 costs.
    (c) Transfer the amount due.

(2) You act for Bill.
    (a) Receive £300.
    (b) Deliver a bill for £50 costs.
    (c) Transfer the amount due.

(3) You act for Charles.
    (a) Receive £600.
    (b) Pay cheque £70.
    (c) Deliver a bill for £80 costs.
    (d) Transfer the amount due.

(4) You act for Dennis.
    (a) Receive £90.
    (b) Pay petty cash £10.
    (c) Deliver a bill for £30 costs.
    (d) Transfer the amount due.

(5) You act for Ethel.
    (a) Receive £400.
    (b) Pay cheque £50.
    (c) Pay petty cash £6.
    (d) Deliver a bill for £70 costs.
    (e) Transfer the amount due.

(6) You act for Frances.
    (a) Receive £80.
    (b) Pay by cheque £10.
    (c) Pay petty cash £1.
    (d) Deliver a bill for £20 costs.
    (e) Transfer the amount due.

B. BANK TRANSFERS—OFFICE ACCOUNT TO CLIENT ACCOUNT

6. This becomes necessary where a solicitor has inadvertently committed a breach of the Rules by overdrawing sums held on behalf of a client.

Example 1
Receive £300 from A.B. Client
Withdraw £400 from Clients' Bank Account on his behalf.

A.B. Client (CL1)							
		OFFICE ACCOUNT			CLIENT ACCOUNT		
		DR	CR	Balance	DR	CR	Balance
	Cash					300	300
	Cash				400		100[DR]

7. IF THE LEDGER ACCOUNT—CLIENT ACCOUNT—HAS A DEBIT BALANCE, THE SOLICITOR HAS COMMITTED A BREACH OF THE RULES, which must be rectified immediately. This is done by withdrawing the appropriate amount from the Office Bank Account and paying it into the Clients' Bank Account. It can be done by a Bank Transfer.

8. The bank will transfer £100 from the Office Bank Account to the Clients' Bank Account.

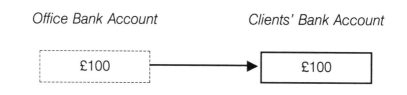

9. **The double-entries**
   There are two steps:

   (1) Payment of office money;
   (2) Receipt of clients' money.

Step 1—Payment of Office Money

   DEBIT ledger account of client—OFFICE ACCOUNT
   CREDIT Cash Account—OFFICE ACCOUNT

Step 2—Receipt of clients' money

   CREDIT ledger account of client—CLIENT ACCOUNT
   DEBIT Cash Account—CLIENT ACCOUNT

Step 1: Payment of Office Money

A.B. Client (CL1)							
		OFFICE ACCOUNT			CLIENT ACCOUNT		
		DR	CR	Balance	DR	CR	Balance
	Cash					300	300
	Cash				400		100DR
	Cash. Transfer	**100**		100			

Cash							
		OFFICE ACCOUNT			CLIENT ACCOUNT		
		DR	CR	Balance	DR	CR	Balance
	A.B. Client. Transfer		**100**				

Step 2: Receipt of clients' money

A.B. Client (CL1)							
		OFFICE ACCOUNT			CLIENT ACCOUNT		
		DR	CR	Balance	DR	CR	Balance
	Cash					300	300
	Cash				400		100^{DR}
	Cash. Transfer	100		100		**100**	—

Cash							
		OFFICE ACCOUNT			CLIENT ACCOUNT		
		DR	CR	Balance	DR	CR	Balance
	A.B. Client. Transfer		100		**100**		

10. Exercises

Show Cash Account and Clients' Ledger.

(1) You act for Graham.
 (a) Receive £40 clients' money.
 (b) Pay £50 clients' money.
 (c) Repair the breach.

(2) You act for Henry.
 (a) Receive £700.
 (b) Pay £1,000 clients' money.
 (c) Repair the breach.

(3) You act for Ian.
 (a) Receive £2,000.
 (b) Pay £2,500 clients' money.
 (c) Repair the breach.

C. LEDGER TRANSFERS

11. You act for two different clients: Barnaby and Laurence. You receive £600 from Laurence—clients' money.

Laurence (CL2)							
		OFFICE ACCOUNT			CLIENT ACCOUNT		
		DR	CR	Balance	DR	CR	Balance
	Cash					600	600

12. You now receive instructions from Laurence to cease holding £500 of this sum on his behalf and to hold it on behalf of Barnaby. This needs a transfer between the two ledger accounts of the two clients.

13. *In the Bank* there is no movement of money at all. Contrast the other two types of transfer (Bank Transfers) where there was a movement of money between the bank accounts.

14. The Double-Entry is:

DEBIT Laurence—CLIENT ACCOUNT
CREDIT Barnaby—CLIENT ACCOUNT
Note that there is *no* entry on any Cash Account.

15. Under Rule 11 SAR, where clients' money is transferred from one client ledger account to another client ledger account, an entry must be made "in a record of sums transferred". This entry is in addition to the double-entry mentioned above. The way of achieving all the necessary entries is to use a special sheet. This sheet may be called a "Transfer Sheet". The Transfer Sheet is made up in a similar way to the ledger card.

(a) DEBIT the ledger account of the client *from whom* the money is being transferred. The computer will also record this on the Transfer Sheet.

Laurence (CL2)							
		OFFICE ACCOUNT			CLIENT ACCOUNT		
		DR	CR	Balance	DR	CR	Balance
	Cash Barnaby. Transfer					600	600
					500		100

Transfer Sheet							
		OFFICE ACCOUNT			CLIENT ACCOUNT		
		DR	CR	Balance	DR	CR	Balance
	Laurence				**500**		

(b) CREDIT the ledger account of the client *to whom* the money is being transferred. Again, the computer will record this on the Transfer Sheet.

Barnaby (CL3)							
		OFFICE ACCOUNT			CLIENT ACCOUNT		
		DR	CR	Balance	DR	CR	Balance
	Laurence. Transfer					**500**	500

Transfer Sheet						
		OFFICE ACCOUNT			CLIENT ACCOUNT		
		DR	CR	Balance	DR	CR	Balance
	Laurence Barnaby				500	**500**	100 500

It should be noted that the double-entry consists of the entries made on the two client ledger accounts (*i.e.* Laurence and Barnaby). The entries which appear on the Transfer Sheet are not in this case part of the double-entry at all. They are made in order to comply with Rule 11.

16. **Exercises**
Show Clients' Ledger.

(1) Receive £40 on behalf of John. Transfer £20 to Kevin's account.

(2) Receive £700 on behalf of Lesley. Transfer £400 to Mary's account.

(3) You act for Nick.
    (a) Receive £300.
    (b) Deliver a bill for £40 costs.
    (c) Pay £50 clients' money.
    (d) Transfer amount due to OFFICE ACCOUNT.
    (e) Transfer the balance of clients' money to the account of Olive—another client.
    Show Cash Account and Clients' Ledger.

(4) You act for Peter, on whose behalf you hold £10 clients' money. Transfer £5 to Robert's account. Transfer £7 to Robert's account—use clients' money and so break the Rules. Repair the breach. Show Cash Account and Clients' Ledger.

Chapter 9

VALUE ADDED TAX

A. The General Law

1. The charge to tax

(a) VAT is charged when
    (i) a taxable person,
    (ii) in the course of furtherance of a business carried on by him,
    (iii) makes a taxable supply.
(b) All three conditions must be satisfied, so that no VAT is chargeable if
    (i) the person making the supply is not a taxable person or
    (ii) the supply is not made in the course or furtherance of a business or
    (iii) the supply is not taxable.
(c) Thus if a solicitor is a taxable person and in the course of his business he makes a taxable supply to another person (*e.g.* a client), the solicitor must charge that person with VAT. The supply made by the solicitor is called his OUTPUT and the tax charged is called OUTPUT TAX.

2. Taxable person

(a) He is a person who
    (i) is registered; or
    (ii) is required to register.
(b) A person is required to register if the value of his taxable supplies exceeds a certain annual figure (which is updated annually).
(c) This is an important definition. Supplies are classified for VAT purposes as being either Taxable or Exempt. In this case, the relevant test is the number of Taxable outputs (or supplies) made by a solicitor in a year; any Exempt supplies are ignored. Another point to notice is that the legislation refers to the annual value of the solicitor's output (or turnover), not to his profit.
(d) The result is that a solicitor is taxable if
    (i) he is required to register (*i.e.* if taxable outputs exceed the annual figure) and he does register, or
    (ii) he does not need to register (*e.g.* his taxable outputs are of a small amount) but he has actually registered, or
    (iii) he ought to register (his taxable supplies exceed the annual figure), but he does not actually register.

3. Business includes any trade, profession or vocation
This definition is similar to the definition of "business" for income tax purposes and the effect is that a solicitor's practice is caught by the definition. It is most

unlikely that a solicitor will not be a registered person and thus when, in the course of his business, he makes a taxable supply to clients, he will have to charge them with VAT.

4. **Taxable supply**

(a) Any supply other than an exempt supply is taxable.

(b) Supplies may be divided into two categories, taxable and exempt. Taxable supplies may in turn be divided into two further categories: those taxable at the *standard rate* and those taxable at *zero rate*.

(c) Supplies taxable at the standard rate
Basically any supply which is not taxable at zero rate and is not exempt will be taxable at the standard rate.

(d) Zero rate supplies include:
  (i) Books;
  (ii) International services;
  (iii) Transport.

(e) Exempt supplies include:
  (i) Insurance;
  (ii) Postal services;
  (iii) Burial and cremation;
  (iv) Finance
  The giving of tax advice is treated as the supply of legal services and not the supply of financial services, with the result that it is taxable.
  If a solicitor arranges a loan for a client and makes a specific charge to the client for arranging and negotiating the loan, this is a supply of financial services (*i.e.* exempt).
  If a solicitor places money on deposit with a bank and later the bank pays the solicitor interest on such money, this is treated as a supply of finance by the solicitor to the bank for which the bank pays a fee (*i.e.* the interest) and this is an exempt supply (finance) by the solicitor to the bank.

(f) *Supply*
  (i) If the supplier is a taxable person, he must charge VAT on any supply unless the supply is exempt. This will cover supplies of goods or services made by the solicitor in the course of his business, *e.g.* the giving of legal advice (supply of legal services). However, it is not only the supply of legal services which is caught but *ANY* supply made by the solicitor in the course of carrying on his business. Thus it will include the giving of other advice (not legal advice), or the disposal of a fixed asset, *e.g.* sale of an unwanted desk.
  (ii) The word "supply" includes sale, hire-purchase, hire, and exchange.
  (iii) *Gift of goods*
  A gift of goods is taxable but a gift of services is not a supply at all for VAT purposes. Thus if a solicitor makes a gift of goods to a client, VAT is chargeable, whereas if a solicitor performs a service for a client (*e.g.* drafts a will) and makes no charge, then no VAT is chargeable.
  (iv) *Private use of goods*
  If business goods are put to private use outside the business, this is treated as a taxable supply made by the solicitor, *e.g.* the solicitor

a. uses an asset owned by the firm for private purposes (*e.g.* takes a desk home);
b. lends a business asset to a friend;
c. allows an employee to use an asset of the firm over a weekend.

5. **Offices**

(a) Where a person, in the course of carrying on a trade, profession or vocation, accepts any office, any services supplied by him as holder of the office are treated as supplied in the course of a business carried on by him.
(b) The situations in which this is relevant are where a solicitor
  (i) becomes the trustee of a trust; or
  (ii) becomes a director in a company.
(c) The test is whether the solicitor obtained the office as a result of carrying on his practice and it would seem most unlikely that the solicitor could avoid having to charge VAT except in the case of his own private family trusts or companies.
(d) A solicitor also has to charge VAT on oath fees.

6. **Input tax**

(a) In the same way that a solicitor charges output tax to clients on taxable supplies made by him, so too the solicitor is charged with and has to pay VAT on taxable supplies made to him by taxable persons. Thus a solicitor will have to pay VAT on his expenses and on any fixed asset bought by him, provided in both cases that the supply was a taxable supply and the supplier was a taxable person. The supply made to the solicitor is called his input and the tax charged to the solicitor is called his input tax.
(b) A taxable person is entitled to a credit for input tax paid by him and to deduct that amount from any output tax which he has charged his customers, clients, etc.
(c) Each year is divided into four quarterly periods. At the end of each quarter, the solicitor must account to Customs & Excise for the total output tax in respect of supplies made by him, less the total input tax in respect of supplies received by him.

Example; In one quarter, you charge clients £100,000 costs plus VAT of £10,000. You disposed of a surplus machine for £100 plus £10 VAT. You paid, in respect of running expenses of the firm which were subject to VAT, £6,000 plus £600 VAT and bought a new machine for £2,000 plus £200 VAT.

	£	£
OUTPUT TAX		
Costs	10,000	
Machine	10	10,010
INPUT TAX		
Expenses	600	
New Machine	200	800
DUE TO CUSTOMS & EXCISE		9,210

(d) *Zero-rated supplies*

A person who makes taxable supplies is entitled to deduct all input tax paid in the quarter. For this purpose, it is unnecessary to distinguish between zero-rated supplies and standard rated supplies. If it so happens that in any quarter the figure for input tax exceeds the figure for output tax, the supplier is entitled to a refund from Customs & Excise. This is likely to occur if a supplier buys an extremely expensive fixed asset in one period and/or the supplier's outputs are wholly or mainly zero-rated supplies.

(e) If a supplier makes only exempt supplies, then he is not allowed to recover any input tax paid.

(f) *Disallowed inputs*

In all cases, a supplier is not allowed to claim back any input tax in respect of the following purchases:

(i) Motor cars;

(ii) Business entertaining expenses except for reasonable entertainment of overseas customers.

7. **Partial exemption**

(a) If a solicitor makes only taxable supplies, whether wholly standard or a mixture of standard and zero-rated supplies, he is allowed to deduct all his input tax from his output tax.

(b) If a solicitor makes only exempt supplies, he is not allowed to deduct any input tax from his output tax.

(c) If a solicitor makes partly taxable and partly exempt supplies, then he is "partially exempt".

(d) *De minimis*

A partially exempt person may deduct all his input tax as if he only made taxable supplies provided that the value of his exempt supplies is small. In order to determine this there are several different tests, *e.g.* was the value of his exempt supplies less than £200 per month?

(e) If the solicitor's exempt outputs are above the *de minimis* limit, he will be unable to deduct (and so recover) the total of the input tax which he has paid in a particular quarter. The amount of input tax which he can deduct is basically the proportion which his taxable outputs bears to his total outputs. Thus if, in one quarter, the outputs of a solicitor are made up of 75 per cent exempt outputs and 25 per cent taxable outputs, then 75 per cent of the solicitor's input tax is disallowed and he can only deduct 25 per cent of his input tax from his total output tax.

Example

OUTPUTS (excluding VAT)	£
Exempt ¾	7,500
Taxable ¼	2,500
	10,000

INPUT TAX	
Total Input Tax	4,000
Disallowed ¾	3,000
Deductible ¼	1,000

(f) It is, however, possible for a completely different method to be agreed on an individual basis between a business and Customs & Excise.

8. **Value of supply**

Any price quoted by a supplier to a customer or client is deemed to include VAT unless the supplier makes it clear to the customer or client that the contrary is the case. Thus if a solicitor tells a client that the firm's charges are £100, then the solicitor will have to calculate that sum which, with the addition of VAT, equals £100.

9. **Time—the tax point**

When a solicitor charges a client with VAT, the VAT becomes a debt payable by the client to the solicitor. Similarly, the solicitor has to account to Customs & Excise for the VAT and this is a debt owed by the solicitor to Customs & Excise. The importance of deciding the tax point in a transaction is that it fixes the time at which the debt arises between the solicitor and Customs & Excise. Thus if a solicitor is charging a client with £10 VAT, once the tax point has arisen this £10 becomes a debt payable by the client to the solicitor; in turn the solicitor now owes a debt of £10 to Customs & Excise, which the solicitor will have to pay to Customs & Excise at the end of the accounting quarter, subject to any right to deduct and set off input tax.

The rules for determining the timing of the tax point are complex. If a supplier is supplying goods, the basic tax point is the date when the goods are made available to the purchaser. A solicitor, however, does not supply goods but services. The basic tax point with services is the time when the services are completed. In practice, this is almost impossible to identify. Fortunately, however, there are three alternative tax points.

The first of these is where the supplier issues a tax invoice to the customer or client before the basic tax point arises and the second is where the supplier issues a tax invoice within 14 days after the basic tax point. In the case of solicitors, Customs & Excise have approved a general extension of the 14-day period to three months. The effect is that if a solicitor issues a tax invoice to the client at any time during the transaction or within three months after the transaction has ended, then the date of the tax invoice will be the tax point.

The third exception is that where a supplier receives payment before the basic tax point arises, then the date that the supplier receives payment is treated as the tax point.

If therefore a solicitor sends all clients a tax invoice at the time of making a charge to them, this will fix the tax point as at the date of that invoice. If, however, no tax invoice is sent, then the tax point will be the date when the solicitor receives payment.

If there is a continuous supply of services (*e.g.* a solicitor does work for a trust which is billed on a regular basis) the tax point will be the date of each tax invoice or the date when the solicitor receives payment, whichever is the earlier.

10. **VAT invoices**

The VAT invoice is the centrepiece of the administrative system. Whenever a taxable person makes a taxable supply (and so charges VAT) to another taxable person, the supplier must provide the customer or client with a tax invoice within 30 days after the time of the supply. One of the reasons for this is that a taxable person is not allowed to claim a credit in respect of input tax unless he is in possession of a tax invoice addressed to him charging him with the VAT. It should be noticed that there is no obligation to give a tax invoice to a customer or client who is not a taxable person.

Thus a solicitor's firm should ensure that when it is charged with VAT in respect of any supplies to the firm, a tax invoice is received and the original carefully preserved. So far as concerns the outputs of a solicitor's firm, to comply with the law the firm only needs to issue a tax invoice to those clients who are taxable persons and who could claim a tax credit in respect of the VAT charged to them. Having a system where some clients are issued with a tax invoice and some are not could cause administrative difficulties and therefore it may prove simpler to issue all clients with a VAT invoice whether or not they are taxable persons. In addition, if a VAT invoice is issued it will fix the tax point (see above). Finally, a copy of the VAT invoice should be retained; this copy will provide evidence of the firm's outputs to substantiate the tax return made to Customs & Excise at the end of the quarter.

VAT invoices must show the following information:

(a) An identifying number;
(b) The solicitor's name, address and VAT registration number;
(c) The time of supply;
(d) The client's name and address;
(e) The type of supply;
(f) A description which identifies the services supplied;
(g) The total charge made, excluding VAT;
(h) The rate of any cash discount offered;
(i) The total VAT payable.

When a solicitor sends a tax invoice to a client, the solicitor should describe the type of supply as "supply of legal services".

11. **Records**

A taxable person must keep records of all transactions connected with his business which affect his tax position and enable him to complete his tax return. Thus a taxable person must keep

(a) a record of all taxable goods and services *received*, both standard and zero-rated supplies, but not exempt supplies.
(b) a record of all supplies *made*, whether standard-rated, zero-rated, or exempt.

If, therefore, the solicitor issues tax invoices in respect of all supplies made by him and keeps a copy of that invoice, then these copies will be sufficient records of all the solicitor's outputs, whether taxable or exempt. Similarly, in respect of taxable inputs, the solicitor should obtain and keep all invoices received. Note that to "issue" a tax invoice, the supplier must give or send it to the customer or client; it is not sufficient simply to prepare it.

At the end of each quarter, a taxable person must make a return not later than one month after the end of the quarter. Before preparing the VAT return, the supplier must summarise his records in a *"VAT Account"* showing:

(a) total output tax for the period;
(b) total input tax for the period;
(c) the balance, whether tax payable or tax reclaimed.

B. Basic Entries

12. When a trader buys and sells goods which are subject to VAT, the tax (input or output) is generally recorded, separately from the value of the goods, on an account called "The Customs and Excise Account" or "*VAT* Account". Thus, if the trader buys goods from A Supplier for £50 plus £5 VAT, the entries are:

DEBIT Purchases Account with the value (tax exclusive) of the purchase
DEBIT Customs & Excise Account with the VAT—input tax
CREDIT A Supplier with the total (inclusive of VAT)

Example

```
            Purchases                          A Supplier
    ─────────────────────          ─────────────────────────
    A Supplier  50                              Purchases  50
                                                VAT         5



          Customs & Excise
    ─────────────────────
    A Supplier   5
```

Similarly, if the trader sells goods to A Customer for £60 plus £6 VAT, the entries are:

CREDIT Sales Account with the value (tax exclusive) of the sale
CREDIT Customs & Excise Account with the VAT—output tax
DEBIT A Customer with the total (tax inclusive)

Example

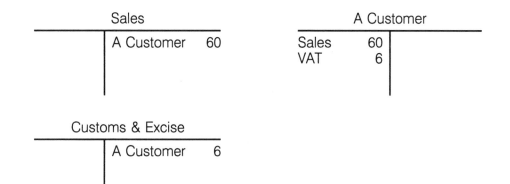

```
             Sales                             A Customer
    ─────────────────────          ─────────────────────────
              A Customer   60       Sales    60
                                    VAT        6



          Customs & Excise
    ─────────────────────
              A Customer    6
```

13. The Customs & Excise Account records the VAT *whenever there is an input or an output* for tax purposes:

  (a) Input tax—DEBIT the Customs & Excise Account.
  (b) Output tax—CREDIT the Customs & Excise Account.

  In a solicitor's accounts the Customs & Excise Account is kept in the Nominal Ledger, *i.e.* OFFICE ACCOUNT. There is no Customs and Excise Account in CLIENT ACCOUNT.

14. Inputs

  These arise when a solicitor pays for something (*e.g.* an expense) which is subject to VAT:

  DEBIT the appropriate ledger account with the tax exclusive amount
  DEBIT Customs & Excise Account with the VAT—input tax
  CREDIT Cash Account—OFFICE ACCOUNT—with total payment

Example
Pay for stationery £8 plus 80p VAT.

Stationery (NL9)				
		DR	CR	Balance
	Cash	8–		

Customs & Excise (NL11)				
		DR	CR	Balance
	Cash. Stationery	0·80		

Cash							
		OFFICE ACCOUNT			CLIENT ACCOUNT		
		DR	CR	Balance	DR	CR	Balance
	Stationery		8				
	VAT		0·80				

15. If, on making a payment, no input tax deduction is claimed, no entry is made on the Customs & Excise Account and the relevant ledger account is debited with the total payment.

Example (a)
Pay rates £160. There is no VAT on rates.

Rates (NL7)				
		DR	CR	Balance
	Cash	160 –		

Example (b)
Pay £5,500 for a new motor car plus £550 VAT. The input tax on this is disallowed.

Motor Cars (NL21)				
		DR	CR	Balance
	Cash	6,050 –		

16. **Exercises**

(1) Pay £50 plus £5 VAT on telephone bills. Pay £40 plus £4 VAT for typewriter. Pay £30 plus £3 VAT on stationery.

(2) Pay £5 on train fare, pay £4 on postage stamps, pay £10 on water rates, pay £8 interest on bank loan. There is no input tax payable in respect of any of these items. Pay £70 plus £7 VAT for entertaining a client—the VAT is disallowed as an input.

17. **Outputs**

A solicitor normally has a tax point for output tax when he sends a bill to a client charging the client with the costs.

Example
Charge A.B. Client £70 costs.

A.B. Client (CL1)							
		OFFICE ACCOUNT			CLIENT ACCOUNT		
		DR	CR	Balance	DR	CR	Balance
	Costs	70 –		70 –			

18. The double-entry for the VAT is:

DEBIT the ledger account of client—OFFICE ACCOUNT
CREDIT Customs & Excise Account

Example
Record the VAT output tax of £7.

A.B. Client (CL1)							
		OFFICE ACCOUNT			CLIENT ACCOUNT		
		DR	CR	Balance	DR	CR	Balance
	Costs	70 –		70			
	VAT	**7** –		77 –			

Customs & Excise (NL11)				
		DR	CR	Balance
	A.B. Client		**7** –	

C. Payments on Behalf of a Client—Methods of Treatment

19. During the course of a transaction, a solicitor often makes payments on behalf of a client and obtains reimbursement from the client usually at a later date. These payments may be:

(a) *taxable* (*i.e.* when the solicitor makes the payment it is subject to VAT, *e.g.* counsel's fees); or
(b) *non-taxable* (*i.e.* not subject to VAT, *e.g.* court fees).

20. For VAT purposes, there are two ways of dealing with such payments:

(a) the Principal Method;
(b) the Agency Method.

(a) The Principal Method
In this case, the original supplier is deemed to supply the goods or services to the solicitor. The solicitor is then deemed to supply the goods or services to the client. Thus, if the relevant item involved the purchase of tools, the ironmonger would be deemed to sell the tools to the solicitor who would be deemed to resell them to the client.
(b) The Agency Method
In this case, the original supplier is deemed to supply the goods or services direct to the client. All the solicitor does is to pay the supplier's bill on the client's behalf. Thus, the ironmonger would be deemed to sell the tools direct

to the client. The solicitor merely pays the ironmonger's bill (as the client's agent) and gets reimbursement from the client.

21. **Non-taxable payments**

An item is subject to VAT if a taxable person in the course of his business makes a taxable supply. Thus, a payment made by a solicitor will not be taxable in any one of the three following cases:

(a) supply to the solicitor by an *unregistered supplier* (*i.e.* not registered for VAT).
(b) supply to the solicitor by a supplier but supplied *not in the course of the business*.
(c) supply to the solicitor of an *exempt supply*.

If the solicitor adopted the Principal Method for (a) or (b) above, the solicitor would not pay VAT to the supplier but when he claimed reimbursement from the client he would have to charge the client with VAT. This is because the solicitor would be a taxable person who would make a taxable supply in the course of his business.

Example
An unregistered supplier supplies services to you for £150—no VAT (supplier not registered). You now, in turn, resell the services to the client for £150. You must add VAT, *i.e.* the total amount due from the client would be £150 plus VAT £15 = £165.

If the solicitor adopted the Agency Method, the solicitor would pay no VAT to the supplier and would merely claim reimbursement of the sum paid on behalf of the client.

Example
As above. You would pay the supplier £150 and would obtain reimbursement of this sum only (no VAT) from the client.

In either event then, the solicitor ought to use the Agency Method and not the Principal Method so as to save the client money.

With item (c)—an exempt supply—if the solicitor adopted the Principal Method the solicitor would pay no VAT to the supplier but, this time, when claiming reimbursement from the client, would not have to charge VAT. Although a taxable person and in business, the solicitor is now making an *exempt supply* to the client. This does, however, mean that the solicitor has an output for VAT purposes and it is an exempt one. Because of the system for disallowing a proportion of input tax as a deduction from output tax in respect of partially exempt traders, it is in the solicitor's interest to avoid exempt outputs as far as possible. If the Agency Method is used, the solicitor has no input or output (the supply is deemed to be made direct to the client) and so the solicitor again always ought to use the Agency Method. Customs & Excise permit solicitors to treat payments on an agency basis provided certain conditions are satisfied, namely:

(a) the solicitor acted as the agent of the client when paying the third party; and
(b) the client actually received and used the services provided by the third party (this condition usually prevents the solicitor's own travelling and subsistence

expenses, telephone bills, postage, and other payments being treated on the agency basis) (see *post*, page 116); and

(c) the client was responsible for paying the third party; and
(d) the client authorised the solicitor to make the payment on his behalf; and
(e) the client knew that the services paid by the solicitor would be provided by a third party; and
(f) the outlay is separately itemised when the solicitor invoices the client; and
(g) the solicitor recovers only the exact amount paid to the third party; and
(h) the services which the solicitor pays for are clearly additional to the supplies which the solicitor makes to the client.

In most cases, there should be no problem with treating payments made to third parties as being made as the agent of the client; the solicitor will be able to debit the client with the precise amounts paid out and to exclude these amounts when calculating any VAT due on the solicitor's supply to the client. (It should be noticed that if a solicitor treats a payment on the agency basis, the solicitor must keep evidence (such as a copy invoice) to enable the solicitor to show that he was entitled to exclude the payment from the value of his own supplies to the client.) However, it is sometimes the practice for all or some of the costs incidental to a supply to the client, such as travelling expenses, to be treated as disbursements and shown or charged separately on the bill/invoice issued to the client. Thus sometimes solicitors send bills to clients showing their profit costs (or fees) and under "Disbursements" list items such as "Postages, fares, and telephone calls".

Example

	£
COSTS	100
DISBURSEMENTS	
Postages and fares	20
	120

Where these costs have been incurred by the solicitor in the course of making his own supply to the client, they must be included in the value of that supply when VAT is calculated, with the result that VAT will be charged on the total amount including those incidental costs (see *post*, page 116).

22. **Conclusion**
With non-taxable payments, always use the Agency Method, except for incidental costs, *e.g.* postages, fares, and telephones.

23. **Taxable payments—Agency Method**
A feature of the VAT system is that a registered supplier can claim a deduction for input tax if he has a tax invoice *addressed to him* charging him with VAT. Thus, if a solicitor receives a tax invoice from a supplier, which tax invoice is addressed to the client, the solicitor will be unable to claim any input tax deduction in respect of VAT. In such a case, if the solicitor decided to use the Principal Method, although he would not be able to claim any input tax deduction because the tax invoice was not addressed to him, the solicitor would still have an output for VAT purposes and

have to charge the client VAT. The Principal Method is thus inappropriate and the solicitor should always use the Agency Method.

24. **Taxable payments—Principal Method**

When a solicitor receives a tax invoice from a supplier addressed to him, the client is unable to claim any input tax deduction in respect of it (the invoice being addressed to the solicitor). If the solicitor used the Agency Method in such a case, the solicitor would also be unable to claim the input tax as a deduction. If, however, he used the Principal Method, the solicitor would claim an input tax deduction when paying the supplier, and he would then have an output (with output tax) when charging the client. He would now have to send his own tax invoice for the item resold to the client, which invoice would be addressed to the client, and thus the client in an appropriate case could now claim a deduction for the VAT.

Example
Supplier sends you a bill for £250 plus VAT (*i.e.* a total of £275). You pay the supplier and claim £25 input tax deduction. You then charge the client with the item: £250 plus VAT (*i.e.* £275). This means you have an output of £25 and send the client a tax invoice in respect of it.

If the supply to the client was in respect of the client's business, *e.g.* collection of bad debts, and the client is a taxable person, he will want to claim the input tax deduction in respect of it. In such a case, therefore, the Principal Method must be used. In order to avoid any problems of classification and to achieve a uniform practice, it is suggested that the solicitor should always use the Principal Method where the supplier's invoice is addressed to the solicitor. In addition, before the Agency Method could be used, the eight conditions set out in paragraph 21, above, would have to be satisfied. Finally, the solicitor must keep evidence not only to show that he was entitled to exclude the payment from the value of his own supplies to the client, but also to show that he did not reclaim input tax on the supply by the third party. This would probably be administratively very difficult to do if he did not use the Agency Method in such cases.

25. **Conclusion**

If the supplier's tax invoice is addressed to the *client*, use the *Agency Method*.
If the supplier's tax invoice is addressed to the *solicitor*, use the *Principal Method*.

D. Payments—Double-entries—Inputs

26. **Non-taxable payments**

(a) Method of treatment: Agency Method.
(b) Office or clients' money may be used.
(c) DEBIT ledger account or card of client—OFFICE or CLIENT ACCOUNT, as appropriate.
(d) CREDIT the Cash Account.

Example

Pay court fees £7 on behalf of A.B. Client.

A.B. Client (CL1)						
		OFFICE ACCOUNT			CLIENT ACCOUNT	
		DR	CR	Balance	DR	CR	Balance
	Cash: Court fees	7 –		7 –			

The credit entry will appear on the Cash Account.

27. **Taxable payments—supplier's invoice addressed to client**

(a) Method of treatment: Agency Method.
(b) Office or clients' money may be used.
(c) DEBIT ledger account or card of client—OFFICE or CLIENT ACCOUNT, as appropriate—with *TOTAL PAYMENT*. There is no entry on the Customs & Excise account because on the Agency Method the solicitor is not claiming any input.
(d) CREDIT the Cash Account.

Example

Pay surveyor's fee £40 plus VAT, Agency Method, on behalf of A.B. Client.

A.B. Client (CL1)						
		OFFICE ACCOUNT			CLIENT ACCOUNT	
		DR	CR	Balance	DR	CR	Balance
	Cash. Survey fee	44 –		44 –			

The credit entry will appear on the Cash Account.

28. **Taxable payments—invoice to solicitor**

(a) Method of treatment: Principal Method.
(b) OFFICE MONEY ONLY MUST BE USED. Since the solicitor is using the principal method, his business will be claiming the deduction for the input tax. This is clearly a matter for OFFICE ACCOUNT only and CLIENT ACCOUNT is not concerned in any way. (See also note (d) below.)
(c) DEBIT the ledger account of the client—OFFICE ACCOUNT—with the tax exclusive amount.
(d) DEBIT the VAT on the Customs & Excise Account. This debit is in respect of the input tax, which the solicitor will be claiming as a deduction against his

output tax. The Customs & Excise account exists in OFFICE ACCOUNT only and this is another reason why clients' money and CLIENT ACCOUNT could not be used. The solicitor could not credit the Cash Account—CLIENT ACCOUNT—and debit the VAT in an Office Ledger Account.

(e) CREDIT Cash Account—OFFICE ACCOUNT—with total payment.

Example

Pay counsel's fee £90 plus VAT, Principal Method, on behalf of A.B. Client.

A.B. Client (CL1)		OFFICE ACCOUNT			CLIENT ACCOUNT		
		DR	CR	Balance	DR	CR	Balance
	Cash. Counsel	**90** –					

Customs & Excise (NL11)		DR	CR	Balance
	Cash	**9** –		

Cash		OFFICE ACCOUNT			CLIENT ACCOUNT		
		DR	CR	Balance	DR	CR	Balance
	A.B. Client VAT		**90** **9**				

(f) When a taxable payment is made using the Principal Method, the client would have to be charged with the VAT at the appropriate time. His ledger account at present fails to show the VAT and thus it is helpful to make some note in the details column (*e.g.* "VAT" is written in). This should be done on the ledger account of the client but only in respect of a taxable payment when the Principal Method is used.

29. **Exercises**

(1) Make the following payments on Adam's behalf. Use the Principal Method:
Pay by cheque £1 plus VAT.
Pay by cheque £2 plus VAT.
Pay Petty Cash £3 plus VAT.
Pay cheque £4 plus VAT.
Pay Petty Cash £5 plus VAT.

(2) Repeat exercise (1) using the Agency Method.

(3) Make the following payments on Bill's behalf:
    Pay cheque £1 plus VAT—Principal Method.
    Pay cheque £2 plus VAT—Agency Method.
    Pay cash £3 plus VAT—Principal Method.
    Pay cash £4 plus VAT—Agency Method.
    Pay cheque £5 plus VAT—Principal Method.

(4) You act for Carol. Receive £400 client's money.
    Pay (cheque) £50 plus VAT—Principal Method.
    Pay (cheque) £40 plus VAT—Agency Method.
    Pay £30 no VAT.

(5) You act for Dick. Receive £700.
    Pay (cheque) £100 no VAT.
    Pay (cheque) £20 plus VAT—Principal Method.
    Pay (petty cash) £8 no VAT.
    Pay (cheque) £60 plus VAT—Agency Method.
    Pay (petty cash) £4 plus VAT—Principal Method.

(6) You act for Edward. Receive £600.
    Pay (cheque) £400 plus VAT—Agency Method.
    Pay (petty cash) £3 no VAT.
    Pay (cheque) £150 no VAT.
    Pay (cheque) £10 plus VAT—Principal Method.
    Pay (cheque) £50 no VAT.

E. Output Entries

30. At the time of the tax point for output tax,[1] the solicitor ought to make entries to record the VAT.

31. An entry can be made in the *Bills Delivered Book* but the simplest system is merely to file a copy of the tax invoice (as with profit costs when filing the bill was sufficient).[2]

32. DEBIT the ledger account or card of the client in the Clients' Ledger—OFFICE ACCOUNT.

33. CREDIT the Customs & Excise account with the total VAT output tax.

---

[1] See *post*, p. 86.
[2] In some cases, firms may not send the clients a tax invoice but the entries must still be made.

Example
March 5. Deliver a bill to Violet for £160 plus VAT.

Violet (CL4)							
		OFFICE ACCOUNT			CLIENT ACCOUNT		
		DR	CR	Balance	DR	CR	Balance
Mar 5	Costs VAT	160 – * **16 –**		160 176 –			

*The credit entry appears on the Costs Account.

Customs & Excise (NL11)				
		DR	CR	Balance
Mar. 5	Violet		**16 –**	

34. **Exercises**

Show Clients' Ledger only.

(1) Deliver a bill to Fred for £70 costs plus VAT. Receive payment.

(2) Deliver a bill to George for £90 costs plus VAT. Receive payment.

(3) You act for Harold. Pay £40 no VAT. Deliver a bill for £60 costs plus VAT. Receive payment.

(4) You act for Ian. Pay £80 no VAT. Deliver a bill for £120 costs plus VAT £12. Receive payment.

35. The amount of VAT to be debited to the ledger account of a client is the total output tax on the transaction. This is not simply the VAT on the profit costs but the VAT on *all the solicitor's outputs*, i.e.:

(a) the Profit Costs;
  plus
(b) taxable payments made on the Principal Method on the client's behalf.

Example
You act for A.B. Client.

(a) Pay £4, no VAT, by cheque.
(b) Pay £80 plus VAT by cheque, Principal Method.
(c) Deliver a bill, which includes a charge for costs of £160 plus VAT.
(d) Receive amount due from A.B. Client.

		A.B. Client (CL1)					
		OFFICE ACCOUNT			CLIENT ACCOUNT		
		DR	CR	Balance	DR	CR	Balance
(a)	Cash	4 –		4 –			
(b)	Cash. VAT	80 –		84 –			
(c)	Costs	160		244 –			
	VAT	24 –[3]		268 –			
(d)	Cash		268 –				

36. **Exercises**

(1) You act for Jane. On her behalf pay by cheque £10 plus VAT—Principal Method. Deliver a bill for £60 costs plus VAT. Receive the amount due.

(2) You act for Kate. Pay cheque £20 plus VAT—Principal Method. Deliver a bill for £70 costs plus VAT. Receive the amount due.

(3) You act for Lucy. Pay cheque £3 plus VAT—Principal Method. Deliver a bill for £80 costs plus VAT. Receive the amount due.

(4) You act for Mary. Pay cheque £20 no VAT. Pay cheque £30 plus VAT—Principal Method. Deliver a bill for £40 plus VAT. Receive the amount due.

(5) You act for Nancy. Pay cheque £90 plus VAT—Principal Method. Pay cash £10 no VAT. Deliver a bill for £20 plus VAT. Receive the amount due.

(6) You act for Olivia. Pay cheque £1 no VAT. Pay cheque £20 plus VAT—Principal Method. Pay cash £3 plus VAT—Principal Method. Pay cash £4 no VAT. Deliver a bill for £50 plus VAT. Receive the amount due.

F. The Timing of the Tax Point—Output

37. The normal tax point for the solicitor's output is the date of the bill. Thus, along with the bill, the solicitor should send the client a tax invoice,[4] which will include all the taxable outputs in the transaction, *i.e.*:

---

[3] Taxable outputs are: Costs £160 + Taxable payment £80 = £240 @ 10% = £24.
[4] In some firms it may prove practical not to send tax invoices to clients except on request.

(a) profit costs;
   plus
(b) Principal Method taxable payments.

38. If a solicitor receives a tax invoice in his favour for an item from a supplier (*i.e.* the solicitor is to use the Principal Method) and the client is charged for the item in the bill before the solicitor pays the supplier, the tax point for the output is still the date of the bill. Thus, even though not paid, the item should be included on the tax invoice and the client debited with the VAT.

Example
   June 1: Receive supplier's invoice for £50 plus VAT in respect of A.B. Client.
   June 2: Send client a bill including costs £60 plus the £50 item plus VAT.

A.B. Client (CL1)							
		OFFICE ACCOUNT			CLIENT ACCOUNT		
Date	Details	DR	CR	Balance	DR	CR	Balance
Jun 2	Costs	60 –		60 –			
	VAT	11 –		71 –			

Note: Only the input TAX is debited at this time. The payment (tax exclusive) of £50 is debited when actually paid.

Example (continued)
   June 7. Receive the amount due from A.B. Client (*i.e.* £121).
   June 8. Pay supplier.
   June 9. Transfer to office account the amount due.

A.B. Client (CL1)							
		OFFICE ACCOUNT			CLIENT ACCOUNT		
Date	Details	DR	CR	Balance	DR	CR	Balance
Jun 2	Costs	60 –		60 –			
	VAT	11 –		71 –			
Jun 7	Cash					121 –	121 –
Jun 8	Cash. Supplier						
	VAT	50		121			
Jun 9	Cash. Transfer		121 –	—	121 –		—

Cash							
		OFFICE ACCOUNT			CLIENT ACCOUNT		
Date	Details	DR	CR	Balance	DR	CR	Balance
Jun 7	A.B. Client				121		
Jun 8	A.B. Client		50				
	VAT		5*				
Jun 9	A.B. Client.						
	Transfer	121				121	

*The debit entry appears in the Customs and Excise Account.

39. **Exercises**

Show Clients' Ledger.

(1) You act for Peter. Pay (cheque) £100 plus VAT—Principal Method. Receive reimbursement from Humphrey.

(2) You act for Rachel.
   May 1. Receive £800.
   May 2. Pay (cheque) £300 plus VAT—Principal Method.
   May 3. Transfer amount due to OFFICE ACCOUNT.

Chapter 10

MISCELLANEOUS POSTINGS

A. ABATEMENTS

1(a). Sometimes, after a bill has been sent to a client, the charge for profit costs is reduced. If this is so, a reduction will also be made in the VAT charge.

Example
A.B. Client is charged £200 costs plus VAT (£220). Later, the bill is reduced by £30 plus VAT (£33), *i.e.* balance due £187.

(b) When a reduction is made, send the client a credit note showing:

 (i) the reduction exclusive of tax;
 (ii) the rate and amount of tax;
 (iii) the total of the reduction.

This negatives the VAT invoice previously sent in respect of the amount reduced.[1]

(c) A preliminary entry for the abatement can be made in a number of ways, *e.g.*

 (i) by entry in a formal *Abatements and Allowances Book* or
 (ii) by filing a copy of the credit note in an informal Abatements Book.

(d) **Posting to the accounts**
   The entries are the reverse of those for charging costs when a bill is delivered. All the entries are in OFFICE ACCOUNT.

 (i) The reduction—excluding VAT.

CREDIT the ledger account of the client.
DEBIT the Costs Account

 (ii) VAT.

CREDIT the ledger account of the client
DEBIT the Customs & Excise Account

---

[1] If the firm's practice is not to send VAT invoices except when requested, the credit note is only necessary where a tax invoice has previously been sent.

Example
January 2. You act for Barnaby. Deliver a bill for £200 plus VAT.
January 5. Reduce Barnaby's bill by £30 plus VAT.

Barnaby (CL3)							
		OFFICE ACCOUNT			CLIENT ACCOUNT		
Date	Details	DR	CR	Balance	DR	CR	Balance
Jan 2	Costs	200 –		200 –			
	VAT	20 –		220 –			
Jan 5	Abatement		**30 –**	190			
	VAT		**3 –**	187 –			

Costs				
Date	Details	DR	CR	Balance
Jan 2	Barnaby		200 –	
Jan 5	Barnaby	**30 –**		

Customs & Excise (NL11)				
Date	Details	DR	CR	Balance
Jan 2	Barnaby		20 –	
Jan 5	Barnaby	**3 –**		

B. Bad Debts

2(a). If an account owing from a client is written off, in general the whole sum *including VAT* is written off; there is no tax credit.

Example
A.B. Client owes the firm £44 (costs £40, VAT £4), which is to be written off.

(b) CREDIT the ledger account of the client—OFFICE ACCOUNT
(c) DEBIT Bad Debts Account

A.B. Client (CL1)							
		OFFICE ACCOUNT			CLIENT ACCOUNT		
Date	Details	DR	CR	Balance	DR	CR	Balance
Dec 31	Balance	44 –		44 –			
Jan 5	Bad Debts		**44 –**				

Bad Debts (NL6)				
Date	Details	DR	CR	Balance
Jan 5	A.B. Client	**44 –**		44 –

(d) Sometimes there may be a tax credit for the bad debt,[2] in which case the entries are:

> CREDIT the ledger account of the client—OFFICE ACCOUNT—with the *TOTAL*.
> DEBIT Bad Debts Account with the *TAX EXCLUSIVE* amount.
> DEBIT Customs & Excise Account with the VAT.

Example

A.B. Client (CL1)							
		OFFICE ACCOUNT			CLIENT ACCOUNT		
Date	Details	DR	CR	Balance	DR	CR	Balance
Dec 31	Balance	44 –		44 –			
Jan 5	Bad Debts		**40 –**	4 –			
	VAT		**4 –**	–			

Bad Debts (NL6)				
Date	Details	DR	CR	Balance
Jan 5	A.B. Client	**40 –**		

Customs & Excise (NL11)				
Date	Details	DR	CR	Balance
Jan 5	A.B. Client	**4 –**		

---

[2] At the time of writing, the tax credit is allowed basically if one year has passed since the date of supply to the client, *i.e.* the date the bill was sent.

C. Splitting

3(a). Sometimes a cheque is received comprising partly clients' money and partly office money—a composite cheque. In such a case either:

  (i) split the cheque, *i.e* pay the clients' money portion into the Clients' Bank Account, and the office money portion into the Office Bank Account; or
  (ii) pay the whole cheque into the Clients' Bank Account and then transfer the office money from the Clients' Bank Account to the Office Bank Account.

(b). DO NOT PAY THE WHOLE CHEQUE INTO THE OFFICE BANK ACCOUNT AND THEN TRANSFER THE CLIENTS' MONEY TO THE CLIENTS' BANK ACCOUNT.

(c). **Double-entries if cheque is "split"**

  (i) CREDIT ledger account of client—CLIENT ACCOUNT—with the clients' money
       DEBIT Cash Account—CLIENT ACCOUNT—with the clients' money
  (ii) CREDIT ledger account of the client—OFFICE ACCOUNT—with the office money
       DEBIT Cash Account—OFFICE ACCOUNT—with the office money

Example
Laurence owes you £50.
Receive £60 and split the cheque.

		Laurence (CL2)					
		OFFICE ACCOUNT			CLIENT ACCOUNT		
		DR	CR	Balance	DR	CR	Balance
	Balance	50 –		50 –			
	Cash		**50 –**	**—**		**10 –**	**10 –**

		Cash					
		OFFICE ACCOUNT			CLIENT ACCOUNT		
		DR	CR	Balance	DR	CR	Balance
	Laurence	**50**			**10**		

Note: It is sufficient to enter both the £50 and the £10 on the same line.

(d) **Double-entries if cheque is "not split"**
  (i) CREDIT ledger account of the client—CLIENT ACCOUNT—with total receipt
       DEBIT Cash Account—CLIENT ACCOUNT—with total receipt
  (ii) DEBIT ledger account of the client—CLIENT ACCOUNT—with the office money

CREDIT Cash Account—CLIENT ACCOUNT—with the office money
(iii) CREDIT ledger account of the client—OFFICE ACCOUNT—with the office money
DEBIT Cash Account—OFFICE ACCOUNT—with the office money

Example
Barnaby owes you £70.
Receive £90. Do not split the cheque.

		Barnaby (CL3)					
		OFFICE ACCOUNT			CLIENT ACCOUNT		
		DR	CR	Balance	DR	CR	Balance
	Balance	70 –		70 –			
(1)	Cash. You					90 –	90 –
(2)	Cash. Transfer		70 –	–	70 –		20 –

		Cash					
		OFFICE ACCOUNT			CLIENT ACCOUNT		
		DR	CR	Balance	DR	CR	Balance
(1)	Laurence				90		
(2)	Laurence. Transfer	70				70	

D. Cheques Payable to a Third Person

4. If a cheque is received not payable to the solicitor but payable to a third person and the cheque is sent on to that third person, there is no need to make any entries at all. However, it is probably unwise to have no record of the receipt and despatch of the cheque. The recording can be done on the file of the papers and correspondence kept for the client, or it can be kept in the accounts themselves. If it is decided to keep the record in the accounts, the double-entry would be:

CREDIT ledger account of client—CLIENT ACCOUNT
DEBIT ledger account of client—CLIENT ACCOUNT
No entry would be made on the Cash Account.

E. Indorsed Cheques, etc.

5. If clients' money is received in cash and immediately paid over in the course of a transaction, or is received by cheque but similarly indorsed over, there is no need to pay such money into a Clients' Bank Account (Rule 9 SAR). However, for the purposes of the book-keeping, there is still a receipt of clients' money. NOTWITH-

STANDING THEREFORE THAT THE MONEY WAS NOT PAID INTO ANY BANK
ACCOUNT, THE FULL ENTRIES TO RECORD A RECEIPT AND A PAYMENT OF
CLIENTS' MONEY MUST BE MADE, *i.e.*:

   (a) CREDIT ledger account of the client—CLIENT ACCOUNT
       DEBIT Cash Account—CLIENT ACCOUNT
   (b) DEBIT ledger account of the client—CLIENT ACCOUNT
       CREDIT Cash Account—CLIENT ACCOUNT

Since, however, no money was ever actually paid into the clients' bank account,
some note of this should be made beside the Cash Account entries to save trouble
when preparing a bank reconciliation statement (*e.g.* in the details column).

Example
You act for A.B. Client. You receive a cheque for £5,000, which you indorse over.

		A.B. Client (CL1)					
		OFFICE ACCOUNT			CLIENT ACCOUNT		
		DR	CR	Balance	DR	CR	Balance
	Cash. Cheque indorsed				5,000 –	5,000 –	

		Cash					
		OFFICE ACCOUNT			CLIENT ACCOUNT		
		DR	CR	Balance	DR	CR	Balance
	A.B. Client. Cheque indorsed				5,000 – *	5,000 – *	

F. Returned Cheques

6(a). If a cheque comprising clients' money is received from a client, banked, but
later dishonoured, the entries are:

   DEBIT the ledger account of the client—CLIENT ACCOUNT[3]
   CREDIT Cash Account—CLIENT ACCOUNT

---

[3] This assumes that the cheque received from the client was paid into CLIENT ACCOUNT. If the
cheque was paid into OFFICE ACCOUNT, the entries would, of course, be in OFFICE ACCOUNT.

Example
February 1. Receive £40 from A.B. Client.
February 5. Cheque dishonoured.

A.B. Client (CL1)							
Date	Details	OFFICE ACCOUNT			CLIENT ACCOUNT		
		DR	CR	Balance	DR	CR	Balance
Feb 1	Cash					40 –	40 –
Feb 5	Cash. Cheque dishonoured				**40 –**		—

The credit entry will appear on the Cash Account.

(b). A solicitor may receive a cheque from a client and wish to draw against it before it has been cleared. This is permissible. If, however, the client's cheque is dishonoured, a breach of the Rules may now have been committed and, if so, must be rectified (see *ante*, page 63).

(c) *Example*

You act for Violet.
March 1. Receive £400.
March 2. Pay £300 clients' money.
March 5. Violet's cheque is dishonoured. You have thus broken the Rules and you repair the breach.

Violet (CL4)							
Date	Details	OFFICE ACCOUNT			CLIENT ACCOUNT		
		DR	CR	Balance	DR	CR	Balance
Mar 1	Cash. You					400 –	400 –
Mar 2	Cash				300 –		100 –
Mar 5	Cash. Cheque dishonoured				**400 –**		300 – DR
	Cash. Transfer	300 –		300 –		300 –	—

7. **Exercises**
Show Clients' Ledger.

(1) You act for Dust. Deliver a bill for £400 plus VAT. Reduce the bill by £20 plus VAT.

(2) Lizzie owes you £47. Receive £60 and split the cheque.

(3) Repeat Exercise 2, but do not split the cheque.

(4) You act for Meff. Send him a bill for £800 plus VAT. Reduce the bill by £50 plus VAT. Receive £900 and split the cheque.

(5) Repeat Exercise 4 but do not split the cheque.

(6) You act for Saunders.
    (a) Receive a cheque from him for £50 payable to Edgar, who is not a client. You send the cheque to Edgar.
    (b) Receive a cheque from Saunders for £600 payable to you and indorse it over to Fry. Show Cash Account and Clients' Ledger.

(7) You act for Griffiths. Receive a cheque from him for £8,000 which you indorse over to Hare. Then receive a cheque from Griffiths for £200 payable to you. Later this cheque is dishonoured. Show Cash Account and Clients' Ledger.

(8) You act for Rudge.

May 1. Receive £5,000.
May 2. Pay £1,000 out of clients' money.
May 5. Rudge's cheque is dishonoured. Repair the breach.
Show Cash Account and Clients' Ledger.

Chapter 11

REVISION EXERCISES

Show Clients' Ledger only. Your costs are shown exclusive of VAT in each case.

(1) You act for Bill. Receive £400. Pay cheque £50. Pay cash £6. Deliver a bill (costs £70). Transfer the amount due.

(2) You act for Carol. Pay cheque £80 (no VAT). Pay cheque £90 plus VAT—Principal Method. Pay cash £2. Pay cash £10 plus VAT—Principal Method. Deliver a bill (costs £300). Receive the amount due.

(3) You act for David. Pay cash £3 plus VAT—Principal Method. Pay cheque £400 plus VAT—Principal Method. Pay cheque £50 plus VAT—Agency Method. Pay cheque £60. Deliver a bill (costs £700). Receive the amount due.

(4) You act for Ethel. Pay cheque £80 plus VAT—Agency Method. Pay cash £9. Pay cheque £125 plus VAT—Principal Method. Pay cheque £20. Pay cash £3 plus VAT—Principal Method. Deliver a bill (costs £42). Receive the amount due.

(5) You act for George. Receive £70. Pay cheque £8. Pay cheque £9 plus VAT—Agency Method. Pay cheque £10 plus VAT—Principal Method. Deliver a bill (costs £20). Transfer the amount due.

(6) You act for Henry. Receive £80. Pay cheque £20 plus VAT—Principal Method. Pay cash £1. Pay cheque £11. Deliver a bill (costs £30). Transfer the amount due.

(7) You act for Kate. Pay cheque £80. Pay cheque £90 plus VAT—Principal Method. Deliver a bill which includes a charge for costs of £100, plus a taxable payment on the Principal Method not yet paid, of £20, plus VAT. Receive the amount due. Pay the £20 plus VAT by cheque—Principal Method. Transfer the amount due.

(8) Carambas, Solicitors, are instructed by the Phantom Co Ltd, to appear on their behalf, in a tax matter, before the Special Commissioners. The following events take place:

April 4. Payment of £11 (including VAT £1) by cheque drawn in respect of the reproduction of documents. This payment is to be treated as an input of Carambas.

April 9. Received the sum of £200 from Phantom Co Ltd on account of costs generally.

May 8. Paid fee of £88 (including VAT £8) to expert witness A.N. Accountant. This disbursement is to be treated as an agency disbursement.

May 26. The amount due to Jakes for transcripts (£44 including VAT £4) is paid out of CLIENT ACCOUNT.

May 31. The bill of costs in respect of the appeal is rendered to Phantom Co Ltd, showing profit costs of £500 (excluding VAT).

June 21. The balance of moneys due from Phantom Co Ltd is received and the requisite transfer is made from CLIENT ACCOUNT to OFFICE ACCOUNT.

You are required to show the ledger account of Phantom Co Ltd as it appears in the books of Carambas.

(Part II Qualifying Examination, August 1975).

(9) Inn, Flate & Co, Solicitors, deal with the following events:

November 3. Paid sundry disbursements of £126 in respect of the estate of Cashe, deceased, in which account there was a credit balance on client account of £84.

November 5. Paid a disbursement on behalf of Guy Forkes of £22 (no VAT). Forkes had already paid £100 on account of costs.

November 6. A bill of costs is sent to Forkes showing profit costs £80 plus VAT and the disbursement of £22.

November 8. Received a cheque from Fred (£450) on account of costs generally.

November 16. Paid surveyor on behalf of Fred, the sum of £100 (including VAT), the cheque being drawn on CLIENT ACCOUNT.

November 17. The bank notified the firm that the cheque from Fred has been returned unpaid by the paying bankers.

November 20. Received completion moneys (£31,710) on sale of a house which is being made by the executors of Cashe, deceased.

November 23. A cheque is received drawn in favour of Brown for £1,243. The previous month a fee had been agreed with Brown of £60 plus VAT, which amount had been received by the firm. An abatement of this fee £20 plus VAT is now made. The amount due to Brown is paid by cheque, and the account is then closed.

November 27. Paid by cheque, the sum of £1,200 on behalf of Tree, and received later the same day from Tree, a cheque for £1,000 in partial satisfaction. The balance is to be transferred from the account of the executors of Cashe, deceased, in accordance with their instructions, Tree being a beneficiary under the will.

November 28. Cheque received from Guy Forkes, settling the amount due by him to the firm in full.

Write up the client's ledger cards together with the Cash Account, showing all relevant entries. All accounts are to be balanced except the Cash Account.

(Part II Qualifying Examination, February 1981—adapted.)

Chapter 12

COSTS

1. At the heart of the Rules lies the distinction between clients' money and office money. When receiving money from a client, it is vitally important to determine whether this money belongs to the firm (office money) or whether it is clients' money. Equally important is the question of cash flow. Many solicitors firms have an overdraft on OFFICE ACCOUNT and, unless the cash position is carefully controlled, the firm may end up paying more interest to the bank on the overdraft than it ought to. Control can be achieved by:

(a) wherever possible, paying all disbursements out of clients' money;
(b) when receiving money, paying it direct into the OFFICE ACCOUNT, if permissible;
(c) transferring money from CLIENT ACCOUNT to OFFICE ACCOUNT as early as possible;
(d) sending out bills of costs to clients as early as possible.

Unfortunately the law governing this is complex. The relevant authorities are:

(a) the Solicitors' Accounts Rules 1991;
(b) the Solicitors' Act 1974;
(c) the Law Society's *Guide to Professional Conduct of Solicitors*;
(d) Cordery, *Law relating to Solicitors*.

2. The Solicitors' Accounts Rules

(a) Rule 9(2) provides that a solicitor must pay into OFFICE ACCOUNT money received which is expressly paid to the solicitor in respect of costs, where a bill or other written intimation has been delivered, or expressly paid as an agreed fee, or paid in full or partial repayment of money spent by the solicitor on behalf of the client.
(b) Rule 7(a) provides that a solicitor may (following the procedure in Rule 8) transfer to OFFICE ACCOUNT clients' money properly required for or towards payment of the solicitor's costs where there has been delivered to the client a bill or other written intimation.

In Rule 2, "costs" is defined as including "fees, charges, disbursements, expenses and remuneration". It also includes costs where the solicitor "has incurred a liability but shall exclude the fees of counsel or other lawyer, or of a professional or other agent, or of an expert instructed by the solicitor".

Notice that this definition of "costs" can include both the fee which a solicitor charges to the client for handling a file and professional disbursements, *i.e.* the payments which a solicitor makes on behalf of the client during the transaction.

3. **Fees**

At what time during a transaction is a solicitor entitled to payment of his or her professional fees from the client?

(a) As the relationship between solicitor and client is contractual, the basic answer to the question is at the time specified in the contract. Unless otherwise agreed, the contract is an entire one, *i.e.* performance by the solicitor is a condition precedent to the client's liability to pay (*Re Hall and Barker* (1878) 9 Ch.D. 538). This means that in most circumstances the solicitor will have to finish the job before sending a bill to the client and receiving payment. If the solicitor wishes to avoid this situation, it will normally have to be a term of the contract that the client should pay earlier. Usually the terms of the contract between the solicitor and the client (known as the retainer) are agreed during the first interview. It is therefore important from a commercial point of view that, at this interview, the solicitor agrees with the client when payment or payments are to be made. This is also now necessary as a matter of professional practice (Rule 15 Solicitors' Practice Rules 1990).

(b) At this stage, therefore, the law can be summarised as follows:

　(i) At the first interview, the solicitor and the client can agree on a fee for the whole transaction and the date at which the fee is to be paid. This could provide for payment at once before work commences or at any time or times during the transaction. Notice Sections 59–63 Solicitors' Act 1974, for the procedure for enforcing this. When these sums are received, they must be paid into OFFICE ACCOUNT in accordance with Rule 11(2).

　(ii) Alternatively, the solicitor can wait until the transaction is completed and then send a bill to a client, charging the client with the fees which, when paid, will also have to be paid into the OFFICE ACCOUNT under Rule 11(2).

(c) It is also possible that a solicitor may agree with a client either at the initial interview or during the course of the transaction that the client should make payments on account. In addition, Section 65(2) Solicitors' Act 1974, provides: "If a solicitor who has been retained by a client to conduct contentious business requests the client to make a payment of a sum of money, being a reasonable sum on account of the costs incurred or to be incurred in the conduct of that business, and the client refuses or fails within a reasonable time to make that payment, the refusal or failure shall be deemed to be a good cause whereby the solicitor may, upon giving reasonable notice to the client, withdraw from the retainer." This provision only applies to "contentious business", *i.e.* litigation matters where proceedings have actually been begun (*e.g.* by the issue of a writ or the commencement of arbitration proceedings). Section 65(2) also allows the solicitor to determine the retainer if the client fails to pay a reasonable sum in these circumstances even though the contract is an entire one.

4. **Bills of costs**

(a) There are two types of bills: a statute bill and a bill on account.
(b) A statute bill is a final bill for the work covered by it and a solicitor is only entitled to deliver such a statute bill:
　(i) at the end of the matter;

(ii) when the client has terminated the instructions;

(iii) when the solicitor has ended the retainer for some good cause, *e.g.* the client has failed to comply with a reasonable demand for payment under section 65(2);

(iv) when the client has asked for, or agreed to, the delivery of such a bill;

(v) at a "natural break" in protracted, complicated or lingering litigation. What exactly constitutes a "natural break" is a question of fact and rather obscure. The Law Society has recommended that it is wiser not to rely on this ground for delivering a bill except in the clearest of cases.

A statute bill is a final bill for the work covered by it. Thus, if given before the end of the retainer, the solicitor will not be able to send a further bill for work covered by the first one. The client can challenge the bill and have it taxed, but if the client fails to pay the solicitor may sue on it. The solicitor must, however, make it clear when delivering the bill that it is a complete bill in respect of the work specified in it. When the client pays such a bill, the solicitor will be able to pay it into OFFICE ACCOUNT.

(c) The solicitor can deliver a "bill on account" at any time during the retainer because in substance it is only a demand for payment on account of a statute bill to be delivered later. If the client fails to pay, the solicitor cannot sue on it and the client has no right to demand taxation in respect of it. Instead, the client can compel the solicitor to deliver a statute bill. Again, when the client pays such a bill, the solicitor should pay such money into OFFICE ACCOUNT. A bill on account can only be sent in respect of costs already incurred and not in respect of costs to be incurred in the future.

(d) Rules 9(2)(c) and 7(a)(iv) also refer to a "written intimation". A written intimation is not a bill but merely notification to the client of how his or her money is being applied. A written intimation can only cover costs which have been actually incurred and not anticipated future costs. If the solicitor sends the client a written intimation and the client expressly sends money in satisfaction, such money must be paid into OFFICE ACCOUNT. Similarly, if the solicitor already holds clients' money and sends a written intimation, the money can be transferred from CLIENT ACCOUNT to OFFICE ACCOUNT. However, the solicitor should also bear in mind VAT implications. If the client is registered for VAT and the supply of services is to the client in a business capacity, it will be necessary to send a tax invoice to the client and in these circumstances it may be more convenient to render a bill on account.

5. **Professional disbursements**

(a) *Payment of disbursements*

In order to manage cash flow effectively, wherever possible a solicitor ought to use clients' money to pay disbursements, especially where the disbursement is a substantial one.

(b) *Reimbursement*

If a solicitor holds no clients' money, any disbursement paid will have to be made out of OFFICE ACCOUNT. However, when the client reimburses the solicitor, such money must be paid into OFFICE ACCOUNT.

If the solicitor made the payment out of OFFICE ACCOUNT, notwithstanding the fact that clients' money was held, the solicitor is entitled to transfer the appropriate sum from CLIENT ACCOUNT to OFFICE ACCOUNT.

(c) If a solicitor receives money from a client in respect of a future disbursement, this must be paid into CLIENT ACCOUNT. This includes counsel's fees, agent's fees, stamp duty, land registration fees, etc.

(d) If, therefore, a solicitor receives money from a client in respect of:
  (i) a future disbursement, such money should go normally into CLIENT ACCOUNT;
  (ii) a past disbursement, such money should normally go into OFFICE ACCOUNT.

(e) There is an exception to d(ii), above, under the Solicitors' Accounts (Legal Aid Temporary Provision) Rule 1992. The Legal Aid Board makes payments to solicitors in block (*i.e.* covering several matters), and it therefore may be difficult within a few hours for the solicitor to work out precisely to which matters the money relates and how much of it is clients' money and how much of it is office money. The Rule therefore allows the solicitor to put all the money received into OFFICE ACCOUNT temporarily. The solicitor then has 14 days in which to work out how much of the money received is in fact clients' money and to make the necessary transfer to CLIENT ACCOUNT.

(f) Although the basic principle is that money received to reimburse the solicitor for disbursements already paid out of OFFICE ACCOUNT should be paid into OFFICE ACCOUNT, there are two situations in which the solicitor is allowed to pay the money into CLIENT ACCOUNT:
  (i) The first of these is where the money received from the client comprises partly the reimbursement for the disbursement already paid and partly clients' money. In this case, the solicitor is allowed under Rule 5 either to split the money received or to pay the whole amount into CLIENT ACCOUNT and make the necessary transfer to OFFICE ACCOUNT: see page 92);
  (ii) There is also a special rule (Rule 5a). Under this Rule, where all the money received from the client is money belonging to the solicitor—*i.e.* office money only—the solicitor is allowed to pay the whole sum into CLIENT ACCOUNT provided it is transferred to OFFICE ACCOUNT within seven days. This could be useful where the solicitor has difficulty in working out immediately whether it is wholly office money or a mixed receipt, *i.e.* partly office and partly clients' money. This may arise where the solicitor has difficulty in determining whether some disbursements have or have not at that time been paid.

(g) Despite the existence of these exceptions in (e) and (f) above, it cannot be too strongly emphasised that the better way is to pay the money directly into the correct account in the first place. In its *Guide to Solicitors*, the Law Society says that if solicitors follow a policy of posting payments to the correct account first time, not only will solicitors find this simpler but it also "carries with it both organisational and financial benefits".

Chapter 13

INTEREST ON CLIENTS' MONEY

A. Accounting to the Client for Interest

Specially designated deposit

1. If a solicitor receives clients' money which he anticipates holding for longer than a few days, he may place such money in a specially designated deposit bank account. This is a deposit account at a bank and so interest will be earned on money deposited in it. "Specially designated" means that it is reserved exclusively for clients' money belonging to one particular client. Thus, if the solicitor wishes to place clients' money belonging to three different clients in specially designated deposit bank accounts, three such bank accounts will be needed, one for each client.

2. IF CLIENTS' MONEY IS PLACED ON SPECIALLY DESIGNATED DEPOSIT, ANY INTEREST EARNED BELONGS TO THAT PARTICULAR CLIENT AND IS CLIENTS' MONEY.

3. In order to record what moneys are placed on separate designated deposit, a separate Cash Account is needed. This is reserved for clients' money placed on deposit and will be called "*Deposit Cash Account*". This will have "Office" and "Client" account columns, although the Office Account columns will "never" be used.

4. **Placing money on deposit**

   (a) When the clients' money is received from or on behalf of the client, it can first be paid into the ordinary current bank account for clients' money; the double-entry is:

CREDIT ledger account of client—CLIENT ACCOUNT
DEBIT Cash Account—CLIENT ACCOUNT

Example
Receive £8,000 from A.B. Client on May 1.

A.B. Client (CL1)							
Date	Detail	OFFICE ACCOUNT			CLIENT ACCOUNT		
		DR	CR	Balance	DR	CR	Balance
May 1	Cash					8,000 –	8,000 –

(b) The second step is to transfer the money from the ordinary current bank account for clients' money to the specially designated deposit account. This is done by a bank transfer, thus reducing the amount in the current account.

The double-entry to record this is:
    CREDIT Cash Account—CLIENT ACCOUNT
    DEBIT Deposit Cash Account—CLIENT ACCOUNT

Example
Transfer the £8,000 to a specially designated account.

Cash							
Date	Details	OFFICE ACCOUNT			CLIENT ACCOUNT		
		DR	CR	Balance	DR	CR	Balance
May 1	A.B. Client Deposit Cash Specially designated Re A.B. Client				8,000	8,000	

Deposit Cash Re A.B. Client (DC1)							
Date	Details	OFFICE ACCOUNT			CLIENT ACCOUNT		
		DR	CR	Balance	DR	CR	Balance
May 1	Cash. Transfer from Current Account				8,000		8,000

(c) THERE IS NO ENTRY ON THE LEDGER ACCOUNT OF THE CLIENT. However, it may be unwise to have no note that the money is on deposit and therefore some note could be made on the ledger account, *e.g.* by writing in the words "On Deposit" in an appropriate place.

If clients' money belonging to more than one client is placed on deposit, the same Deposit Cash Account could be used. However, since the two different amounts are in different bank accounts, the solicitor ought to record them separately. Thus the solicitor would have a separate bank account in respect of each client on whose behalf he had placed the money on deposit represented by a separate Deposit Cash Account.

5. **Interest**

At the appropriate time, the bank will account to the solicitor for the interest earned by the money on deposit. The usual way in which this is done is to credit the appropriate bank account. Thus, if £8,000 belonging to A.B. Client has been placed on deposit, the interest which such money earned should be credited to that deposit account, thus increasing the balance in that bank account.

The double-entry is:
CREDIT the ledger account of the client—CLIENT ACCOUNT
DEBIT Deposit Cash Account—CLIENT ACCOUNT

Example
The bank credits A.B. Client's deposit account with £50 interest on June 1.

Date	Details	OFFICE ACCOUNT			CLIENT ACCOUNT		
		DR	CR	Balance	DR	CR	Balance
May 1	Cash. You					8,000 –	8,000 –
Jun 1	Deposit Cash. Interest					**50 –**	**8,050 –**

A.B. Client (CL1) On Deposit

The debit entry will appear on the relevant Deposit Cash Account (*i.e.* the one for A.B. Client).

6. When the money is withdrawn from the deposit account, either to send to the client or to spend on his behalf, it must first be transferred from the deposit bank account to the current bank account for clients' money by a bank transfer.

The double-entry to record this is:
CREDIT deposit Cash Account—CLIENT ACCOUNT
DEBIT Cash Account—CLIENT ACCOUNT

Example

Transfer the £8,050 held for A.B. Client back to current account.

Cash							
Date	Details	OFFICE ACCOUNT			CLIENT ACCOUNT		
		DR	CR	Balance	DR	CR	Balance
Jun 2	Deposit Cash. Specially designated Re A.B. Client				8,050		

Deposit Cash Re A.B. Client (DC1)							
Date	Details	OFFICE ACCOUNT			CLIENT ACCOUNT		
		DR	CR	Balance	DR	CR	Balance
May 1	Cash. Transfer from Current Account				8,000		8,000
Jun 1	Interest				50		8,050
Jun 2	Cash. Transfer to Current Account					8,050	—

THERE IS NO ENTRY ON THE LEDGER ACCOUNT OF THE CLIENT, but the note attached to it when the money was first placed on deposit should be removed. The client's money is now ready for withdrawal in the normal way.

7. **Exercises**

(1) You act for Laurence.
   January 2. Receive £5,000.
   January 3. Place in a specially designated account.
   September 1. The bank credits the deposit account with interest of £30.
   September 3. Remove amount in the deposit account to current account.
   September 4. Return the amount due to Laurence.

(2) You act for Barnaby.
   February 1. Receive £2,000 and place it in a specially designated account.
   August 1. Bank credits the deposit account with interest of £42.
   October 2. Close deposit account by transfer to current account and draw cheque on Barnaby's behalf for £2,000 payable to Jacob.
   October 3. Bank credits current (client) account with interest of £18.
   October 4. Send Barnaby the interest due.

(3) You act for Violet.
  March 1. Receive £4,500 and place it in a specially designated account.
  April 1. Bank credits deposit account with interest of £14.
  April 2. You send Violet a bill charging her £20 costs plus VAT.
  April 3. Transfer the £4,514 to current account.
  April 4. Send Violet the amount due and transfer the costs.

Money not specially designated

8. Even if a solicitor anticipates when receiving clients' money that the money will be held for a considerable time, the solicitor does not have to place such money in a specially designated deposit bank account. The money can be placed in the ordinary current bank account for clients' money.

9. If a solicitor does receive clients' money, does not place it in a specially designated deposit account, and holds such money for a long time, the solicitor has to pay the client the interest which the client would have received had such money been specially designated.

10. **Note**

(a) The obligation to pay interest arises whether the holding of the money for a long time was foreseeable or not.
(b) There are two tests:
   (i) the amount of clients' money held; and
   (ii) for how long it is held.
   The Solicitors' Accounts Rules 1991 contain a table, which indicates when interest must be paid.
(c) The solicitor has to pay the interest out of his own money (*i.e.* office money).

11. In order to record the payment of interest in such cases, the solicitor needs an account called *Deposit Interest Payable Account*. This is a nominal account; it records the *Expense* to the business of paying interest to clients (similar to the expense of paying interest to a bank on an overdraft). This account exists in OFFICE ACCOUNT only.

12. If the only transaction involved is sending the interest to the client, draw a cheque on the OFFICE ACCOUNT and record this:

DEBIT Deposit Interest Payable Account
CREDIT Cash Account—OFFICE ACCOUNT

Example
Send A.B. Client £60 interest.

Deposit Interest Payable (NL12)				
		DR	CR	Balance
	Cash. Re A.B. Client	**60 –**		

The credit entry will appear on the Cash Account—OFFICE ACCOUNT.

THERE IS NO ENTRY ON THE LEDGER ACCOUNT OF THE CLIENT but a note could be made on the account that interest has been sent.

13. If, at the same time as sending the client interest, the solicitor is sending clients' money to him, the solicitor needs to send the client two cheques.

   (a) Send a clients' account cheque in respect of the clients' money, *i.e.*:

   DEBIT ledger account of client—CLIENT ACCOUNT
   CREDIT Cash Account—CLIENT ACCOUNT

   (b) Send an office account cheque for the interest, *i.e.*:

   DEBIT Deposit Interest Payable Account
   CREDIT Cash Account—OFFICE ACCOUNT

THERE IS NO ENTRY ON THE LEDGER ACCOUNT OF THE CLIENT to record the interest, but again some note can be made on the ledger account of the client, if desired.

14. Alternatively, the solicitor could send one cheque drawn on CLIENT ACCOUNT for the whole amount, if he first transfers the interest from the Office Bank Account to the Clients' Bank Account. This involves a bank transfer, *i.e.*:

   (a) withdrawing the money from the office bank account; and
   (b) receiving the money in the clients' bank account.

   Step 1—Withdrawing the money from OFFICE ACCOUNT
   DEBIT Deposit Interest Payable Account
   CREDIT Cash Account—OFFICE ACCOUNT

   Step 2—Receiving the money in CLIENT ACCOUNT
   CREDIT the ledger account of the client—CLIENT ACCOUNT
   DEBIT Cash Account—CLIENT ACCOUNT

Step 3—sending the client the total due to him
DEBIT the ledger account of the client—CLIENT ACCOUNT
CREDIT Cash Account—CLIENT ACCOUNT

Example

Step 1

Deposit Interest Payable (NL12)				
		DR	CR	Balance
	Cash. Re A.B. Client	60 –		

Cash							
		OFFICE ACCOUNT			CLIENT ACCOUNT		
		DR	CR	Balance	DR	CR	Balance
	Deposit Interest Payable		60				

Step 2

A.B. Client (CL1)							
		OFFICE ACCOUNT			CLIENT ACCOUNT		
		DR	CR	Balance	DR	CR	Balance
	Balance Cash. Deposit Interest					3,000 – **60 –**	3,000 – **3,060 –**

Cash							
		OFFICE ACCOUNT			CLIENT ACCOUNT		
		DR	CR	Balance	DR	CR	Balance
	Deposit Interest Payable. A.B. Client		60		**60**		

Step 3

A.B. Client (CL1)							
		OFFICE ACCOUNT			CLIENT ACCOUNT		
		DR	CR	Balance	DR	CR	Balance
Balance						3,000 –	3,000 –
Cash. Deposit Interest						60 –	3,060 –
Cash. You					3,060		—

Cash							
		OFFICE ACCOUNT			CLIENT ACCOUNT		
		DR	CR	Balance	DR	CR	Balance
Deposit Interest Payable			60				
A.B. Client					60		
A.B. Client						3,060	

This procedure can be used as an alternative to that in 13 above, and whenever a solicitor wishes to hold the interest in CLIENT ACCOUNT for the client.

15. **Exercises**
Show Cash Account and Clients' Ledger.

(1) You act for Laurence. Receive £5,000. Return to Laurence £5,000 plus interest of £30. (Send two cheques).

(2) You act for Barnaby. Receive £7,000. Pay £7,000 on Barnaby's behalf to X and send Barnaby interest of £60.

(3) You act for Sue. Receive £5,000. Return to Sue £5,000 plus interest of £30. (Send one cheque.)

(4) You act for Violet. Receive £4,500. Pay on Violet's behalf £4,400. Charge her with £120 costs plus VAT. Allow her interest on the £4,500 of £43. Transfer the costs, etc., due to OFFICE ACCOUNT and send Violet the balance. Show only Violet's account.

B. GENERAL DEPOSIT

16. At any given time, a solicitor will be holding a fair amount of clients' money. Although on an average day the solicitor may be withdrawing clients' money for one client, this will usually be balanced by a receipt on behalf of another client. Consequently, in the normal course of events throughout a year, there will always be a minimum amount held in the Clients' Bank Account, *e.g.* £50,000. Some days the balance will be higher but normally never lower.

17. In such circumstances, instead of keeping all the clients' money in the current bank account, the solicitor can keep some of it in a separate deposit bank account, *e.g.* £40,000 in a general deposit bank account and the rest (*e.g.* £10,000) in the Clients' Current Bank Account.

18. **Note:**

   (a) A daily watch will need to be kept on the current account to make sure it is never overdrawn. So long as withdrawals are matched by the receipts, this will not occur—a safety margin could be left (*e.g.* £10,000).
   (b) THE MONEY ON DEPOSIT IS NOT ALLOCATED TO ANY PARTICULAR CLIENT. This placing of money on deposit has nothing to do with any of the clients. It is purely between the solicitor and his bank.
   (c) THE INTEREST EARNED BY SUCH MONEY ON DEPOSIT BELONGS TO THE SOLICITOR, *i.e.* office money. This is allowed by section 33 of the Solicitors' Act 1974.
   (d) The deposit bank account is a Clients' Bank Account, *i.e.* in the title the word "client" must appear and it is subject to the Solicitors' Accounts Rules 1991.

19. To record when clients' money is placed on general deposit, another Deposit Cash Account is needed.

20. When clients' money is placed on general deposit, there is a bank transfer from the ordinary current account for clients' money (thus reducing the balance) to the General Deposit Account for clients' money. To record this:

CREDIT Cash Account—CLIENT ACCOUNT
DEBIT Deposit Cash Account (general deposit)—CLIENT ACCOUNT

Example

You hold £10,000 in the current Clients' Bank Account
Transfer £8,000 to a General Deposit Clients' Bank Account.

Cash							
		OFFICE ACCOUNT			CLIENT ACCOUNT		
		DR	CR	Balance	DR	CR	Balance
	Balance Deposit Cash. General Deposit				10,000	**8,000**	10,000 2,000

Deposit Cash General Deposit							
		OFFICE ACCOUNT			CLIENT ACCOUNT		
		DR	CR	Balance	DR	CR	Balance
	Cash. Transfer from Current Account				**8,000**		8,000

21. Interest

Since any interest received is office money, instructions must be given to the bank to credit such interest to the Office Bank Account and not to the General Deposit Account for clients' money. When any interest is credited by the bank to the Office Bank Account, the double-entry is:

CREDIT Deposit Interest Receivable Account
DEBIT Cash Account—OFFICE ACCOUNT

The Deposit Interest Receivable Account is a nominal account recording a miscellaneous source of income for the solicitor, and is either a Nominal or a Private Ledger Account.

Example

Bank credits £700 interest to Office Bank Account.

Deposit Interest Receivable (PL6)				
		DR	CR	Balance
	Cash		700 –	700 –

The debit entry will appear on the Cash Account—OFFICE ACCOUNT.

22. **Exercises**

(1) You hold £20,000 in Clients' Bank Account. Place £15,000 on general deposit. Bank credits £52 interest. Transfer £2,500 from deposit to current account. Bank credits £34 interest. Show all the entries.

(2) You hold £18,000 in current (clients') account. Place £14,000 on general deposit. Receive £8,300 from A (not specially designated). Return to A £8,300 plus £58 interest. Bank credits the Office Bank Account with interest of £108 in respect of money on general deposit. Show the (main) Cash Account only.

(3) (a) You receive £4,500 from Adams which you place in a specially designated account.
      (b) Your bank pays £70 into your OFFICE ACCOUNT in respect of interest on your general client deposit account.
      (c) You pay Brown £500 which you have held for him for some considerable time together with £25 interest thereon.
      (d) Repay Adams the £4,500 together with £100 interest that it has earned.

Show the clients' ledger and the (main) Cash Account.

(4) The following events occur:

May 1. You open a general Clients' Deposit Bank Account and transfer into it £30,000 from the Clients' Bank Account. (You may assume that you have sufficient clients' money).
May 2. You receive £10,000 on behalf of Simon. He is abroad, but has left instructions that it is to be placed on deposit pending his return.
May 3. You receive £20,000 on behalf of Andrew. He cannot be contacted for some time.
September 1. The bank informs you that £35 and £25 interest has been earned on the general Clients' Deposit Account and the account of Simon respectively, and credited as appropriate.
September 2. Simon returns and is sent the sum due to him.
September 3. Andrew returns home and is sent the sum standing to the credit of his account plus £15 interest (one cheque).

Show the (main) Cash Account entries. There is no need to show entries in the "Balance" columns.

Chapter 14

MISCELLANEOUS ITEMS

A. MISCELLANEOUS SUNDRY DISBURSEMENTS

1. In the course of a transaction on behalf of a client, a solicitor incurs numerous small items of expenditure such as postage stamps, telephone calls and fares. It is obviously unrealistic to keep a note of each item as it is spent in order to charge it specifically to the client. Thus, one would not keep a record of every postage stamp used in a transaction on a particular client's behalf. When it comes to charging the client for acting for him, some firms adopt the practice of making a nominal charge for these items; other firms make no charge whatsoever, regarding these items as general overhead expenses which are covered in the charge for profit costs. If, however, a solicitor does decide to make a specific charge for any of these sundry disbursements, *e.g.* fares, separate from the charge for profit costs, VAT must be added on at the standard rate. This is so, notwithstanding that, when the solicitor paid for the item concerned, no VAT was paid, *e.g.* postage stamps, fares.

2. When expenditure is incurred in respect of any of these items, the whole of the expenditure is normally debited to the relevant nominal account recording the expense.

Example
September 1. Buy a set of postage stamps at £30.
September 2. Pay the quarterly telephone bill of £860.
September 5. Pay £1 in respect of fares.

Postages and Telephones (NL40)				
Date	Details	DR	CR	Balance
Sept 1	Petty Cash. Stamps	30 –		30 –
Sept 2	Cash. Telephone bill	860 –		890 –

Fares (NL8)				
Date	Details	DR	CR	Balance
Sept 5	Petty Cash. Fares to court	1 –		1 –

3. If an item of an exceptionally high amount is paid on behalf of an individual client, then instead this may be debited to his ledger account in the normal way.

Example
Pay on behalf of A.B. Client £500 air fare to Cloud-Cuckoo Land.

A.B. Client (CL1)							
		OFFICE ACCOUNT			CLIENT ACCOUNT		
		DR	CR	Balance	DR	CR	Balance
	Cash. Air fare	500 –		500 –			

4. If the solicitor decides to make a specific charge to the client for miscellaneous sundry disbursements in addition to the profit costs charge, the simplest way to deal with this in the accounts is to add the sundry disbursement charge to the profit costs charge and enter the total figure, *i.e.*:

DEBIT the ledger account of the client—OFFICE ACCOUNT—with the total of costs plus sundry disbursements
CREDIT Costs Account and Customs & Excise Account

Example
Charge A.B. Client £100 profit costs plus £5 in respect of sundry disbursements.

A.B. Client (CL1)							
		OFFICE ACCOUNT			CLIENT ACCOUNT		
		DR	CR	Balance	DR	CR	Balance
	Costs 100 Sundries 5 VAT	105[1] 10·50		105 – 115·50			

---

[1] The credit entry appears on the Costs Account.

5. **Exercises**

Prepare clients' ledger. Your costs are quoted exclusive of VAT.

(1) You act for Simon. Pay fares £300—this is to be charged to the client. Deliver a bill (costs £400). Receive the amount due.

(2) You act for Andrew. Pay fares £3. Deliver a bill (costs £100 plus sundry disbursements—including fares—£8). Receive the amount due.

B. One Party Paying Another's Legal Costs

6. On some occasions, one party agrees to pay the legal costs of another party. In litigation matters, the court often orders the losing party to pay all or part of the winning party's costs. In such cases it is essential to distinguish between:

(a) the party whose bill is being paid; and
(b) the party who is paying the bill.

7. The VAT invoice is always addressed by the solicitor to his client, *i.e.* the person to whom he gives the legal advice—the party whose bill is being paid. Thus, if Solicitor A has a Client, B, Solicitor A would address his bill and tax invoice to Client B. This is so, even if the bill is actually being paid by another party, C.

8. Normally the party paying the bill pays the whole of the VAT.

9. The party paying the bill may, however, pay the tax-exclusive amount, but will normally do this only where the client whose costs are being paid can claim an input tax deduction in respect of the VAT, *i.e.*:

(a) the client whose costs are being paid is in business;
(b) the services were supplied to his business rather than to him personally;
(c) the business is registered for VAT;
(d) the business deals in taxable as opposed to exempt supplies.

Where the business client, whose bill is being paid, is partially exempt and partially taxable, it may be agreed that a portion of the VAT will be paid by the other party.

Example 1
You act for Laurence. His bill is £100 plus VAT.
The other side, Barnaby, is paying Laurence's bill.
Normally, Barnaby pays £110.

Example 2
You act for Violet in a business matter.
She deals only in taxable supplies.
Her bill amounts to £200 plus VAT. Jacob is paying the bill.
Jacob would pay £200, Violet the £20 VAT.

10. **Exercises**
   Prepare Clients' Ledger.

   (1) You act for James. Pay £50. Deliver a bill (costs £70 plus VAT), the total plus disbursements to be paid by Mick—not a client of yours. Receive payment from Mick.

   (2) You act for Matthew. Pay £10. Deliver a bill (costs £40 plus VAT). Paul—not a client of yours—is ordered to contribute £36 plus VAT towards Matthew's costs. Receive the amount due from both Matthew and Paul.

   (3) You act for John. Pay £30. Deliver a bill (costs £80 plus VAT). Luke, not a client, is to pay John's costs exclusive of VAT. Receive payment from John and Luke.

11. Sometimes this situation can occur where the same solicitor is acting for both parties, *e.g.* when the solicitor is acting for the purchaser of a house, the purchaser is buying the house with the aid of a mortgage, and the solicitor also acts for the mortgagee.

   (a) The first step is to charge the client whose bill is being paid with his costs in the normal way.

   Example
   Charge Laurence with £80 costs plus VAT (eventually to be paid by Barnaby).

Laurence (CL2)							
		OFFICE ACCOUNT			CLIENT ACCOUNT		
		DR	CR	Balance	DR	CR	Balance
	Costs	80 –		80 –			
	VAT	8 –		88 –			

   (b) The second step is to record that these costs are paid or to be paid by the client paying the bill.

   The double-entry is:
   CREDIT the ledger account of the client who is being paid—OFFICE ACCOUNT
   DEBIT the ledger account of the client paying the bill—OFFICE ACCOUNT

Example

Laurence (CL2)							
		OFFICE ACCOUNT			CLIENT ACCOUNT		
		DR	CR	Balance	DR	CR	Balance
	Costs	80 –					
	VAT	8 –		88			
	Barnaby		**88**	—			

Barnaby (CL3)							
		OFFICE ACCOUNT			CLIENT ACCOUNT		
		DR	CR	Balance	DR	CR	Balance
	Laurence	**88 –**		88 –			

(c) An alternative way of recording this is to transfer clients' money from Barnaby's account to Laurence's account and then make the necessary transfer from CLIENT ACCOUNT to OFFICE ACCOUNT. This, however, cannot be done unless clients' money is held on behalf of Barnaby.

Example
January 2. Receive £90 from Barnaby.
January 3. Charge £60 costs plus VAT to Laurence, payable by Barnaby.
January 4. Make the necessary transfers.

Laurence (CL2)							
Date	Details	OFFICE ACCOUNT			CLIENT ACCOUNT		
		DR	CR	Balance	DR	CR	Balance
Jan 3	Costs	60					
	VAT	6		66 –			
Jan 4	Barnaby					**66**[1]	66 –
	Cash. Transfer		66 – [2]	—	66 – [2]	—	

[1] For this entry the Transfer Sheet was used.
[2] For these entries the Cash Account was used.

Barnaby (CL3)							
Date	Details	OFFICE ACCOUNT			CLIENT ACCOUNT		
		DR	CR	Balance	DR	CR	Balance
Jan 2	Cash.					90 –	90 –
Jan 4	Laurence				**66** – [3]		24 –

[3] For this entry the transfer sheet was used.

12. **Exercises**
Prepare Clients' Ledger.

(1) You act for Philip and Bartholomew. Pay £50 on behalf of Philip. Deliver a bill to him for £70 costs plus VAT. The total due is to be paid by Bartholomew. Receive the money due from Bartholomew.

(2) You act for Thomas and Jude. Pay £10 on behalf of Thomas, £20 on behalf of Jude. Deliver a bill to Thomas for £40 costs plus VAT and to Jude for £50 costs plus VAT. Jude is to pay the total due in both cases. Receive the amount due from Jude.

C. AGENCY

13. A solicitor may have a transaction which is to be executed some distance from his own office and he may therefore instruct a local solicitor to act on his behalf. Such a transaction needs to be looked at from two points of view;

(a) that of the instructing solicitor; and
(b) that of the agent solicitor.

14. **The agent solicitor**
He treats the instructing solicitor as his client and therefore will probably have a ledger account drawn up in the name of that solicitor. Sometimes, the agent solicitor when making a charge for profit costs will allow a small commission to the instructing solicitor for introducing the business. In such a case, only the net charge for profit costs is entered into the accounts and the commission is totally omitted.

Example
You are instructed by Jones & Co of Sheffield to act on their behalf in the local county court. You charge them £10 but allow them commission of 2 per cent.

Jones & Co (CL10)							
		OFFICE ACCOUNT			CLIENT ACCOUNT		
		DR	CR	Balance	DR	CR	Balance
	Costs	9·80		9·80			
	VAT	0·98		10·78			

15. **The instructing solicitor**

(a) Where the instructing solicitor pays the agent solicitor's charges, these are entered in a nominal account called Agency Expenses Account. Thus the entries are:

DEBIT Customs & Excise Account with the VAT
DEBIT Agency Expenses Account with the balance
CREDIT Cash Account—OFFICE ACCOUNT—with the total

Example
You pay Godfrey & Co of Birmingham their charges of £10 less a commission of 2 per cent plus VAT for acting for you in the local magistrates' courts.

Agency Expenses (NL20)				
		DR	CR	Balance
	Cash Godfrey & Co	9·80		9·80

Customs & Excise (NL11)				
		DR	CR	Balance
	Cash Godfrey & Co	0·98		0·98

The two credit entries will appear on the Cash Account.

(b) When the solicitor later charges his own client with profit costs for acting for him, he will take into account the work done by the local agent and add on the local agent's fee to his own charge.
(c) Under Rule 10 of the Solicitors' Practice Rules 1990, a solicitor must account to a client for any commission received of more than £20. Thus, if the commission is £20 or less, the solicitor can normally retain it. If it is more than £20, the solicitor must disclose the amount of the commission to the client and obtain the client's consent before the solicitor can retain it.

Example

At the end of the transaction, you decide to charge £30 profit costs in respect of your own work. The total charge of profit costs would therefore be £40 (being £30 in respect of your work and £10 in respect of your agent's work). Note that the full charge of £10 will be made to the client; the 2 per cent commission can be retained by you.

A.B. Client (CL1)							
		OFFICE ACCOUNT			CLIENT ACCOUNT		
		DR	CR	Balance	DR	CR	Balance
	Costs	40		40 −			
	VAT	4		44 −			

(d) Sometimes the agent solicitor incurs a disbursement on behalf of the instructing solicitor and therefore obtains reimbursement for such disbursement together with payment of his fees. When the instructing solicitor pays the agent solicitor, the instructing solicitor should ensure that the account of his client is debited with the disbursements. The simplest set of double-entries to record this is:

DEBIT Customs & Excise Account with the VAT
DEBIT Agency Expenses Account with the agent solicitor's profit costs
DEBIT the ledger account of the client with the disbursements
CREDIT Cash Account—OFFICE ACCOUNT—with the total payment

Example

You pay Godfrey & Co £13.78 (profit costs £10 less a commission of 2 per cent plus VAT and a disbursement of £3).

A.B. Client (CL1)							
		OFFICE ACCOUNT			CLIENT ACCOUNT		
		DR	CR	Balance	DR	CR	Balance
	Cash. Godfrey & Co Disbursement	3 −		3 −			

Agency Expenses (NL20)				
		DR	CR	Balance
	Cash. Godfrey & Co	9·80		9·80

Customs & Excise (NL11)		DR	CR	Balance
	Cash. Godfrey & Co	0·98		0·98

Cash		OFFICE ACCOUNT			CLIENT ACCOUNT		
		DR	CR	Balance	DR	CR	Balance
	A.B. Client. Disbursement. Agency Expenses. Godfrey & Co VAT		3 9·80 0·98				

16. **Exercises**

Prepare Clients' Ledger.

(1) You act as agent for Peter & Co Solicitors. Charge them £20 costs less commission of 5 per cent plus VAT. Receive the amount due.

(2) You act as agent for Benjamin & Co Solicitors. Pay court fee £6. Deliver bill (costs £30 less commission of 5 per cent). Receive the amount due.

(3) You act for Jeremy. Pay court fee £10. Pay counsel £30 plus VAT—use the Agency Method. Pay local agents, McGregor & Co their fee of £20 less commission of 5 per cent plus VAT. Deliver a bill (costs—your work £40, agents' work £20, total £60). Receive the amount due.

(4) You act for Jackson. Pay counsel £50—use the Principal Method. Pay local agents, McGregor & Co, their fee of £30 less 5 per cent commission plus VAT plus £6 court fee paid by them. Deliver a bill in which costs in respect of work done by you (*i.e.* exclusive of the local agents' work) are shown at £50 plus VAT. Receive the amount due. Show both Clients' Ledger and Agency Expenses Account.

(5) You act for Tom. Pay court fee £7. Pay local agents, McGregor & Co, their fee of £18 less 5 per cent commission plus VAT, together with a witness fee of £9 (no VAT) paid by them. Deliver a bill—total costs £40 plus VAT. Receive the amount due. Show both Clients' Ledger and Agency Expenses Account.

(6) You are acting for Thomasina in the collection of a debt from Pickles. You instruct Bland & Co, another firm of solicitors, to act as your agent. The following events occur:

January 2. Thomasina sends £75 generally on account of costs and disbursements.

January 4. Pickles sends a cheque for £900 to you.

January 5. Bland & Co pay counsel's fees of £16.50 (inclusive of VAT): requesting a receipted fee note in favour of you.

January 8. Bland & Co send a bill showing a profit costs figure of £50 (excluding VAT) after allowing £5 commission.

January 9. Pay Bland & Co's bill, on receipt that day, the cheque reaching them on January 11.

January 10. Deliver a bill to Thomasina having calculated the profit costs for your own work at £40, and account to Thomasina for the sum due, transferring costs and disbursements to Office Bank Account.

Show:

(a) the entries in your ledgers;

(b) the entries in the Clients' Ledger of Bland & Co.

D. INSURANCE COMMISSIONS

17. From time to time, a solicitor may introduce a client to an insurance company and thus bring business to the company. In such a case, the insurance company will pay the solicitor a commission for the introduction of the business. In order to record the earnings of such commissions, a new account or card is opened in the Nominal Ledger (or Private Ledger) called the *Insurance Commission Receivable Account*. This is a nominal account recording miscellaneous income.

18. If the only financial transaction is the receipt of the commission from the insurance company then the double-entry is:

CREDIT Insurance Commission Receivable Account[1]
DEBIT Cash Account—OFFICE ACCOUNT.

Example
You receive £18 commission from the Short Life Insurance Company.

Insurance Commission Receivable (PL7)				
		DR	CR	Balance
	Cash		18 –	18 –

---

[1] At the time of writing, insurance commission is EXEMPT VAT.

		Cash					
		OFFICE ACCOUNT			CLIENT ACCOUNT		
		DR	CR	Balance	DR	CR	Balance
	Insurance Commission	18					

19. Sometimes the solicitor receives instructions from the insurance company to collect the first premium on the insurance policy from the client who requested the insurance, to deduct the commission from such premium and to send only the balance to the insurance company. This may happen in a conveyancing transaction where the solicitor is acting for a purchaser of a house. In such a case, the following are the steps which should occur:

(a) the premium is collected from the client purchaser, *i.e.*:

CREDIT ledger account of the client—CLIENT ACCOUNT
DEBIT Cash Account—CLIENT ACCOUNT

(b) make a transfer of the premium from the client taking out the insurance to a ledger account in the clients' ledger for the insurance company, *i.e.*:

DEBIT ledger account of the client taking out the insurance—CLIENT ACCOUNT
CREDIT the ledger account of the insurance company—CLIENT ACCOUNT
Under Rule 2 (SAR), the insurance company is a "client" because the solicitor is now holding clients' money on behalf of the company.

(c) charge the insurance company with the commission, *i.e.*:

DEBIT the ledger account of the insurance company—OFFICE ACCOUNT
CREDIT the Insurance Commission Receivable Account

(d) make a bank transfer of the amount due from CLIENT ACCOUNT to OFFICE ACCOUNT;

(e) send the balance of clients' money due to the insurance company.

Example

July 1. Receive £10,000 from A.B. Client in respect of purchase of a house which sum includes a premium of £20 due to the Short Life Insurance Co.

July 2. Transfer the premium of £20 from A.B. Client's ledger account to the ledger account of the insurance company.

July 3. Charge the insurance company £3 commission (exempt VAT).

July 4. Transfer to OFFICE ACCOUNT the £3 due.

July 5. Send balance due to insurance company.

A.B. Client (CL1)							
Date	Details	OFFICE ACCOUNT			CLIENT ACCOUNT		
		DR	CR	Balance	DR	CR	Balance
Jul 1	Cash.					10,000 –	10,000 –
Jul 2	Short Life Insurance. Transfer. Premium				**20 –**		9,980 –

Short Life Insurance Co (CL6)							
Date	Details	OFFICE ACCOUNT			CLIENT ACCOUNT		
		DR	CR	Balance	DR	CR	Balance
Jul 2	A.B. Client. Transfer Premium					**20 –**	20 –
Jul 3	Commission	3 –		3 –			
Jul 4	Cash. Transfer		3	—	3		17
Jul 5	Cash				17 –		—

Insurance Commission Receivable Account (PL7)				
Date	Details	DR	CR	Balance
Jul 3	Short Life.		3 –	

Cash							
Date	Details	OFFICE ACCOUNT			CLIENT ACCOUNT		
		DR	CR	Balance	DR	CR	Balance
Jul 1	A.B. Client				10,000		
Jul 4	Short Life Transfer	3				3	
Jul 5	Short Life					17	

20. Note, again, the effect of Rule 10 of the Solicitors' Practice Rules 1990 (see *ante*, page 121). If the commission received by the solicitor is more than £20, the solicitor may have to account to the client for it. If this is so, when the commission is received from the insurance company it is clients' money.

Example
While acting for Paul, you arrange an insurance for him with the Theta Insurance Co. You receive a commission of £300 from the Theta Insurance Co and decide to account to Paul for it. This is a receipt of clients' money on behalf of Paul, *i.e.*:

CREDIT ledger account of Paul—CLIENT ACCOUNT
DEBIT Cash Account—CLIENT ACCOUNT

21. **Exercises**
Show Clients' Ledger.

(1) Receive £34 insurance premium in respect of the Gamma Insurance Co. Charge £5 commission. Send balance to the company.

(2) Receive £41 from Delta, a client. You then receive instructions that this sum is to be held in respect of a premium due to the Zeta Insurance Co. Send the money to the Insurance Company less commission of £16. Do not show Delta's account.

(3) You act for the Sigma Insurance Co. Charge them £7 commission in respect of an insurance. Receive a premium of £28 to hold on behalf of the company. Charge a commission of £5 in respect of this amount. Send the balance due to the company and transfer the amount due to OFFICE ACCOUNT from CLIENT ACCOUNT.

(4) Harry, Peter and Tom, are solicitors, and they deal with the following events:

January 2. Brown (not a client) pays cash (£104) to the firm, who act as agents for the Nonpay Insurance Co Ltd. Commission currently due to the firm on that agency amounts to £43.
January 7. The firm acts for Black in respect of the sale of Black's house and also acts for the mortgagees of Black, the Savall Building Society. A bill of costs is rendered to the building society for acting for it on the redemption; these costs are £20 plus VAT and are to be borne by Black.
January 10. Cheque received drawn in favour of White, for £1,250 (which is endorsed over to the firm). Bill of costs is sent to White in respect of debt collection, showing fee of £40 plus VAT.
January 14. The firm acts for Yellow in a court action, having already paid the counsel's fee of £100 plus VAT (the Principal Method was used). The firm had appointed local agents, and their bill showed profit costs of £120 less agency commission £20 plus VAT and an agency disbursement which consisted of a court fee of £12. A bill of costs is sent to Yellow in which costs in respect of work done by Harry, Peter and Tom (*i.e.* exclusive of the agents' work) are shown at £100 plus VAT.
January 17. The net amount due to Nonpay Insurance Co Ltd is paid, being the gross premium received (£104) less commission of £15 and prior

commission due (£43). Transfer the requisite amount from CLIENT ACCOUNT to OFFICE ACCOUNT.

January 18. Received amount due from Yellow, and paid the amount due to the local agents who acted in his court action. Transfer the requisite amount from CLIENT ACCOUNT to OFFICE ACCOUNT.

Write up the Clients' Ledger Accounts, together with the Cash Account, showing all relevant entries. All accounts are to be balanced, except the Cash Account.

(Solicitors' Final Examination, Summer 1980)

Chapter 15

CONVEYANCING

A. DEPOSITS

1. It is common practice for a purchaser to pay 10 per cent of the purchase price on or before the exchange of contracts, as a deposit. Sometimes this deposit is paid to the estate agents who negotiated the sale but often it is paid to one of the solicitors. This will usually be the solicitor acting for the vendor who will have to record the receipt. The entries he makes depend on whether he holds the deposit:

  (a) as agent for the vendor;
  (b) as stakeholder.

2. **Agent for the vendor**
   In this case the money belongs to the vendor immediately and so the entries are:

CREDIT the ledger account of the vendor—CLIENT ACCOUNT
DEBIT Cash Account—CLIENT ACCOUNT

Example
You act for A.B. Client who is selling his house. On exchange of contracts receive £2,000 as agent for the vendor.

A.B. Client (CL1)							
		OFFICE ACCOUNT			CLIENT ACCOUNT		
		DR	CR	Balance	DR	CR	Balance
	Cash. Deposit					2,000 –	2,000 –

3. **Stakeholder**
   When the deposit is received as stakeholder, the money is temporarily neither that of the vendor nor that of the purchaser until the relevant matter is completed when it immediately belongs to the vendor. To record this an account is opened in the Clients' Ledger called "Stakeholder Account."
   On the receipt of the stake, the relevant entries are:

CREDIT Stakeholder Account—CLIENT ACCOUNT
DEBIT Cash Account—CLIENT ACCOUNT

On completion of the transaction a Ledger Transfer must be made from the Stakeholder Account to the account of the vendor, *i.e.*:

DEBIT Stakeholder Account—CLIENT ACCOUNT
CREDIT the ledger account of the vendor—CLIENT ACCOUNT

Example
You act for A.B. Client who is selling his house.
   May 1. Receive deposit of £2,000 to hold as stakeholder.
   June 1. Completion takes place.

Stakeholder (CL11)							
Date	Details	OFFICE ACCOUNT			CLIENT ACCOUNT		
		DR	CR	Balance	DR	CR	Balance
May 1	Cash. Deposit Re A.B. Client					2,000 –	2,000 –
Jun 1	A.B. Client. Transfer				**2,000[1] –**		

A.B. Client (CL1)							
Date	Details	OFFICE ACCOUNT			CLIENT ACCOUNT		
		DR	CR	Balance	DR	CR	Balance
Jun 1	Stakeholder. Transfer					**2,000[1]**	2,000 –

[1] Note: The Transfer Sheet is used for these two entries.

Interest on any money held by a solicitor in his or her capacity as a stakeholder must be paid to the person to whom the stake is eventually paid, *e.g.* the vendor, in accordance with the Solicitors Accounts Rules 1991 Part III.

B. MORTGAGES

4. When a client is buying a house with the aid of a mortgage, sometimes the same solicitor will act for both the client purchaser and the mortgagee, and sometimes there will be a different solicitor acting for the mortgagee.

5. If the solicitors acting for the purchaser are not also acting for the mortgagee, they will not receive the mortgage advance until they actually arrive at completion. Therefore, they will need to consider how to deal with the payment of the completion moneys to the vendor. The simplest solution to adopt is to provide that the mortgagee's solicitors make their draft for the mortgage advance payable

direct to the vendor's solicitors. In this case, all the purchaser's solicitors have to do is to draw a draft for the balance of the purchase price, also made payable to the vendor's solicitors.

Example
Your client is buying a house for £20,000 with the aid of a mortgage of £15,000. On the completion, the mortgagee's solicitors will be bringing a draft for £15,000 which can be made payable to the vendor's solicitors. All you need to do is to bring a draft for the balance of £5,000.

6. If the mortgagee's solicitors make their draft payable to the purchaser's solicitors, then this could be indorsed over to the vendor's solicitors. The one thing that the purchaser's solicitors will not be able to do is to draw a draft for all the completion moneys on CLIENT ACCOUNT, because their client will only have provided the balance of the purchase price after allowing for the mortgage advance, and thus the solicitors will be holding insufficient clients' money for that particular client.

7. On completion, the deeds, etc., will all be handed over to the mortgagee's solicitors. If, therefore, the conveyance requires stamping and/or the documents require registration at the Land Registry, these matters will now have to be attended to by the mortgagee's solicitors on behalf of the purchaser. The stamp duty and the land registry fees are payable, however, by the purchaser. In such a case, the relevant amounts could either be deducted from the mortgage advance and only the net amount handed over by the mortgagee's solicitors or, alternatively, the purchaser's solicitors could hand the mortgagee's solicitors cheques in respect of these items, using clients' money if sufficient funds are available.

8. It is customary for it to be agreed that the purchaser will pay the legal costs of the mortgagee. In such a case it is common for the mortgagee's solicitors to deduct this sum from the mortgage advance.

9. Where one solicitor acts for both the purchaser and mortgagee:

(a) if the solicitor who acts for the purchaser receives the mortgage advance from the mortgagee before completion takes place, then that solicitor is also acting for the mortgagee. This is as a result of Rule 2 SAR; the solicitor is now holding clients' money on behalf of the mortgagee;

(b) the solicitor must have a separate account in his Clients' Ledger for the mortgagee and credit the mortgage advance to that ledger account. The money does not yet belong to the purchaser and so must not yet be credited to the ledger account of the purchaser. The mortgage advance only belongs to the purchaser as from the day of completion. On that day, therefore, the solicitor can make a transfer of the mortgage advance from the account of the mortgagee to the account of the purchaser;

(c) under Rule 11(3), where a solicitor acts for both borrower and lender in a conveyancing transaction and receives from the lender a mortgage advance, the solicitor is not obliged to open a separate ledger account for both borrower and lender in respect of such advance provided that:

(i) the funds belonging to each client are clearly identifiable; and

(ii) the lender is an institutional lender which provides mortgages in the normal course of its activites.

This rule only applies to a mortgage advance (not a mortgage redemption). It is optional, not compulsory. A difficulty with this rule is that it conflicts with one of the basic concepts of the Rules: namely, that each client's ledger should show clearly on whose behalf clients' money is held. For this reason, and because it is optional, all the exercises and examples in this book will be done the traditional way and Rule 11(3) will not be used. In order to understand the subject, you will probably find it easier, in the end, to ignore Rule 11(3) for the time being.

Example

Completion moneys due to vendor: £20,000 (paid on January 15).
Mortgage advance: £15,000 (received on January 14).
A.B. Client to provide: £5,000 (received on January 11).

A.B. Client (CL1)							
Date	Details	OFFICE ACCOUNT			CLIENT ACCOUNT		
		DR	CR	Balance	DR	CR	Balance
Jan 11	Cash					5,000 –	5,000 –
Jan 15	Building Society. Transfer					15,000 –[1]	20,000 –
	Cash. completion				20,000 –	.	—

Building Society (CL7)							
Date	Details	OFFICE ACCOUNT			CLIENT ACCOUNT		
		DR	CR	Balance	DR	CR	Balance
Jan 14	Cash					15,000 –	15,000 –
Jan 15	A.B. Client. Transfer				15,000 –[1]	—	

(d) alternatively, on completion no transfer is made and entries are merely:

DEBIT ledger account of mortgagee—CLIENT ACCOUNT—with mortgage advance
DEBIT ledger account of purchaser—CLIENT ACCOUNT—with the balance
CREDIT Cash Account—CLIENT ACCOUNT—with total payment

---

[1] Note: the Transfer Sheet is used for these two entries.

A.B. Client (CL1)							
Date	Details	OFFICE ACCOUNT			CLIENT ACCOUNT		
		DR	CR	Balance	DR	CR	Balance
Jan 11	Cash					5,000 –	5,000 –
Jan 15	Cash. Completion				5,000 –		—

Building Society (CL7)							
Date	Details	OFFICE ACCOUNT			CLIENT ACCOUNT		
		DR	CR	Balance	DR	CR	Balance
Jan 14	Cash					15,000	15,000
Jan 15	Cash. Completion				15,000		—

Cash							
Date	Details	OFFICE ACCOUNT			CLIENT ACCOUNT		
		DR	CR	Balance	DR	CR	Balance
Jan 11	A.B. Client				5,000		
Jan 14	Building Society				15,000		
Jan 15	A.B. Client Completion.					5,000	
	Building Society. Completion					15,000	

(e) **Costs**

The solicitor is basically acting for two clients in three transactions:
  (i) for the purchaser in the purchase of the house;
  (ii) for the purchaser in the grant of a mortgage;
  (iii) for the mortgagee in the receipt of the mortgage.
In theory, therefore, the solicitor is entitled to make three charges for profit costs, one for each item. In practice, however, where the same solicitor acts for both purchaser and mortgagee it is customary not to charge twice for the mortgage transactions. Thus the solicitor could either:
  (i) charge the purchaser for acting for the purchaser in connection with the purchase and the mortgage, *i.e.* solicitor waives the charge for acting for the mortgagee[1]; or
  (ii) charge the purchaser for acting on the purchase, and charge the mortgagee for acting in connection with the mortgage, *i.e.* solicitor waives the charge for acting for the purchaser on the mortgage.

[1] This procedure is questionable. It is arguable that the solicitor did the work for the mortgagee and would probably have difficulty in justifying the charge to the purchaser if challenged.

If the solicitor elects to charge the purchaser with the mortgage costs, he must:

DEBIT the ledger account of the *purchaser*—OFFICE ACCOUNT—with the total profit costs (purchase plus mortgage)

If the solicitor elects to charge the mortgagee with such costs, he must:

DEBIT the ledger account of the *purchaser*—OFFICE ACCOUNT—with the purchase costs, and
DEBIT the ledger account of the *mortgagee*—OFFICE ACCOUNT—with the mortgage costs

Note that this is still so, even if the purchaser is to pay the mortgage costs.[2]

C. CLIENT BUYING AND SELLING HOUSES SIMULTANEOUSLY

10. Frequently it happens that a client is buying a house and simultaneously selling another house, in which case the solicitor will attempt to arrange completion to take place on the same day. In such a case, it is advisable to provide for the sale to take place before the purchase so that the proceeds of sale can be used for the purchase. If the solicitor decides to complete the purchase first, he may be unable to use clients' money for the purchase because he holds insufficient clients' money on behalf of his client.

Example
You act for A.B. Client who is selling one house for £20,000 and buying a second house for £25,000. You receive £5,000 from the client two days before completion. If the sale is completed first, the £20,000 proceeds of sale together with the £5,000 previously received from the client are available in CLIENT ACCOUNT for the use on the purchase. If, however, the purchase is completed first, since only £5,000 clients' money is held on behalf of the client, at least £20,000 will have to be drawn from OFFICE ACCOUNT.

	£
(a) Completion of sale first:	
1. Received from A.B. Client	5,000
2. Proceeds of sale	20,000
3. Available for purchase	25,000
(b) Completion of purchase first:	£
1. Received from A.B. Client	5,000
2. Borrowed from OFFICE ACCOUNT	20,000
3. Available for purchase	25,000
4. Proceeds of sale used to repay OFFICE ACCOUNT	20,000

---

[2] For entries see *ante*, p. 122.

D. STATEMENTS

11. At some time in most transactions, and in particular in conveyancing, the solicitor will have to account to the client for all moneys paid and received during the transaction and either ask the client to send the balance due to the solicitor or send the balance due to the client.

12. It is usual to send the statement to the client at the same time as sending the bill of costs. In conveyancing, when acting for a client who is buying a house, the statement is usually sent to the client just before completion so that the solicitor can collect from the client the necessary amount due in order to finish off the whole transaction. If the only transaction is the sale of the client's house, then the usual time to send the statement (and the bill) is after completion has taken place, when the solicitor is sending the balance due to the client.

13. The statement can be in any form; it is important to realise that it does not have to be laid out in any particular way. The relevant criteria are:

   (a) In the statement the solicitor must account for all moneys received and paid on behalf of the client; nothing must be left out.
   (b) The statement must conclude with the correct amount due to the client or the correct amount due to the solicitor.
   (c) The statement must be laid out neatly and should be relatively easy to follow.

14. A simple system would be to send a statement divided into two sides.

   (a) On one side (*e.g.* the left-hand side), list all the items charged to the client in chronological order, *e.g.*
      (i) payments made on behalf of the client;
      (ii) payments to be made on behalf of the client;
      (iii) profit costs charged to the client.
   (b) On the other side (*e.g.* the right-hand side), list in chronological order all receipts whether from the client direct or from third persons on the client's behalf.
   (c) The difference between the two sides will be the balance due either from the client or to the client.

Example
You act for Paul who is buying a house for £50,000. He is borrowing £30,000 from a building society, the loan being secured by a mortgage. You also receive instructions to act for the building society.

February 1. Pay search £10.
March 11. Receive a cheque from Paul for the deposit of 10 per cent.
March 14. Send your own cheque to the vendor's solicitors for £5,000. You receive a completion statement from the vendor's solicitors showing the purchase price less the deposit, *i.e.* a balance due on completion of £45,000.
April 1. Send Paul a bill in which your costs are shown at £200 plus VAT; you also charge him £40 for land registry fees. You also prepare a bill in respect of your charges for acting for the building society; these costs are £50 plus VAT and are to be paid by Paul. You expect to receive the mortgage advance of £30,000 from the building society on April 13. Completion is due to take place on April 14.

Prepare a statement for sending to Paul on April 1.

Paul: Purchase of . . .

Feb. 1	Local Search	10	Mar. 11	Deposit	5,000
Mar. 14	Deposit	5,000	Apr. 13	Mortgage advance	30,000
Apr. 1	Costs	200		BALANCE DUE	15,325
	VAT	20			
	L.R. fees	40			
	Mortgage costs	55			
Apr. 14	Completion	45,000			
		50,325			50,325

15. If you are acting for a client who is purchasing one house and selling another, it would be more helpful to the client if the figures in respect of the sale and purchase were shown separately.

Example (continued)
You are selling Paul's existing house for £34,000 and on completion you have to redeem a mortgage on it for £20,000.

March 11. Receive the deposit of £3,400 to hold as stakeholder.
April 1. Send Paul a bill (costs £60 plus VAT). Your charges for acting for the building society are £10 plus VAT, which costs are to be paid by Paul.

Paul: Sale of . . . and Purchase of . . .

PURCHASE of . . .

	£		£
Search	10	On account	5,000
Deposit	5,000	Mortgage advance	30,000
Costs	200		
VAT	20		35,000
L.R. fees	40	Balance	15,325
Mortgage costs	55		
Completion	45,000		
	50,325		50,325

SALE of . . .

Costs	60	Deposit	3,400
VAT	6	Completion	30,600
Mortgage redemption	20,000		
Mortgage costs	11		
	20,077		
Balance	13,923		
	34,000		34,000

SUMMARY

Purchase	15,325	Sale	13,923
		BALANCE DUE	1,402
	15,325		15,325

16. It must be emphasised that there is no single method of presentation which has to be used. The method used in paragraph 15, above, adopts an account form. It would be equally acceptable to use a vertical form of presentation.

Example (continued)

Paul: Sale of . . . Purchase of . . .

PURCHASE of . . .

	£	£	£
Payments			
Search	10		
Deposit	5,000		
Completion	45,000		
Costs	200		
VAT	20		
L.R. fees	40		
Mortgage costs	55		
		50,325	
Receipts			
On account	5,000		
Mortgage advance	30,000		
		35,000	
			15,325
SALE of . . .			
Receipts			
Deposit	3,400		
Completion	30,600		
		34,000	
Payments			
Costs	60		
VAT	6		
Mortgage redemption	20,000		
Mortgage costs	11		
		20,077	
			13,923
BALANCE DUE			1,402

17. **Exercises**

(1) You act for Oliver who is selling Whiteacre for £60,000. It is at present subject to a mortgage of £20,000 which is to be discharged on completion. On June 1, you receive the 10 per cent deposit from the purchaser's solicitors to hold as stakeholder. On June 10, you receive instructions to act for the mortgagee, Pat, in the discharge of the mortgage, Pat's costs to be paid by Oliver. On July 1, you complete the sale and the discharge of the mortgage, the purchaser's solicitors handing over to you a draft for the balance of the purchase price; there are no apportionments. On July 4, you send Oliver a bill together with the balance due in his favour and also send Pat the amount due to her. Your bill to Oliver comprises the following item: costs for acting for Oliver in relation to the sale of the house £140 plus VAT. You also charge Pat £30 plus VAT for acting for her. Prepare the statement to be sent to Oliver.

(2) You receive instructions to act for Robert who is buying a house for £70,000. He is borrowing £30,000 from a building society, the loan being secured by a mortgage. You are not acting for the building society. On February 2, you make a search for £15. On March 3, you receive the 10 per cent deposit from Edward and you send your own cheque to the vendor's solicitors for this amount on March 4, when contracts are exchanged. You then receive a completion statement from the vendor's solicitors showing that £63,000 is due on completion. The mortgagee's solicitors tell you that their costs, payable by Robert, amount to £66 including VAT but that they will deduct this from the mortgage advance. On April 1, you send Oliver a bill in which your costs are shown at £340 (purchase £300, mortgage £40) plus VAT. After completion you will be paying Land Registry fees of £80. Prepare a statement for sending to Robert before completion.

(3) You receive instructions to act for Sarah who is selling Greenacre for £80,000 and buying Blueacre for £110,000. There is at present a mortgage of £9,000 on Greenacre in favour of Tom which will have to be discharged on completion and Sarah is borrowing £20,000 from Tom to be secured by a mortgage on Blueacre. September 1. Pay search fees £10. October 2. Receive a cheque from Sarah for £11,000. October 6. Exchange contracts. Send your cheque for £11,000 to the solicitors for the vendor of Blueacre and receive a cheque from the solicitors for the purchaser of Greenacre for £8,000 in respect of the deposit which you are to hold as stakeholder. You receive a note from the solicitors acting for the vendor of Blueacre that the amount due on completion is £99,000. You receive a note from Tom to send him £9,230 after completion of the sale of Greenacre in order to redeem the mortgage thereon. October 31. Pay £8 search fees. You send Sarah a bill together with a statement. You are charging her £450 for acting on the purchase and £350 for acting on the sale plus VAT. You are also going to have to pay stamp duty of £550 after completion. Your charges for acting for Tom in respect of the mortgage on Blueacre are £99 and these costs are to be paid by Sarah.

Prepare the statement to be sent to Sarah before completion.

E. Exercises on Conveyancing

18. Prepare entries in the Clients' Ledger (ignore interest unless the question specifically states to the contrary):

 (1) You act for Albert who is selling Blackacre for £20,000.

    January 2. Receive £2,000 deposit on exchange of contracts to be held as vendor's agent.
    February 1. Receive balance of sale price £18,000.
    February 2. Send Albert a bill for £300 costs plus VAT, transfer the amount due to OFFICE ACCOUNT and send the balance due to Albert.

 (2) You act for Brian who is buying a house for £10,000.

    September 1. Pay £1.85 search fees by cheque.
    October 1. Brian sends a cheque for the 10 per cent deposit direct to the estate agents to hold as stakeholders.
    October 14. Pay £1.50 out of petty cash search.
    October 15. Send Brian a bill including a charge for £200 costs plus VAT.
    October 29. Receive from Brian £9,223.35, being the balance of the purchase price plus payment of your bill.
    November 1. Complete the purchase.

 (3) You act for Charles who is buying a house for £18,000.

    May 1. Pay search £1.85 petty cash.
    May 16. Receive a cheque from Charles for the deposit of 10 per cent and send your own cheque to the vendor's solicitors for this amount.
    June 9. You send a bill to Charles comprising costs of £135.00 and land registry fees of £40.00.
    June 19. You receive Charles' cheque for the amount due to complete the matter (*i.e.* the balance of the purchase price plus payment of your bill).
    June 24. Complete the purchase.
    June 25. Pay the land registry fees.

    Your fees are quoted exclusive of VAT.

 (4) You act for William on the purchase of a house. The following events take place.

    January 13. Paid search fees £4.
    January 19. Received from William the deposit of £3,000.
    January 22. Paid survey fee £165 (including VAT £15). The invoice is addressed to William.
    January 27. Exchanged contracts and paid deposit to vendor's solicitors as stakeholders.
    February 9. Completion statement received from vendor's solicitors showing £27,000 due.
    February 12. Paid search £2.

February 13. Sent financial statement to William showing balance of money which will be due from him on completion of the purchase, together with bill of costs (profit costs £220 inclusive of VAT £20).

February 15. William sends cheque for the full amount due.

February 17. Purchase completed.

February 20. Paid stamp duty £72.

(5) You receive instructions to act for Edward who is buying a house for £10,000. He is borrowing £8,000 from a building society, the loan being secured by a mortgage. On January 2, make a search for £6 petty cash. On January 3, Edward pays the 10 per cent deposit direct to the estate agents. On January 10, you make a further search for £4 petty cash. You then receive a completion statement from the vendor's solicitors showing that £9,000 is due on completion. The mortgagee's solicitors tell you that their costs, payable by Edward, amount to £55.00 but that they will deduct this from the mortgage advance. On January 20, you send Edward the bill in which costs are shown at £150 (purchase £140, mortgage £10) plus VAT. You ask him to send you a cheque for the amount due in order to complete the whole of the transaction and this is received on January 30. You complete on February 10, when the mortgagee's solicitors hand over a draft for the net mortgage advance direct to the vendor's solicitors. You hand over a draft to the vendor's solicitors for the balance of the purchase price. Prepare Edward's Ledger Account.

(6) You act for the Fishy Building Society who are lending £8,000 to Edward in order to enable Edward to buy a house. You do not act for Edward. Your costs, payable by Edward, amount to £50 plus VAT and this will be deducted from the mortgage advance. On February 9, you receive the gross mortgage advance from the building society. On February 10, you complete the mortgage and hand over the net advance. Prepare the ledger account of your client.

(7) You receive instructions to act for George who is buying a house for £25,000. He is borrowing £15,000 from the Grim Building Society, the loan being secured by a mortgage. You also receive instructions to act for the building society. On April 1, you make a search for £7 by cheque. George sends a cheque for the deposit of £2,000 direct to the estate agents. You then receive a completion statement from the vendor's solicitors showing that £23,000 is due on completion. On May 8, you send George a bill in which costs are shown at £400 for the purchase plus VAT (no charge is being made for acting for George in connection with the grant of the mortgage). You also prepare a bill in respect of your charges for acting for the Grim Building Society and your costs are £70 plus VAT; these costs are to be paid by George. You ask George to send you a cheque for the amount due in order to be able to finish off the matter and this is received on May 17. On May 18, you receive the mortgage advance from the Building Society. You complete the transaction on May 19.

(8) You act for Henry who is buying a house for £50,000 with the aid of a mortgage of £10,000 from the Ink Building Society for whom you also act.

June 1. Make a search for Henry £3 petty cash.

June 20. A cheque is received from Henry for the 10 per cent deposit which is indorsed over to the vendor's solicitors.

June 30. Make a search for £4 petty cash on behalf of Henry.

July 1. Send Henry a bill charging him £200 for acting on the purchase; you also charge him £100 for stamp duty and £20 for land registry fees. Add VAT where appropriate. You are charging the building society £30 plus VAT for acting in connection with the mortgage, such costs to be paid by Henry.

July 15. Receive the amounts due from Henry and the building society in order to be able to complete the matter.

July 16. Complete the purchase.

July 17. Pay stamp duty.

July 18. Pay land registry fees.

(9) You act for John who is selling his house for £10,000. It is at present subject to a mortgage of £5,000 which is to be discharged on completion. On May 1, you receive the 10 per cent deposit from the purchaser's solicitors to hold as stakeholder. On May 10, you receive instructions to act for the mortgagee, Kate, in the discharge of the mortgage, Kate's costs to be paid by John. On June 1, complete the sale and the discharge of the mortgage, the purchaser's solicitors handing over to you a draft for £9,000. On June 2, you send John a bill, together with the balance due in his favour, and also send Kate the amount due to her. Your bill comprises the following item: costs for acting for John in relation to the sale of the house £50. You also charge Kate £20 for acting for her. Your costs are quoted exclusive of VAT. Prepare the entries in your Clients' Ledger.

[*Time limit for Questions 10–13: 1 hour each*]

(10) You act for Mary in the purchase of "Piccadilly Circus" for £20,000 and the sale of "Buckingham Palace" for £15,000.

January 2. Make searches for £4 by cheque.

February 2. Pay the estate agents £2,000 deposit on the purchase of "Piccadilly Circus". The purchaser of "Buckingham Palace" sends a cheque for a deposit of £1,500 to Noddy & Co, the estate agents who negotiated the sale thereof.

February 15. Receive £5,500 on account from Mary.

March 1. You complete the sale of "Buckingham Palace" and then complete the purchase of "Piccadilly Circus"—there are no apportionments.

March 2. Pay stamp duty of £180 and land registry fees of £70.

March 3. Receive a cheque from Noddy & Co for £1,100, being the deposit on the sale of "Buckingham Palace" less their commission.

March 8. Send Mary a bill, which includes an item of £150 for profit costs plus VAT, transfer the amount due to OFFICE ACCOUNT, and send Mary the balance due, if any.

Show the entries in your Clients' Ledger.

(11)   You are instructed to act for Mrs Dick who is selling "The Habendum" for £40,000 and buying "The Testatum" for £58,000. There is at present a

mortgage of £3,000 on "The Habendum" in favour of the Gibson Building Society which will have to be discharged on completion. In order to finance the purchase of "The Testatum" Mrs Dick is borrowing £15,000 from the Tyler Building Society.

The deposit in respect of the sale is paid direct by the purchaser to the estate agents who negotiated the sale and Mrs Dick pays the deposit in respect of "The Testatum" direct to the estate agents. You calculate that the amount due from the purchasers of "The Habendum" on completion is to be £36,000. You receive a note from the solicitors acting for the vendor of "The Testatum" that the amount due on completion is £52,200. You receive a note from the Gibson Building Society to send them exactly £3,000 after completion of the sale of "The Habendum" in order to redeem the mortgage thereon. You receive a note from the Tyler Building Society that their legal costs will amount to £115 which will be deducted from the mortgage advance and in addition you are instructed that the land registry fees payable are also to be deducted from the mortgage advance.

On March 1 you make a search and pay £10 out of petty cash.

On May 1 Mrs Dick pays £5,000 on account. You inform the Tyler Building Society that the land registry fees payable and deductible from the mortgage advance are £440. On May 5 you complete the purchase and the sale. You also send the amount due to the Gibson Building Society.

On May 8 you send Mrs Dick a bill of costs together with a statement. You are charging her £400 for acting on the purchase and £200 for acting on the sale plus VAT. The costs for acting in the mortgage redemption charged to the Gibson Building Society, but payable by Mrs Dick, are £20 plus VAT.

Transfer the amount due to OFFICE ACCOUNT.

Prepare the entries in your Clients' Ledger and the statement sent on May 8 to Mrs Dick.

(12) George & Co, acted for Hotspur (for whom they had not previously acted) on the sale of "Blackwater" and the purchase of "Greenmead." Below is a diary of events:

August 27. Notified of proposed purchase at £65,000.
August 31. Notified of proposed sale at £40,000. Paid local search fees £3. H.M.L.C.R. search fees £1.
September 3. Instructions received from Whinshire Building Society to act in connection with advance to Hotspur of £25,000 on security of "Greenmead" and life policy for £2,500. The initial fire insurance premium of £10 and life policy premium of £150 are to be deducted from the advance.
September 17. Exchanged contracts for sale of "Blackwater" and received 10 per cent deposit as agent for vendor. Also exchanged contracts for purchase of "Greenmead" and paid 10 per cent deposit to Mowbray & Co, the vendor's solicitors as stakeholders. The balance required for the deposit being advanced by George & Co.

September 23. Mowbray & Co sent completion statement showing balance of purchase money.

September 30. Sent financial statement to Hotspur, together with bill of costs showing costs on sale £60, costs on purchase £74, plus VAT. The mortgagee's costs are £16 plus VAT and it has been agreed that these will be borne by Hotspur.

October 12. Hotspur sent a cheque for amount required.

October 16. Paid H.M.L.C.R. fees £1 out of petty cash.

October 17. Received net advance cheque from building society.

October 18. Completed sale of "Blackwater". Completed purchase of "Greenmead".

October 19. Paid stamp duty on conveyance £325 and land registry fees £20.

October 30. Transferred amount due to OFFICE ACCOUNT and closed files.

    1. Prepare the financial statement sent to Hotspur on October 1.

    2. Write up clients' ledger accounts showing all the necessary entries to deal with the above events.

(Part II Qualifying Examination, February 1969—adapted)

(13) Black, Bobb & Co, are solicitors, and they deal with the following events:

November 3. Paid by cash: (i) search fees £2 in respect of the purchase of "The Padd" by Smith; (ii) agency disbursements £11 (including VAT) on behalf of solicitors representing Brown, by whom they have been requested to act as agents.

November 9. Paid survey fee £165 (including VAT £12) in respect of "The Padd".

November 11. Instructions received from Highrate Building Society to act for them in granting an advance of £7,000 to Smith on security of "The Padd".

November 15. Cheque for £2,400 received from solicitors for Bungo who had been disputing a debt owed to Brown.

November 16. Received from Nonsuch Bank cheque for £2,500 as bridging loan on behalf of Smith.

November 18. Cheque for £2,246 sent to solicitors for Brown, together with bill of costs showing:

	£
Professional charge	144
Less: Agency commission allowed	14
	130
Add: VAT	13
	143
Add: Agency disbursements (including VAT)	11
	154

November 20. Exchanged contracts for the purchase of "The Padd" and paid 10 per cent deposit (£2,500) to the vendor's solicitors who are to act as stakeholders. On the same day, contracts are exchanged for the sale of

Smith's house "Coslot" and a deposit of 10 per cent (£1,600) was received, Black, Bobb & Co acting as stakeholders.

December 5. Received completion statement from vendor's solicitors in respect of "The Padd" showing £22,500 due, being the balance of purchase money.

December 5. Completion statement sent to purchaser's solicitor in respect of "Coslot" showing balance of £14,400 due in respect of the balance of purchase money.

December 6. Received cheque for £7,000 from the Highrate Building Society. The profit costs to be charged in respect of the advance are £44 (including VAT).

December 8. Sent financial statement to Smith showing balance of money which will be due from him on completion of the sale and purchase, together with bill of costs for £1,106 (being search fees, survey fee, stamp duty £250, land registry fees £51, profit costs on sale £90 plus VAT, profit costs on purchase £140 plus VAT, and estate agents commission £385 inclusive of VAT).

December 11. Cheque received from Smith being the balance of purchase money and payment of costs.

December 14. Completed purchase and sale of properties. Net advance transferred from the Highrate Building Society account to Smith's account. Loan of £2,500 repaid to Nonsuch Bank, interest thereon being charged by the bank to Smith's current account with the bank. Transferred £1,600 from Stakeholder Account to Smith's account. Paid stamp duties and land registry fees.

December 15. Paid estate agents' commission £385.

December 31. Transferred costs and disbursements from CLIENT ACCOUNT to OFFICE ACCOUNT.

Ignore interest on the deposit.

Write up the ledger account of Smith and the Agency Account for the solicitors representing Brown, showing all the entries necessary to deal with the above events, and prepare a financial statement suitable for presentation to Smith on December 8, showing how the balance of money due on completion is calculated.

(Part II Qualifying Examination, February 1977—adapted)

Chapter 16

TRUSTS

1. Frequently, a solicitor is asked to act as a trustee to a trust and in such a case will, from time to time, receive money belonging to that trust. It should be noted that where the solicitor is not a trustee himself but is acting for the trustees (*i.e.* they are his clients), then any money received on behalf of that trust, and the trustees, is clients' money. In such a case, the normal rules apply, *i.e.* the money must be paid into the ordinary clients' bank account and a ledger account opened in the clients' ledger in the name of the trustee. Where, however, the solicitor is a trustee himself, certain special considerations apply.

2. Any person who is a trustee must keep proper, faithful and accurate accounts for that trust and such accounts must be kept separately from other matters. Failure to comply with this requirement will render a trustee liable to an action by a beneficiary for breach of trust. Further, a solicitor who is a "controlled trustee" must comply with the Solicitors' Accounts Rules 1991 Part II, otherwise he will be liable to disciplinary proceedings. Consequently, whether a solicitor is a controlled trustee (*e.g.* a sole trustee) or an ordinary trustee (*e.g.* a trustee jointly with a layman who is not an employee in the solicitor's firm), he will need to keep separate records and books of account for each trust of which he is a trustee. Such accounts are, however, outside the scope of this book. In addition, the solicitor ought to have a separate bank account for each trust so as to avoid any problem of mixing moneys belonging to different trusts.

3. If the solicitor receives trust money, he may pay such money into either:

(a) the firm's clients' bank account; or
(b) the bank account of the individual trust.

4. If the money is paid into the firm's clients' bank account, such sum is now governed by the Solicitors' Accounts Rules 1991. Thus, any withdrawal can only be made under Rule 7(b) SAR and the receipt must be properly recorded under Rule 11, *i.e.*:

CREDIT an account in the Clients' Ledger—CLIENT ACCOUNT—in the name of the trust
DEBIT Cash Account—CLIENT ACCOUNT

5. If the money is paid into the bank account for the particular trust, the entries are made in the books of account kept for that particular trust—NO ENTRIES ARE MADE IN THE FIRM'S BOOKS. If the solicitor is a controlled trustee, the money is now governed by the Solicitors' Accounts Rules 1991 Part II.

6. **Withdrawals**

(a) If payment is made out of money held in the firm's CLIENT ACCOUNT under Rule 7(b) SAR, this payment must be properly recorded, *i.e.*:

DEBIT the ledger account in the name of the trust in the clients' ledger—CLIENT ACCOUNT
CREDIT Cash Account—CLIENT ACCOUNT

(b) If the payment is made out of money held in the trust bank account, the withdrawal is recorded in the books of the trust, and NO ENTRY IS MADE IN THE FIRM'S BOOKS.

7. If a solicitor is a trustee of a trust (whether controlled trustee or ordinary trustee) he can pay trust money into his ordinary current account for clients' money. HOWEVER, IF SOME OF THE CLIENTS' MONEY HAS BEEN PLACED ON GENERAL DEPOSIT HE SHOULD NOT DO THIS. It could involve the solicitor in an accidental breach of trust, because it could be alleged that the trust money assisted him to earn the interest, and in such a case a proportionate part of the interest would belong to the trust. Thus, if a solicitor has clients' money on general deposit, and he receives some trust money, either this should be placed in the bank account of the particular trust or yet another bank account in the firm's name—a clients' bank account—should be opened, reserved exclusively for trust money.

Chapter 17

REVISION EXERCISES

Time limit for all these questions is 1 hour except where indicated otherwise. Unless the question states to the contrary please ignore any interest on deposits.

(1) You are forming a new company called NU Ltd. Pay Capital Duty to IRC £300. Pay Companies' Registration Fee £50. You send the client company a bill in which you charge it £200 plus VAT in respect of profit costs. Your bill also includes a disbursement, as yet unpaid, of £40 in respect of the Law Stationer's fees (zero-rated). You receive the amount due from your client company. You pay the Law Stationers £40. Prepare the Clients' Ledger.

[*Time limit: 20 minutes*]

(2) Prepare the ledger account of Albert Hill. Pay £7 for a police report, no VAT. Pay £30 for a medical report. Receive £1,500 from the defendant in full settlement. Deliver a bill to Albert for £75 plus disbursements, plus VAT. Send Albert the balance due to him.

[*Time limit: 15 minutes*]

(3) You acted for Bill in connection with an action against Charles for £2,000. You won and were awarded costs. These were as follows: profit costs £50, counsel's fee £30, court fee £20, conduct money paid in cash to witnesses £5. The amount of the bill payable by Charles is taxed at £40 costs, £25 counsel's fee, £18 court fees, and £5 conduct money. You receive the amount of the claim plus costs from Charles' solicitors and send the balance due to Bill. Prepare Bill's ledger account. (Your costs and counsel's fee are subject to VAT and are quoted exclusive of tax.)

[*Time limit: 25 minutes*]

(4) You act for Romeo, who is divorcing his wife Juliet.

May 1. Receive £40, generally, on account of costs and disbursements.
May 4. Pay enquiry agent £30—no VAT.
May 10. Pay court fees of £20.
May 15. You instruct Fred and Co, local agents, to attend the hearing on your behalf.
June 1. You hear from Fred and Co that your client was granted a decree and Juliet was ordered to pay Romeo's costs. You send Fred and Co a cheque in payment of their fees which were £15 less a commission of 8 per cent plus VAT.

June 10. You pay a witness fee of £20 plus VAT (use the Agency Method) and you pay counsel's fees of £50 plus VAT (use the Principal Method).

July 1. You send your client a bill in which the total charge for profit costs is £75 representing £60 for work done by you and £15 done by your local agents (this includes the taxed costs of £55).

July 11. The proportion of your costs to be paid by Juliet is taxed at £55 and counsel's fees of £40 are also allowed together with court fees of £20.

July 20. You receive from Juliet's solicitors a cheque in respect of the taxed costs.

July 26. Transfer to OFFICE ACCOUNT any balance on CLIENT ACCOUNT.

August 1. You receive the balance due from Romeo.

Prepare Romeo's ledger account. All your charges, etc., are quoted exclusive of VAT.

[Time limit: 30 minutes]

(5) You act for Desmond, who is defending an action brought by Percy. The following events occur:

January 2. Receive £400 on account from your client. It is not specially designated.

January 3. Pay court fees £10 in cash.

February 3. Pay enquiry agent £30 plus VAT; his invoice is addressed to you.

February 4. Pay expert witness £20 plus VAT; his invoice is addressed to Desmond.

February 5. Pay a second witness £9, no tax.

March 6. You lose the case. The other side is awarded £1,000 plus costs.

April 7. The other side's costs and disbursements are taxed at £400 plus £27.20 VAT.

April 18. You send Desmond your bill. This includes an item for profit costs of £200 and counsel's fee of £60 (excluding VAT). You send a statement with your bill showing the amount required from your client to finish this transaction. You inform him that because you have held some money on his behalf on CLIENT ACCOUNT for some time that you are paying him £31 interest. However, instead of sending him the money, you will set this off against the amount owing.

April 29. You receive the amount due from Desmond.

May 1. Pay the other side's solicitors £1,427.20.

May 2. Pay by cheque, counsel's fee £60 plus VAT; use the Principal Method.

May 3. Do any more entries necessary to complete this matter.

Prepare clients' ledger.

(6) You act for George, a widower who has just died. You are one of the executors of the will and the other executor is George's accountant. George's bank has now closed George's account but agrees to advance any necessary money to pay IHT which you are to repay in due course.

May 30. You pay X & Co £200 plus VAT for valuation—use the Principal Method.

June 1. Pay £7 in respect of newspaper advertisements inclusive of VAT—use the Agency Method.

June 2. Receive IHT advance, from the bank—£1,200.

June 3. Pay probate fees £10 by cheque and Inheritance Tax of £1,200.

July 20. Receive £3,400 from George's Building Society Account.

July 21. Receive £800 from George's bank being the balance on George's account as at the date of death.

July 22. Receive assurance policy moneys on George's life of £4,200.

July 24. Pay Income Tax arrears of £600 and repay the £1,200 bank loan.

August 2. Pay legacies of £1,000 each to George's sister Ethel and brother Frank.

August 31. You deliver a bill for £300 profit costs plus £30 general disbursements plus VAT.

The balance of George's estate is to be divided equally between his daughter and son and you send the balance due to each of them.

Prepare clients' ledger.

(7) Prepare the firm's Cash Account from the following information:

April 11. Receive £40 insurance premium on behalf of the Tempest & Flood Insurance Co.

April 15. Send the Tempest & Flood Insurance Co £38, being the premium due to them less commission charged of £2. Transfer the £2 to the OFFICE ACCOUNT.

May 8. You act as a local agent for Dodds & Co of Penzance. Pay enquiry agent a fee of £20 plus VAT (use the Principal Method).

May 9. You send a bill to Dodds & Co which includes an item of £40 for profit costs (this figure is quoted exclusive of VAT).

May 15. Receive the amount due from Dodds & Co.

May 16. You receive £5,000 to hold on behalf of Margaret.

May 18. You send Margaret a bill in which you charge her £140 plus VAT and you send the balance due to her. Transfer the amount due to OFFICE ACCOUNT.

May 20. As a result of a telephone conversation with Margaret, you agree to reduce your fees from £140 to £130 exclusive of VAT.

Do not show the balances.

[*Time limit: 30 minutes*]

(8) Prepare the firm's Cash Account from the following information:

September 5. Receive a cheque from Tom for £800 on account.

September 6. Draw a clients' account cheque on Tom's behalf for £63.

September 7. Receive a cheque for £4,270 to be held on behalf of the Jones Family Trust. You are one of the trustees and decide to pay the cheque into the firm's client bank account.

September 8. Receive a cheque from Simon for £57. He owes you £100 in respect of costs and disbursements.

September 9. Receive a cheque from Michael, a partner in the firm, for £12,340 being the amount required from him to complete the purchase of a house. You are acting for him in the purchase.

September 12. Receive notification from the bank that the cheque received from Tom on September 5 has been dishonoured.

September 13. Draw a cheque on behalf of the Jones Family Trust for £2,500 and transfer to the trust's bank account the balance of £1,770.

September 14: Receive a cheque from Nancy for £8,000 which is immediately indorsed over on her behalf.

Do not show the balances.

[*Time limit: 30 minutes*]

(9) Prepare the firm's Cash Account from the following information:

May 1. You are the trustee of the Albert Deceased Will Trust. You receive a cheque for £10,000 in respect of the trust which you pay into the trust's bank account.

May 2. You withdraw £2,000 from the trust's bank account on behalf of the Albert Deceased Will Trust in respect of purchase of shares.

May 3. You act on behalf of Bill, on whose behalf you are holding £3,000; you have placed this in a specially designated deposit bank account. You receive a note from your bank that interest of £40 in respect of this item has been credited to your office bank account.

May 4. Transfer from your general clients' deposit bank account £500 to your clients' current account.

May 5. You act for Christine. You have held £6,000 on behalf of this client for some time; it has not been specially designated. Return this sum to her together with interest of £42. Send one cheque only.

May 8. Receive £200 from Peter generally on account of costs.

May 9. Receive £14,000 from Robert which is placed in a specially designated bank account.

May 15. Return to Stephen £8,000 clients' money held on his behalf. Since this sum has been held for some time and has not been specially designated, it is decided to send him interest of £50. Send him two cheques.

May 16. You act for Ethel. Receive £200 on account from her.

May 17. Pay on Ethel's behalf stationers' fees £30 plus VAT (use the Principal Method).

May 19. You act for Frances in connection with drafting her will. She calls into the office to sign the will and you agree your fee for this matter at £20. Frances immediately hands you the cash.

May 20. Pay £320 on Peter's behalf.

May 22. Receive £40 cash from Peter in respect of the amount owing.

May 30. Receive notification from the bank that £85 has been credited to your CLIENT ACCOUNT in respect of interest earned by clients' money on general deposit.

Do not show the balances.

(10) The clients' ledger shows the following balances at the close of the entries for yesterday.

	Office A/c £ p	Client A/c £ p
Zebedee	52.35	11.05
William	17.50	
Thomas		50.00
Susan	52.50	
Quentin		40.50
Pauline	62.85	
Oliver Trust	10.50	800.00
Nancy	4.40	45.00
S Building Society		4,400.00

The following events occurred during the course of today's business:

(a) A cheque for £710 was received from Lucy & King, being the deposit on 2, Railway Terrace, which is being sold by Quentin for whom the firm acts. The money is to be held by the firm as stakeholder.

(b) A cheque for £75 payable to the firm was received from Marshire County Council for one month's salary as clerk to the Marshbridge Magistrates' Court, a part-time post filled by one of the firm's partners, Ian.

(c) A cheque for £18 was received from Ian and Jane Ltd on general account of costs in connection with a matter being conducted on their behalf. One of the partners in the firm is the majority shareholder in Ian and Jane Ltd.

(d) A cheque for £20.75 was drawn for Land Registry fees in connection with the purchase of 10, Station Road for Zebedee.

(e) A cheque for £800 was drawn in favour of Violet, the beneficiary under the trust fund held by Trustees of Oliver, who consist of all the partners in the firm.

(f) Susan called in and paid £30 in cash on account of an agreed fee for work done.

(g) A cheque for £612.85 was received from Pauline *re* Fish Hall, being the amount shown on the completion statement sent to her which included costs and disbursements of £62.85. Later in the day, completion took place and a draft for £4,950 drawn on the firm's bank was handed over to Messrs Graham & Hilary, the vendor's solicitors. This sum included £4,400 held for the S Building Society, in connection with an advance to Pauline.

(h) The following cheques were drawn at the end of the day and sent out in the post:

(i) Rotten Insurance Co Ltd £47.50 on behalf of Nancy; premium on an insurance policy issued to Nancy.

(ii) Marshire RDC £127.30: for rates, being £82.80 for the firm's premises and £44.50 for a partner's (Ian's) house.

Draw up the firm's Cash Account to record the above items.

(11) You act for Pauline and Robert who are the executors of the will of Simon deceased. Simon's will has left a pecuniary legacy of £5,000 to a friend, Timothy, and all the rest of his estate to his sole surviving son William. Pauline and Robert tell you that Simon's assets comprise £200 in a bank account, some investments, and a house.

January 2. The executors open a bank account with an overdraft facility of up to £5,000.

February 1. You ascertain that the Inheritance Tax amounts to £4,000; the deceased's bank credits this sum to your CLIENT ACCOUNT and debits the executors' bank account.

February 3. You draw a cheque in favour of the Inland Revenue for the Inheritance Tax and another cheque for £38 in respect of the probate fees.

February 12. Grant of probate received and registered with the bank who transfer all moneys due to the deceased by them to the executors' loan account.

February 20. You receive instructions to sell the deceased's house at an agreed fee of £100.

March 22. Exchange contracts on the sale of the house for £48,000 and receive a 10 per cent deposit to hold as agent for the vendor.

March 25. Investments held on the behalf of the deceased are sold for £700 and you receive the proceeds.

March 26. Pay funeral expenses of £125 and the debts of Simon deceased amounting to £3,100.

April 22. The sale of the house is completed and the balance of the proceeds of sale are received; there were no apportionments. You send a cheque to Pauline and Robert for £3,800 to repay the overdraft on their executors' bank account.

May 3. You deliver a bill in respect of your costs for acting on the probate in the sum of £400 plus VAT. You pay the pecuniary legacy of £5,000 and send a cheque to William for the balance due to him.

Prepare the ledger account of the executors of Simon deceased.

(12) You acted for Mr Hare on the sale of his house, "The Count House" for £15,800 and on the purchase of his new house "Tangerine Cottage" at £30,000. You also received instructions from the Plenty Building Society in connection with an advance of £25,000 which it is to make on the new house. "The Count House" was mortgaged for £11,000 to the Smiles Building Society for whom you do not act. It is your practice to transfer money due to OFFICE ACCOUNT from CLIENT ACCOUNT on the first of each month.

June 2. Contracts exchanged on both properties. Deposit of £1,580 received for "The Count House" to be held as stakeholders. Deposit of £3,000 sent to the vendor's solicitors for "Tangerine Cottage".

June 28. You receive mortgage advance from the Plenty Building Society. Completion statement received for "Tangerine Cottage" showing £27,000 due on completion.

June 29. Purchase of "Tangerine Cottage" completed.

June 30. Sale of "The Count House" completed at mortgagees' solicitors, when a bank draft in their favour for £10,187 was handed over by the purchaser's solicitors; you yourself received a draft for £4,033, the balance due on the sale.

July 18. Pay land registry fees of £80.

July 28. Bill of costs drawn. The profit costs on purchase amounted to £300 (excluding VAT) and general disbursements of £20 were charged. The profit costs on sale amounted to £200 (excluding VAT). Mortgage costs, charged to Plenty Building Society and payable by Mr Hare, are £33.

Prepare the ledger account of Mr Hare in the books of the practice, and the statement sent to Mr Hare on July 28.

(13) You act for Simpson who is selling "Bolt House" for £40,000. It is at present mortgaged to the Whiting Building Society for £35,000. He is buying "Dyer Hall" for £50,000 and will get a new mortgage of £40,000 from the Mercer Building Society. You act for the Mercer Building Society but not the Whiting Building Society.

March 1. Simpson sends you a cheque for the deposit on "Dyer Hall" payable to you.

March 2. You send the deposit to the vendor's solicitors.

March 3. Pay search fees £2 by cheque.

April 1. Receive a cheque for the deposit on the sale which you are to hold as stakeholder.

May 25. Pay search fee of £3, petty cash.

June 1. Receive the mortgage advance from the Mercer Building Society and receive £300 from Simpson.

June 3. Complete the sale of "Bolt House" and redeem the mortgage thereon. You complete the purchase and mortgage of "Dyer Hall".

June 6. Deliver a bill to Simpson for £400 costs (purchase £250, sale £150) and a bill to the Mercer Building Society for £50, both exclusive of tax, the latter bill to be paid by Simpson.

Prepare the entries in your Clients' Ledger, and the statement sent to Simpson on June 6.

(14) You act for Jack who is buying 1, Half Moon Street for £30,000 and selling "The Manor House", Woolton for £20,000. "The Manor House" is subject to a mortgage for £13,000 from the Ernest Building Society and Jack will be borrowing £18,000 on the security of Half Moon Street from the Ernest Building Society. You also act for the building society.

March 1. Jack pays a deposit of £3,000 in respect of Half Moon Street direct to the estate agents and you receive a deposit of 10 per cent in respect of "The Manor House" to hold as stakeholder.

March 3. Make a search £10 cheque.

April 1. You send Jack a bill in which you charge him £100 for acting on the sale, £140 for acting on the purchase plus VAT. You are charging the Ernest Building Society £60 plus VAT for acting on their part.

April 11. Receive £18,000 from the Ernest Building Society and receive from Jack the amount due from him in order to complete the matters.

April 12. Complete the sale of "The Manor House" and then complete the purchase of Half Moon Street. Send to the Ernest Building Society the £13,000 due to them.

Prepare the entries in your Clients' Ledger, and the statement sent to Jack on April 1. The mortgage costs are payable by Jack.

(15) The following balances appeared in the relevant clients' ledger accounts of Tremor, Quake & Co, Solicitors, as at December 1:

Chasm	Office Account	£482	Client Account	£989
Fissure	Office Account	£104	Client Account	£nil

Chasm dies on December 3, and his executors instruct the firm to act in the administration of the estate generally. The estate consists of personalty valued at £62,750 and a house, "Goodinvest", which is valued at £120,000. There is a mortgage on the house (£20,000) and there are other sundry debts amounting to £2,424. Subject to legacies of £5,000 to Chasm's secretary and £1,000 to a local charity, the residue is left to Fissure who is presently purchasing a house, "Epicentre", a matter which is being dealt with by the firm.

During the administration of the estate, the following events take place:

December 10. House insurance premium (£245) on "Goodinvest", now due, and the firm debits the executors' account, the amount being transferred to the account of the insurance company, for whom the firm acts.

December 11. The deceased's bank agrees to advance £22,923 to the executors in respect of inheritance tax payable by the estate. A loan account is opened by the bank for the executors and a cheque for £22,923 is drawn up by the executors, payable to the Inland Revenue, and handed over to Tremor, Quake and Co.
Probate fees of £100 are paid by cheque.

January 4. The grant is received and registered with the bank, which transfers the sum of £12,420 from the deceased's deposit account to the executors' loan account.

January 5. Cheque drawn for £40 plus VAT in respect of statutory advertisements. The cost of the local advertisement (£20 plus VAT) is paid from petty cash. In both cases the disbursement is to be treated as an input of Tremor, Quake & Co.

January 7. The amount invested by the deceased with the Big Bang Building Society is, after registration of the grant, withdrawn by the executors and a sufficient sum to close the executors' loan account with the bank is transferred thereto, the remaining amount of £4,876 being paid into the firm's CLIENT ACCOUNT.

January 11. With the executors' concurrence, the net amount outstanding in Chasm deceased's account at December 1, is transferred to the executors' account.

January 12. Proceeds of life assurance policy amounting to £23,400 received by the firm and placed in a designated deposit account.

January 13. Exchanged contracts for the sale of "Goodinvest" for £120,000, the deposit of £12,000 being received by the firm for them to hold as stakeholders.

January 14. Debts amounting to £2,424, together with funeral expenses of £775, are paid out of CLIENT ACCOUNT.

January 20. Cheque for £1,297 received from the auctioneer in respect of the sale of household contents. Commission of £150 (including VAT) had already been deducted.

January 21. Paid survey fee £276 (inclusive of VAT) in respect of the house "Epicentre" being purchased by Fissure, the local land charges search fee (personal inspection) of £24 being paid out of petty cash.

January 22. The sum of £13,000 is transferred from the executors' designated deposit account to client current bank account. Cheques are drawn in respect of the legacies and handed over to the legatees. The executors agree to make an interim distribution to Fissure, and the sum of £10,000 is transferred to his CLIENT ACCOUNT. The firm then send a cheque for £10,000 to the solicitors acting for the vendor of the house "Epicentre", for them to hold as stakeholders, contracts being exchanged at the same time.

January 27. Completed sale of "Goodinvest". The balance of the purchase money payable by the purchaser is £108,000. The mortgage is to be redeemed by a payment of £20,506 which is inclusive of accrued interest. The mortgagees (Crevice Building Society) are not clients of Tremor, Quake & Co. The purchaser brings two drafts, one payable direct to the mortgagees' solicitor and the other, for the balance, payable to Tremor, Quake & Co. Paid estate agents' commission of £2,510 plus VAT.

January 28. Transferred the sum of £80,000 from client current bank account to the executors' designated deposit account.

January 29. The firm agrees the bills of costs for the sale of the house and the administration of the estate with the executors. Profit costs with regard to the sale are £600 (plus VAT), and with regard to the administration £900 (plus VAT), together with disbursements.

February 1. All moneys due to the firm by the executors are transferred to OFFICE ACCOUNT.

February 4. The executors' designated deposit account is closed and the balance, including interest of £108, is transferred to client current bank account.

February 5. The balance of moneys held by the firm on behalf of the executors, including interest allowed by the firm of £194 (excluding the interest on the designated deposit account but including an amount in respect of interest on the deposit held by the firm as stakeholders), is transferred to the account of Fissure at the request of the executors. Fissure requests that the moneys now due to him be held by the firm on general deposit account pending the completion of his purchase of the house "Epicentre".

You are required to show the ledger accounts of the executors of Chasm, deceased, and of Fissure, recording all the above transactions. Show also the Cash Account (NOT the Designated Deposit Cash Account), recording the entries for the month of January. There is no need to complete the balance columns in the Cash Account.

Ignore all forms of taxation, except the stated amount of Inheritance Tax and VAT.

In making the necessary entries, it is important that the account in which the corresponding entry would be made is clearly identified by the appropriate entry in the details column.

(Solicitors' Final Examination, Winter 1988)

(16) The following balances appeared in the relevant clients' ledger accounts of Oak, Poplar & Co, Solicitors, as at April 1:

Larch	Office Account	£nil	Client Account	£600
Aspen	Office Account	£43	Client Account	£20,232
Willow	Office Account	£nil	Client Account	£1,500

The firm deals with the following events during the months of April and May:

April 1. A designated deposit account is opened by the firm on behalf of Aspen, and the sum of £20,000 is transferred thereto, in accordance with his request.

April 7. After receiving the agreement of Larch, the sum of £250 is transferred to the account of Maple Insurance Limited from the amount held on behalf of Larch in CLIENT ACCOUNT, being an insurance premium due this day.

April 11. Cheque received from Alder, being the deposit on the sale of a house by Aspen, the firm to hold the sum (£5,500) as stakeholders. Exchanged contracts for the sale of Aspen's house, and paid disbursements of £14 (no VAT) on his behalf, out of petty cash the same day.

April 12. Poplar, a partner in the firm, is purchasing a cottage jointly with his wife and they have instructed the firm to act on their behalf in this matter. The firm pays the local land charges search fee (£14) *re* the cottage, from petty cash.

April 15. A bill of costs is received from Wych Elm & Co, a firm of solicitors acting as agents on behalf of the firm in connection with the affairs of Willow. The bill shows profit costs of £800 (excluding VAT) and disbursements of £100 (no VAT). The firm pays the agents' bill and renders its own bill of costs to Willow, showing disbursements of £100 (no VAT) and profit costs of £1,200 plus VAT. Both the profit costs and the disbursements of the agent solicitors, are included in the foregoing amounts.

April 18. Poplar hands over a cheque to the firm's cashier for £4,000, being the deposit on the cottage which he is purchasing jointly with his wife.

April 20. Paid by cheque to Willow, the amount outstanding in his CLIENT ACCOUNT, together with interest allowed by the firm of £42. The account is then closed.

April 25. Contracts are exchanged for the purchase of the Poplars' cottage, the deposit of £4,000 being paid to the vendor's solicitors as stakeholders.

April 27. Banker's draft (£49,500) received from Horse Chestnuts, solicitors, on completion of the sale of Aspen's house. Paid estate agents' fees (£700 plus VAT) the same day, the invoice being addressed to Aspen.

April 28. Aspen agrees with the bill of costs rendered by the firm, showing profit costs of £400 plus VAT and disbursements. The amount due to the firm is transferred to OFFICE ACCOUNT, and Aspen's designated deposit account is closed, interest of £83 having been credited thereto. The balance of moneys now held on behalf of Aspen, including interest allowed by the firm of £106 (inclusive of interest on the deposit held by the firm as stakeholders) is paid over by one cheque, thereby closing the client's ledger account.

April 29. The net amount due to Maple Insurance Limited is paid, being the gross premium received (£250) less commission of £37, the client (Larch) having agreed with the firm's retention of that amount. The account is then closed.

May 3. Larch requests that the firm send a cheque for £1,000 to Rowan, to whom he owes money. The firm sends the cheque, and later the same day, a cheque for £400 is received from Larch in partial satisfaction, together with a cheque for £250 drawn by Spruce (a debtor of Larch) payable to Larch. The latter cheque is indorsed over to Oak, Poplar & Co.

May 9. The bank notifies the firm that the cheque from Spruce has been returned unpaid by the paying bankers.

You are required to show all the relevant entries in the accounts in the clients' ledger (including a stakeholder account, if necessary), recording the above transactions. It is important that the account in which the corresponding entry would be made is clearly identified by the appropriate entry in the details column. All accounts are to be balanced.

Ignore all forms of taxation, except VAT.

(Solicitors' Final Examination, Summer 1988)

(17) Milk decides to sell his house "Churn" for £240,000, and purchase a cottage *"The Dairy" for £120,000.* There is a mortgage on "Churn" of £50,000, the mortgagees being the Cheese Building Society. Both Milk and the Cheese Building Society instruct the same firm of solicitors, Creams, to act on their behalf with regard to the purchase of "The Dairy' and the sale of "Churn" and the redemption of the mortgage thereon. In addition, Butter, a partner in Creams, is purchasing a flat for £100,000 jointly with his wife and they have instructed the firm to act on their behalf in this matter.

The following events and transactions take place:

March 6. Local land charges search fee *re* "The Dairy" (£26) is paid from petty cash.

March 9. Paid survey fee (£300 plus VAT) in respect of "The Dairy", the invoice being addressed to Creams.

March 15. Milk is unable to find the deposit on "The Dairy" as his funds have been invested elsewhere, and after negotiation, and a suitable undertaking has been given by the firm, a cheque for £12,000 is received by the latter from the Round Stilton Co Ltd to be used as a bridging loan.

March 16. Contracts are exchanged for the sale of "Churn", the deposit of £24,000 being received by Creams who are to act as stakeholders. On the same day, contracts are exchanged for the purchase of "The Dairy", the deposit of £12,000 being paid to the solicitors acting for the vendor of the house who are to act as stakeholders.

April 2. Sent completion statement to the purchaser's solicitors in respect of "Churn" showing the balance due in respect of the purchase moneys (£216,000).

April 5. Received completion statement in respect of "The Dairy", showing balance of purchase moneys due (£108,000).

April 9. Received invoice from estate agent addressed to Milk, showing commission due in respect of the sale of "Churn" £3,600 plus VAT.

April 10. Sent bill of costs to Milk, showing total profit costs of £1,100 exclusive of VAT (purchase of "The Dairy" £600, sale of "Churn" £500). The profit costs for acting for the Cheese Building Society (to be borne by Milk) in the redemption of the mortgage, amount to £40 exclusive of VAT.

April 11. Local land charges search fee (£26) *re* Mr and Mrs Butter's flat is paid from petty cash.

April 12. Completed sale of "Churn" and purchase of "The Dairy". Sent cheque for £50,462 redemption moneys to the Cheese Building Society. Repaid loan of £12,000 together with accrued interest of £170, to Round Stilton Co Ltd. Paid stamp duty of £1,200.

April 18. Paid estate agent's commission plus VAT.

April 20. Paid land registry fees of £160. Transferred costs and disbursements from CLIENT ACCOUNT to OFFICE ACCOUNT.

April 24. Butter hands over a bank draft to the firm's cashier for £6,000, being an amount towards the deposit on the flat which he is purchasing jointly with his wife.

April 25. Contracts are exchanged for the purchase of the Butters' flat, the deposit of £10,000 being paid to the vendor's solicitors as stakeholders. The amount required for the balance of the deposit was borrowed from Milk (a relative of Mrs Butter), using funds already held by the firm on his behalf. Independent advice had been obtained by Milk.

May 16. Sent financial statement to Milk, together with a cheque for the balance of moneys held on his behalf, including interest allowed by the firm of £794. The latter amount is inclusive of interest on the deposit held by the firm as stakeholders.

The client's ledger account of Milk is then closed.

You are required to show the ledger accounts of Milk, Mr and Mrs Butter, and the Cheese Building Society, making all the necessary entries to deal with the events and transactions, and to prepare a suitable financial statement showing any balance of money due to Milk after all the transactions have been completed. Milk's transactions are recorded in one ledger account.

Ignore all forms of taxation, except stamp duty and VAT.

In making the necessary entries, it is important that the account in which the corresponding entry would be made is clearly identified by the appropriate entry in the details column.

(Solicitors' Final Examination, Summer 1990)

(18) Bream decides to sell his house "Pike View" for £100,000, and purchase a cottage "Perch Cottage" for £80,000. There is a mortgage on "Pike View" of £12,000, the mortgagees being the Roach Building Society. Both Bream and the Roach Building Society instruct the same firm of solicitors, Gudgeons, to act on their behalf with regard to the purchase of "Perch Cottage" and the sale of "Pike View" and the redemption of the mortgage thereon.

The following events and transactions take place, and you are required to show the ledger accounts of Bream and the Roach Building Society, making all the necessary entries to deal with the events and transactions, and to prepare a suitable financial statement showing any balance of money due to Bream after all the transactions have been completed. Bream's transactions are recorded in one ledger account.

Ignore all forms of taxation, except stamp duty and VAT.

In making the necessary entries, it is important that the account in which the corresponding entry would be made, is clearly identified by the appropriate entry in the details column.

November 4. Received cheque from Bream for £1,000 on account of costs generally.

November 6. Local land charges search fee *re* "Perch Cottage" (£30) is paid from petty cash.

November 8. Paid survey fee (£300 plus VAT) in respect of "Perch Cottage", the invoice being addressed to Gudgeons.

November 15. Bream is unable to find the deposit on "Perch Cottage" from his own resources and Gudgeons agree to advance £7,000 towards the deposit upon exchange of contracts, out of available practice moneys.

November 18. Contracts are exchanged for the sale of "Pike View", the deposit of £10,000 being received by Gudgeons as stakeholders. On the same day, contracts are exchanged for the purchase of "Perch Cottage", the deposit of £8,000 being paid to the solicitors acting for the seller of the house who are to act as stakeholders.

December 2. Sent completion statement to the buyer's solicitors in respect of "Pike View" showing the balance due in respect of the purchase money (£90,000).

December 5. Received completion statement in respect of "Perch Cottage", showing balance of purchase money due (£72,000).

December 9. Received invoice from estate agent addressed to Bream, showing commission due in respect of the sale of "Pike View" £2,000 plus VAT.

December 10. Sent bill of costs to Bream, showing total profit costs of £500 exclusive of VAT (purchase of "Perch Cottage" £350, sale of "Pike View"

£150). The profit costs for acting for the Roach Building Society (to be borne by Bream) in the redemption of the mortgage, amount to £40 exclusive of VAT.

December 16. Completed sale of "Pike View" and purchase of "Perch Cottage". Sent cheque for £12,465 redemption money to Roach Building Society. Paid stamp duty of £800.

December 18. Paid estate agent's commission plus VAT.

December 20. Paid land registry fees of £160. Transferred all sums due from CLIENT ACCOUNT to OFFICE ACCOUNT.

January 16. Sent financial statement to Bream, together with a cheque for the balance of moneys held on his behalf, including interest allowed by the firm of £326. The latter amount has been ascertained after making due allowance for interest payable by Bream on the amount advanced by the firm in respect of the deposit on "Perch Cottage".

The client's ledger account of Bream is then closed.

(Solicitors' Final Examination, Winter 1992)

(19) The clients' ledger of Silver, Zinc & Co, Solicitors, shows the following balances as at April 1:

Executors of Nickel, deceased	Office Account	£nil	Client Account	£125,000
Brass	Office Account	£nil	Client Account	£nil
Antimony	Office Account	£560	Client Account	£nil

Brass has decided to sell his house "Goldmine" for £140,000, and purchase a lodge "Cobalt Lodge" for £100,000, and he instructs the firm to act on his behalf with regard to the purchase and sale of the properties. Brass is also the residuary legatee in the estate of Nickel, deceased, and the amount held in the executors' account represents the net residue to which he is entitled, the sum being held in a designated deposit account.

The following events and transactions take place, and you are required to show all the relevant entries recording these transactions in the accounts in the clients' ledger (excluding the stakeholder account), and to prepare a suitable financial statement showing any balance of money due to Brass on June 1, after all the transactions have been completed.

Ignore all forms of taxation, except stamp duty and VAT.

In making the necessary entries, it is important that the account in which the corresponding entry would be made is clearly identified by the appropriate entry in the details column.

April 2. Received cheque from Antimony (£750) on account of costs and disbursements to date.

April 6. Local land charges search fee *re* "Cobalt Lodge" (£36) is paid from petty cash.

April 8. Paid survey fee (£400 plus VAT) in respect of "Cobalt Lodge", the invoice being addressed to Silver, Zinc & Co.

April 15. The executors of Nickel, deceased, agree to the transfer of the sum of £10,000 from their CLIENT ACCOUNT as an interim distribution in respect of the residuary legacy due to Brass. The sum is transferred to the CLIENT ACCOUNT of Brass forthwith.

April 16. Contracts are exchanged for the sale of "Goldmine", the deposit of £14,000 being received by Silver, Zinc & Co to be held by them as stakeholders. On the same day, contracts are exchanged for the purchase of "Cobalt Lodge", the deposit of £10,000 being paid to the solicitors acting for the seller of the house who are to act as stakeholders.

April 21. Antimony, for whom the firm has been acting in a litigation matter, has settled out of court and has agreed to pay damages of £2,000 together with plaintiff's costs of £1,500 (inclusive of VAT). The firm now renders its own bill of costs to Antimony, showing profit costs £1,200 (plus VAT) together with consultant's fee £1,000 (plus VAT) and other disbursements of £560 (no VAT).

May 4. Antimony sends a cheque for £3,500 made payable to the plaintiff's solicitors, which is sent to the latter the same day.

May 5. Sent completion statement to the buyer's solicitors in respect of "Goldmine" showing the balance due in respect of the purchase money (£126,000). Received completion statement in respect of "Cobalt Lodge", showing balance of purchase money due (£90,000).

May 7. Antimony agrees with the firm's bill costs and sends a cheque to the firm in settlement of the balance due by him.

May 10. Received invoice from estate agent addressed to Brass, showing commission due in respect of the sale of "Goldmine" £2,400 plus VAT.

May 11. Sent bill of costs to Brass, showing total profit costs of £1,000 exclusive of VAT (purchase of "Cobalt Lodge" £600, sale of "Goldmine" £400).

May 12. The bank notifies the firm that the cheque received from Antimony on May 7, has been returned unpaid by the paying bankers.

May 14. The executors of Nickel, deceased, instruct the firm to transfer the balance of the moneys held on their behalf (including interest of £1,875 earned on the designated deposit account) to the client ledger account of Brass. The executors' client ledger account is then closed.

May 18. Completed sale of "Goldmine" and purchase of "Cobalt Lodge". Paid stamp duty of £1,000 *re* "Cobalt Lodge".

May 19. Paid estate agent's commission plus VAT. Received cheque (£4,000) from Tin Lid Insurance Co Ltd, being the proceeds of an endowment policy belonging to Antimony which he has now surrendered. The cheque which he had sent to the firm in respect of their costs is now cancelled by the firm.

May 20. Paid land registry fees of £160 *re* "Cobalt Lodge". The amount due to the firm from Brass in respect of costs and disbursements is now transferred from CLIENT ACCOUNT to OFFICE ACCOUNT, Brass having previously agreed with the firm's bill of costs.

May 25. Paid consultant's fee (£1,000 plus VAT) from OFFICE ACCOUNT, using the agency basis, whereby the disbursement will be treated as an input of the client Antimony. Transferred costs and disbursements from CLIENT ACCOUNT to OFFICE ACCOUNT in respect of Antimony, a cheque for the balance due to him being sent at the same time, thus closing his account.

June 1. Sent financial statement to Brass, together with a cheque for the balance of moneys held on his behalf, including interest allowed by the firm of £534. The latter amount includes interest on the deposit held by the firm as stakeholders.

The clients' ledger account of Brass is then closed.

(Solicitors' Final Examination, Summer 1993)

(20) The clients' ledger of Horse, Blanket & Co, Solicitors, shows the following balances as at October 1:

Skewbald	Office Account	£340	Client Account	£nil
Chestnut	Office Account	£735	Client Account	£1,020

Chestnut dies on October 6, and the executors of his estate instruct the firm of Horse, Blanket & Co to act for them in the administration of the estate. The estate consists of personalty and a house, "The Stables", which is valued at £140,000. There is a mortgage on the house (£30,064) and sundry debts due by the estate of £2,420. The residue of the estate, save for a legacy of £2,000 to Palomino, was bequeathed to Skewbald. Both Palomino and Skewbald are clients of the firm.

The following events and transactions take place:

October 15. The deceased's bank agrees to advance £8,600 to the executors in respect of inheritance tax payable by the estate. A loan account is opened by the bank for the executors and a cheque for £11,358 is drawn by the executors, payable to the Inland Revenue, and handed over to Horse, Blanket & Co. Probate fees of £140 are paid by cheque.

November 2. The grant is received and registered with the bank, which transfers the sum of £2,910 from the deceased's current account to the firm's CLIENT ACCOUNT, thus closing the current account.

November 3. Cheque drawn for £40 plus VAT in respect of statutory advertisement. The cost of the local advertisement (£40 plus VAT) is paid from petty cash.

November 10. Proceeds of life assurance policy amounting to £30,000 received by the firm, and £8,600 is paid to the bank for the credit of the executor's loan account which is then closed.

November 15. Exchanged contracts for the sale of "The Stables" for £140,000, the deposit of £14,000 being received by the firm for them to hold as agents.

November 22. Cheque for £16,476 received from the auctioneer in respect of the sale of household contents. Commission of £1,820 (including VAT) had already been deducted.

December 1. Debts amounting to £2,315, together with funeral expenses of £980, are paid out of CLIENT ACCOUNT.

December 2. With the executors' concurrence, the net amount outstanding on Chestnut's account at October 1, is transferred to the executors' account.

December 3. The amount invested by the deceased with the Last Fence Building Society (£21,046) is, after registration of the grant, withdrawn by the executors and paid into the firm's CLIENT ACCOUNT.

December 8. Palomino requests that the firm sends a cheque for £1,800 to his bookmaker, Stirrups. The firms sends the cheque, and later the same day, a cheque for £1,000 is received from Palomino in part satisfaction.

December 13. Completed sale of "The Stables". The mortgage is redeemed by the payment of £30,463 which is inclusive of accrued interest and a bank draft for the balance of the purchase money (£95,537) is received and banked. The mortgagees (Saddle Building Society) are not clients of Horse, Blanket & Co. Paid estate agents' commission of £2,800 plus VAT. The bank notifies the firm that the cheque from Palomino has been returned by the paying bankers, marked "refer to drawer".

December 16. The firm agrees the bills of costs for the sale of the house and the administration of the estate, with the executors. Profit costs (excluding disbursements) with regard to the sale amount to £400 (excluding VAT), and with regard to the administration £1,800 (excluding VAT). All moneys due to the firm by the executors, are transferred to OFFICE ACCOUNT.

December 17. The executors and Palomino agree that the legacy of £2,000 should be transferred to Palomino's CLIENT ACCOUNT, and after effecting this transaction, the amount due from Palomino to the firm, including an agreed fee for profit costs of £80 plus VAT, is transferred to OFFICE ACCOUNT. The unpaid cheque from Palomino for £1,000 made payable to the firm is cancelled, a cheque for the balance due being forwarded to him.

December 20. At the executors' request, a cheque for £120,000 is sent to Skewbald, and the balance of money on their account plus interest allowed by the firm of £220, is transferred to the account of Skewbald in the books of the firm. Later the same day, the firm is instructed by Skewbald to transfer the sum of £10,000 to a designated deposit account with the bank.

You are required to show the ledger accounts of Chestnut, the executors of Chestnut, deceased, and of Palomino and Skewbald, recording all the above transactions.

Ignore all forms of taxation, except the stated amount of inheritance tax and VAT.

In making the necessary entries, it is important that the account in which the corresponding entry would be made is clearly identified by the appropriate entry in the details column.

(Solicitors' Final Examination, Winter 1994)

Appendix

Answers

General Notes

1. Whenever possible, payments have been made of clients' money. It is not wrong, when clients' money is available, to make payments out of office money but, certainly where the sum involved is substantial, it is impractical to use office money.

2. This was a composite cheque which can either:

   (a) be split; or
   (b) paid into clients' bank account followed by a transfer from CLIENT ACCOUNT to OFFICE ACCOUNT.

3. All petty cash payments must be made out of office money. Clients' money thus could not have been used.

4. The Principal Method of payment has been used in this case, so the VAT item (after the costs charge) will include the VAT on this payment. It would have been perfectly permissible in this case to use the Agency Method instead, in which case the amount debited to the ledger account when making the payment would also have included the VAT (and not the debit for the VAT after the costs debit).

5. This could not have been paid out of CLIENT ACCOUNT, because the Principal Method of payment is used.

6. This must be office money Rule 9(2) SAR.

Chapter 2

Page 19
13.(1)

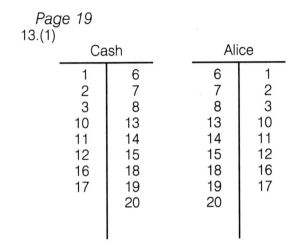

Cash			Alice	
1	6		6	1
2	7		7	2
3	8		8	3
10	13		13	10
11	14		14	11
12	15		15	12
16	18		18	16
17	19		19	17
	20		20	

13.(2)(a)

Purchases		Sales		Bill	
21			26	26	21
22			27	27	22
23			28	28	23
31			34	34	31
32			35	35	32
33			36	36	33

13.(2)(b)

Purchases		Sales		Carol	
41			42	42	41
43			44	44	43
45					45

13.(3)(a)

Purchases		Cash		Dick			
51			51	Cash	51	Purchases	51
52			52		52		52
53			53		53		53

13.(3)(b)

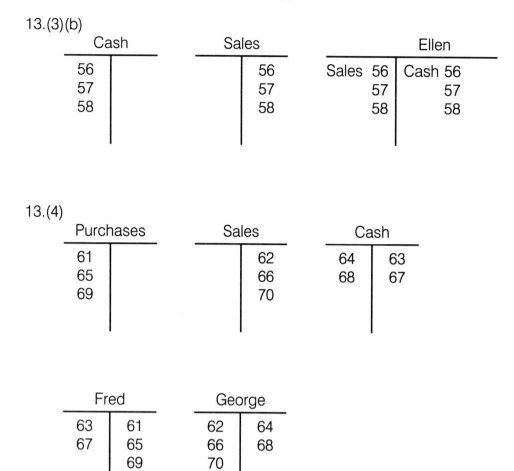

Cash	
56	
57	
58	

Sales	
	56
	57
	58

Ellen	
Sales 56	Cash 56
57	57
58	58

13.(4)

Purchases	
61	
65	
69	

Sales	
	62
	66
	70

Cash	
64	63
68	67

Fred	
63	61
67	65
	69

George	
62	64
66	68
70	

Chapter 3

Page 28

18.(1)

Cash	DR 5,000. 13,000. 1,000. 1,500.
	CR 4,000. 10,000.
Purchases	DR 10,000. 4,000.
	CR —
Capital	DR —
	CR 5,000.
S Ltd	DR 10,000.
	CR 10,000.
A	DR 1,000.
	CR 1,000.
B	DR 2,000.
	CR 1,500.
Sales	DR —
	CR 13,000. 1,000. 2,000.
Trial Balance	DR Cash 6,500. Purchases 14,000. B 500.
	CR Capital 5,000. Sales 16,000.
	Total = 21,000.

18.(2)

Cash	DR 1,500, 3,000. 2,000. 4,000. 750.
	CR 500. 750. 1,500. 25. 150. 1,500
Loan	DR —
	CR 3,000.
Capital	DR —
	CR 1,500.
Fixtures and Fittings	DR 750.
	CR —
Rent	DR 500
	CR —
Purchases	DR 1,500. 2,000.
	CR —
Sales	DR —
	CR 2,000. 4,000. 500. 250.
Wages	DR 150.
	CR —
Electricity	DR 25
	CR —
Tom	DR 1,500.
	CR 2,000.
Rachel	DR 500. 250.
	CR 750.
Trial Balance	DR Cash 6,825. Rent 500. Fixtures and Fittings 750. Purchases 3,500. Wages 150. Electricity 25.
	CR Capital 1,500. Loan 3,000. Sales 6,750. Creditors 500.
	Total = 11,750.

18.(3)

Trial Balance	DR Rent 620. Furniture 250. Rates 35. Sundry Expenses 12. Purchases 3,100. Debtors 915. Cash 908.
	CR Capital 2,200. Sales 2,800. Creditors 840.
	Total = 5,840.

18.(4)

Trial Balance as at December 31	DR Rates 3,000. Premises 28,000. Motor Vehicles 13,000. Fixtures 1,800. Wages 14,000. Purchases 30,000. Postages and Telephones 900. Lighting and Heating 2,800. Debtors 8,600. Cash 2,400.
	CR Capital 40,000. Loan 10,000. Sales 50,000. Creditors 4,500.
	Total = 104,500.

Chapter 5

Page 41
10.(1)

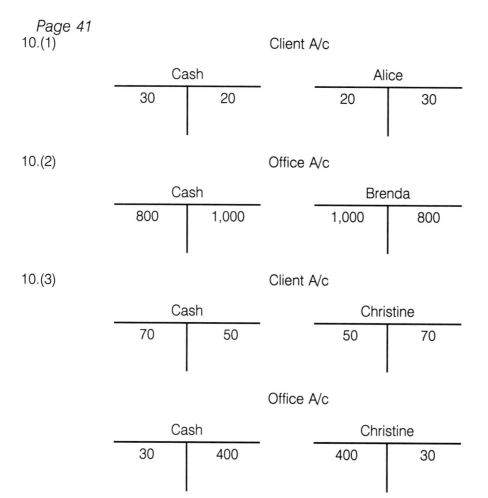

Client A/c

Cash

| 30 | 20 |

Alice

| 20 | 30 |

10.(2)

Office A/c

Cash

| 800 | 1,000 |

Brenda

| 1,000 | 800 |

10.(3)

Client A/c

Cash

| 70 | 50 |

Christine

| 50 | 70 |

Office A/c

Cash

| 30 | 400 |

Christine

| 400 | 30 |

Chapter 7

Page 54
11.(1)

Alpha						
		OFFICE ACCOUNT			CLIENT ACCOUNT	
		DR	CR	Balance	DR	CR	Balance
	Cash					800 –	800 –
	Cash				300 –		500 –
	Cash				400 –		100 –
	Cash				2 –		98 –

Cash						
		OFFICE ACCOUNT			CLIENT ACCOUNT	
		DR	CR	Balance	DR	CR	Balance
	Alpha				800		
	Alpha					300	
	Alpha					400	
	Alpha					2	

11.(2)

Beta						
		OFFICE ACCOUNT			CLIENT ACCOUNT	
		DR	CR	Balance	DR	CR	Balance
	Cash	6 –		6 –			
	Cash	700 –		706 –			
	Cash	45 –		751 –			
	Cash		300 –	451 –			

Cash						
		OFFICE ACCOUNT			CLIENT ACCOUNT	
		DR	CR	Balance	DR	CR	Balance
	Beta		6				
	Beta		700				
	Beta		45				
	Beta	300					

11.(3)

Omega						
		OFFICE ACCOUNT			CLIENT ACCOUNT	
		DR	CR	Balance	DR	CR	Balance
	Cash					38 −	38 −
	Cash				20 −		18 −
	Cash				18 −		—
	Cash	16 −		16 −			
	Cash		9 −	7 −			

Cash						
		OFFICE ACCOUNT			CLIENT ACCOUNT	
		DR	CR	Balance	DR	CR	Balance
	Omega				38		
	Omega					20	
	Omega					18	
	Omega		16				
	Omega	9					

Page 55
16.(1)

Alpha						
		OFFICE ACCOUNT			CLIENT ACCOUNT	
		DR	CR	Balance	DR	CR	Balance
	Petty Cash	4 −		4 −			

Beta						
		OFFICE ACCOUNT			CLIENT ACCOUNT		
		DR	CR	Balance	DR	CR	Balance
	Petty Cash	3·20		3·20			

Gamma						
		OFFICE ACCOUNT			CLIENT ACCOUNT		
		DR	CR	Balance	DR	CR	Balance
	Petty Cash	4·60		4·60			

Petty Cash				
		DR	CR	Balance
	Alpha		4·00	
	Beta		3·20	
	Gamma		4·60	

16.(2)

Delta						
		OFFICE ACCOUNT			CLIENT ACCOUNT		
		DR	CR	Balance	DR	CR	Balance
	Petty Cash	6·00		6·00			
	Cash					18 –	18 –
	Petty Cash*	1·70³		7·70			

* For meaning of superior figures throughout these answers, see General Notes, page 168.

Petty Cash				
		DR	CR	Balance
	Delta		6·00	
	Delta		1·70	

20.(1)

		OFFICE ACCOUNT			CLIENT ACCOUNT		
Alan							
		DR	CR	Balance	DR	CR	Balance
	Cash					100 –	100 –
	Cash				60 –		40 –
	Cash	70 –		70 –			

20.(2)

		OFFICE ACCOUNT			CLIENT ACCOUNT		
Brian							
		DR	CR	Balance	DR	CR	Balance
	Cash					200 –	200 –
	Cash				30 –		170 –
	Cash	400 –		400 –			
	Cash				50 –		120 –

20.(3)

		OFFICE ACCOUNT			CLIENT ACCOUNT		
Charles							
		DR	CR	Balance	DR	CR	Balance
	Cash					300 –	300 –
	Cash				200 –		100 –
	Cash	150 –		150 –			
	Cash				75 –		25 –
	Cash	30 –		180 –			

19.(4)

Donald		OFFICE ACCOUNT			CLIENT ACCOUNT		
		DR	CR	Balance	DR	CR	Balance
	Cash					400 –	400 –
	Cash				100 –		300 –
	Cash	350 –		350 –			
	Cash				150 –		150 –
	Cash				40 –		110 –

Page 58

23.(1)

Ethel		OFFICE ACCOUNT			CLIENT ACCOUNT		
		DR	CR	Balance	DR	CR	Balance
	Cash	100 –		100 –			
	Cash		70 –	30 –			
	Cash					40 –	40 –

23.(2)

Fred		OFFICE ACCOUNT			CLIENT ACCOUNT		
		DR	CR	Balance	DR	CR	Balance
	Cash	200 –		200 –			
	Cash		160 –	40 –			
	Cash					50 –	50 –
	Cash		30 –	10 –			

23.(3)

George							
		OFFICE ACCOUNT			CLIENT ACCOUNT		
		DR	CR	Balance	DR	CR	Balance
	Cash	300 –		300 –			
	Cash					400 –	400 –
	Cash		50 –	250 –			
	Cash	580 –		830 –			
	Cash		800 –	30 –			

Page 60

31.(1)   Harry   OFFICE A/C   Dr. 60
                                   Cr. 60
                     CLIENT A/C   Dr. —
                                   Cr. —

31.(2)   Ian   OFFICE A/C   Dr. 50.40
                                   Cr. 90
                     CLIENT A/C   Dr. —
                                   Cr. —

31.(3)   Joan   OFFICE A/C   Dr. 400.650
                                   Cr. 1,050
                     CLIENT A/C   Dr. —
                                   Cr. —

31.(4)   Kate   OFFICE A/C   Dr. 80.1,500
                                   Cr. 1,580
                     CLIENT A/C   Dr. —
                                   Cr. —

Chapter 8

Page 63

5.(1)

Alice (CL1)							
		OFFICE ACCOUNT			CLIENT ACCOUNT		
		DR	CR	Balance	DR	CR	Balance
(a)	Cash.					100 –	100 –
(b)	Costs	20 –		20 –			
(c)	Cash. Transfer		20 –	—	20 –		80 –

Cash							
		OFFICE ACCOUNT			CLIENT ACCOUNT		
		DR	CR	Balance	DR	CR	Balance
(a)	Alice				100 –		
(c)	Alice. Transfer	20 –				20 –	

5.(2)

Bill (CL2)							
		OFFICE ACCOUNT			CLIENT ACCOUNT		
		DR	CR	Balance	DR	CR	Balance
(a)	Cash. You					300 –	300 –
(b)	Costs	50 –		50 –			
(c)	Cash. Transfer		50 –	—	50 –		250 –

Cash							
		OFFICE ACCOUNT			CLIENT ACCOUNT		
		DR	CR	Balance	DR	CR	Balance
(a)	Bill				300 –		
(c)	Bill. Transfer	50 –				50 –	

5.(3)

Charles (CL3)							
		OFFICE ACCOUNT			CLIENT ACCOUNT		
		DR	CR	Balance	DR	CR	Balance
(a)	Cash. You					600 –	600 –
(b)	Cash				70 –		530 –
(c)	Costs	80 –		80 –			
(d)	Cash. Transfer		80 –	—	80 –		450 –

Cash							
		OFFICE ACCOUNT			CLIENT ACCOUNT		
		DR	CR	Balance	DR	CR	Balance
(a)	Charles				600 −		
(b)	Charles					70 −	
(d)	Charles. Transfer	80 −				80 −	

5.(4)

Dennis (CL4)							
		OFFICE ACCOUNT			CLIENT ACCOUNT		
		DR	CR	Balance	DR	CR	Balance
(a)	Cash. You					90 −	90 −
(b)	Petty Cash	10 −[3]		10 −			
(c)	Costs	30 −		40 −			
(d)	Cash. Transfer		40 −	—	40 −		50 −

Cash							
		OFFICE ACCOUNT			CLIENT ACCOUNT		
		DR	CR	Balance	DR	CR	Balance
(a)	Dennis				90 −		
(d)	Dennis. Transfer	40 −				40 −	

5.(5)

Ethel (CL5)							
		OFFICE ACCOUNT			CLIENT ACCOUNT		
		DR	CR	Balance	DR	CR	Balance
(a)	Cash. You					400 −	400 −
(b)	Cash				50 −		350 −
(c)	Petty Cash	6 −[3]		6 −			
(d)	Costs	70 −		76 −			
(e)	Cash. Transfer		76 −	—	76 −		274 −

Cash						
		OFFICE ACCOUNT			CLIENT ACCOUNT		
		DR	CR	Balance	DR	CR	Balance
(a)	Ethel				400 –		
(b)	Ethel					50 –	
(e)	Ethel. Transfer	76 –				76 –	

5.(6)

Frances (CL6)						
		OFFICE ACCOUNT			CLIENT ACCOUNT		
		DR	CR	Balance	DR	CR	Balance
(a)	Cash					80 –	80 –
(b)	Cash				10 –		70 –
(c)	Petty Cash	1 –		1 –			
(d)	Costs	20 –		21 –			
(e)	Cash. Transfer		21 –	—	21 –		49 –

Cash						
		OFFICE ACCOUNT			CLIENT ACCOUNT		
		DR	CR	Balance	DR	CR	Balance
(a)	Frances				80 –		
(b)	Frances					10 –	
(e)	Frances. Transfer	21 –				21 –	

Page 65

10.(1)

Graham (CL7)						
		OFFICE ACCOUNT			CLIENT ACCOUNT		
		DR	CR	Balance	DR	CR	Balance
(a)	Cash					40 –	40 –
(b)	Cash				50 –		10 – DR
(c)	Cash. Transfer	10 –		10 –		10 –	—

Cash							
		OFFICE ACCOUNT			CLIENT ACCOUNT		
		DR	CR	Balance	DR	CR	Balance
(a)	Graham				40		
(b)	Graham					50	
(c)	Graham. Transfer		10 –		10 –		

10.(2)

Henry (CL8)							
		OFFICE ACCOUNT			CLIENT ACCOUNT		
		DR	CR	Balance	DR	CR	Balance
(a)	Cash					700 –	700 –
(b)	Cash				1,000 –		300 – DR
(c)	Cash. Transfer	300 –		300 –		300 –	–

Cash							
		OFFICE ACCOUNT			CLIENT ACCOUNT		
		DR	CR	Balance	DR	CR	Balance
(a)	Henry				700		
(b)	Henry					1,000	
(c)	Henry. Transfer		300		300		

10.(3)

Ian (CL9)							
		OFFICE ACCOUNT			CLIENT ACCOUNT		
		DR	CR	Balance	DR	CR	Balance
(a)	Cash					2,000 –	2,000 –
(b)	Cash				2,500 –		500 – DR
(c)	Cash. Transfer	500 –		500 –		500 –	—

Cash							
		OFFICE ACCOUNT			CLIENT ACCOUNT		
		DR	CR	Balance	DR	CR	Balance
	Ian				2,000		
	Ian					2,500	
	Ian. Transfer		500		500		

Page 67
16.(1)

John (CL10)							
		OFFICE ACCOUNT			CLIENT ACCOUNT		
		DR	CR	Balance	DR	CR	Balance
	Cash					40 –	40 –
	Kevin				20 –		20 –

Kevin (CL11)							
		OFFICE ACCOUNT			CLIENT ACCOUNT		
		DR	CR	Balance	DR	CR	Balance
	John					20 –	20 –

16.(2)

Lesley (CL12)							
		OFFICE ACCOUNT			CLIENT ACCOUNT		
		DR	CR	Balance	DR	CR	Balance
	Cash					700 –	700 –
	Mary				400 –		300 –

Mary (CL13)							
		OFFICE ACCOUNT			CLIENT ACCOUNT		
		DR	CR	Balance	DR	CR	Balance
	Lesley					400 –	400 –

16.(3)

		OFFICE ACCOUNT			CLIENT ACCOUNT		
		Nick (CL14)					
		DR	CR	Balance	DR	CR	Balance
(a)	Cash					300 –	300 –
(b)	Costs	40 –		40 –			
(c)	Cash				50 –		250 –
(d)	Cash. Transfer		40 –	—	40 –		210 –
(e)	Olive				210 –		—

		OFFICE ACCOUNT			CLIENT ACCOUNT		
		Olive (CL15)					
		DR	CR	Balance	DR	CR	Balance
(e)	Nick.					210 –	210 –

		OFFICE ACCOUNT			CLIENT ACCOUNT		
		Cash					
		DR	CR	Balance	DR	CR	Balance
(a)	Nick				300		
(c)	Nick					50	
(d)	Nick. Transfer	40				40	

16.(4)

		OFFICE ACCOUNT			CLIENT ACCOUNT		
		Peter (CL16)					
		DR	CR	Balance	DR	CR	Balance
	Balance					10 –	10 –
	Robert				5 –		5 –
	Robert				7 –		2 – DR
	Cash	2 –		2 –		2 –	—

Robert (CL17)							
		OFFICE ACCOUNT			CLIENT ACCOUNT		
		DR	CR	Balance	DR	CR	Balance
Peter						5 –	5 –
Peter						7 –	12 –

Cash							
		OFFICE ACCOUNT			CLIENT ACCOUNT		
		DR	CR	Balance	DR	CR	Balance
Peter			2		2		

Chapter 9

Page 77
16.(1)

Cash	DR —	
	CR 50.5.40.4.30.3.	
Postages and	DR 50	
Telephones	CR —	
Typewriters	DR 40	
	CR —	
Stationery	DR 30	
	CR —	
Customs &	DR 5.4.3.	
Excise	CR —	

16.(2)

Cash	DR —	
	CR 5.4.10.8.77.	
Postages	DR 4	
	CR —	
Fares	DR 5	
	CR —	
Water Rates	DR 10	
	CR —	
Interest	DR 8	
	CR —	
Entertaining	DR 77	
	CR —	

Page 83
29.(1)

		OFFICE ACCOUNT			CLIENT ACCOUNT		
		DR	CR	Balance	DR	CR	Balance
	Cash. VAT	1 –		1 –			
	Cash. VAT	2 –		3 –			
	Petty Cash. VAT	3 –		6 –			
	Cash. VAT	4 –		10 –			
	Petty Cash. VAT	5 –		15 –			

(Adam (CL1))

		OFFICE ACCOUNT			CLIENT ACCOUNT		
		DR	CR	Balance	DR	CR	Balance
	Adam		1				
	VAT		0·10				
	Adam		2				
	VAT		0·20				
	Adam		4				
	VAT		0·40				

(Cash)

		DR	CR	Balance
	Cash	0·10		0·10
	Cash	0·20		0·30
	Petty Cash	0·30		0·60
	Cash	0·40		1
	Petty Cash	0·50		1·50

(Customs & Excise (NL11))

		DR	CR	Balance
	Adam		3	
	VAT		0·30	
	Adam		5	
	VAT		0·50	

(Petty Cash)

29.(2)   Adam   Office A/c DR 1·10.2·20.3·30.4·40.5·50
                                CR —
                  Client A/c DR —
                                  CR —
        Cash   Office A/c DR —
                                  CR 1·10.2·20.4·40.
                  Client A/c DR —
                                  CR —
        Petty Cash DR —
                    CR 3·30.5·50.

29.(3)   Bill   Office A/c DR 1.2·20.3.4·40.5.
                                  CR —
                  Client A/c DR —
                                  CR —
        Customs   DR 0·10.0·30.0·50.
         & Excise CR —

Cash						
		OFFICE ACCOUNT			CLIENT ACCOUNT	
		DR	CR	Balance	DR	CR	Balance
	Bill		1				
	VAT		0·10				
	Bill		2·20				
	Bill		5				
	VAT		0·50				

Petty Cash				
		DR	CR	Balance
	Bill		3	
	VAT		0·30	
	Bill		4·40	

29.(4)

Carol (CL3)						
		OFFICE ACCOUNT			CLIENT ACCOUNT	
		DR	CR	Balance	DR	CR	Balance
	Cash					400 –	400 –
	Cash. VAT	50 – [5]		50 –			
	Cash				44 –		356 –
	Cash				30 –		326 –

Cash							
		OFFICE ACCOUNT			CLIENT ACCOUNT		
		DR	CR	Balance	DR	CR	Balance
	Carol				400		
	Carol		50				
	VAT		5				
	Carol					44	
	Carol					30	

Customs & Excise (NL11)				
		DR	CR	Balance
	Cash	5		

29.(5)

Dick (CL4)							
		OFFICE ACCOUNT			CLIENT ACCOUNT		
		DR	CR	Balance	DR	CR	Balance
(a)	Cash					700 –	700 –
	Cash				100 –		600 –
	Cash. VAT	20 – 5		20			
	Petty Cash	8 – 3		28 –			
	Cash				66 –		534 –
	Petty Cash. VAT	4 – 35		32 –			

Cash							
		OFFICE ACCOUNT			CLIENT ACCOUNT		
		DR	CR	Balance	DR	CR	Balance
	Dick				700		
	Dick					100	
	Dick		20				
	VAT		2				
	Dick					66	

Customs & Excise (NL11)				
		DR	CR	Balance
	Cash	2 –		
	Petty Cash	0·40		

Petty Cash				
		DR	CR	Balance
	Dick		8	
	Dick		4	
	VAT		0·40	

29.(6)

Edward (CL5)							
		OFFICE ACCOUNT			CLIENT ACCOUNT		
		DR	CR	Balance	DR	CR	Balance
	Cash					600 –	600 –
	Cash				440 –		160 –
	Petty Cash	3 – ³		3 –			
	Cash				150 –		10 –
	Cash. VAT	10 – ⁵		13 –			
	Cash	50 –		63 –			

Cash							
		OFFICE ACCOUNT			CLIENT ACCOUNT		
		DR	CR	Balance	DR	CR	Balance
	Edward				600		
	Edward					440	
	Edward					150	
	Edward		10				
	VAT		1				
	Edward		50				

Customs & Excise (NL11)				
		DR	CR	Balance
	Cash	1 –		

Petty Cash			DR	CR	Balance
	Edward			3	

Page 85

34.(1)   Fred   OFFICE A/C DR 70.7.
                                 CR 77.
                     CLIENT A/C DR —
                                 CR —

34.(2)   George   OFFICE A/C DR 90.9.
                                 CR 99.
                     CLIENT A/C DR —
                                 CR —

34.(3)   Harold   OFFICE A/C DR 40.60.6.
                                 CR 106.
                     CLIENT A/C DR —
                                 CR —

34.(4)   Ian   OFFICE A/C DR 80.120.12.
                                 CR 212.
                     CLIENT A/C DR —
                                 CR —

Page 86

36.(1)   Jane   OFFICE A/C DR 10.60.7.
                                 CR 77.
                     CLIENT A/C DR —
                                 CR —

36.(2)   Kate   OFFICE A/C DR 20.70.9.
                                 CR 99.
                     CLIENT A/C DR —
                                 CR —

36.(3)   Lucy   OFFICE A/C DR 3.80.8·30.
                                 CR 91·30.
                     CLIENT A/C DR —
                                 CR —

36.(4)   Mary   OFFICE A/C DR 20.30.40.7.
                                 CR 97.
                     CLIENT A/C DR —
                                 CR —

36.(5)   Nancy   OFFICE A/C DR 90.10.20.11.
                                 CR 131.
                     CLIENT A/C DR —
                                 CR —

36.(6)   Olivia   OFFICE A/C DR
                                 1.20.3.4.50.7·30.
                                 CR 85·30.
                     CLIENT A/C DR —
                                 CR —

Page 88
39.(1)

Peter (CL16)							
		OFFICE ACCOUNT			CLIENT ACCOUNT		
		DR	CR	Balance	DR	CR	Balance
	Cash. VAT	100 –					
	VAT	10 –		110 –			
	Cash						
	Humphrey		110 –[6]	–			

39.(2)

Rachel (CL17)							
Date	Details	OFFICE ACCOUNT			CLIENT ACCOUNT		
		DR	CR	Balance	DR	CR	Balance
May 1	Cash					800 –	800 –
May 2	Cash. VAT	300 –[5]		300 –			
May 3	VAT	30 –		330 –			
	Cash. Transfer		330 –	–	330 –		470 –

Chapter 10

Page 95
7.(1)   Dust   OFFICE A/C DR 400.40.
                              CR 20.2.
              CLIENT A/C DR —
                              CR —

7.(2)   Lizzie   OFFICE A/C DR 47.
                              CR 47.
              CLIENT A/C DR —
                              CR 13.

7.(3)

Lizzie (CL2)							
		OFFICE ACCOUNT			CLIENT ACCOUNT		
		DR	CR	Balance	DR	CR	Balance
	Balance	47 –		47 –			
	Cash					60 –	60 –
	Cash. Transfer		47 –	–	47 –	–	13 –

7.(4)

		OFFICE ACCOUNT			CLIENT ACCOUNT		
Meff (CL3)							
		DR	CR	Balance	DR	CR	Balance
	Costs	800					
	VAT	80		880			
	Abatement		50	830			
	VAT		5	825			
	Cash		825	—		75 —	75 —

7.(5)

		OFFICE ACCOUNT			CLIENT ACCOUNT		
Meff (CL3)							
		DR	CR	Balance	DR	CR	Balance
	Costs	800 —					
	VAT	80 —		880 —			
	Abatement		50 —	830 —			
	VAT		5 —	825 —			
	Cash					900 —	900 —
	Cash. Transfer		825 —	—	825 —		75 —

7.(6)

		OFFICE ACCOUNT			CLIENT ACCOUNT		
Saunders (CL4)							
		DR	CR	Balance	DR	CR	Balance
(b)	Cash. You Cheque indorsed to Fry				600 —	600 —	

		OFFICE ACCOUNT			CLIENT ACCOUNT		
Cash							
		DR	CR	Balance	DR	CR	Balance
(b)	Saunders. Cheque indorsed to Fry				600 —	600 —	

Note: (a) No double-entries needed. See page 93.

7.(7)

Griffiths (CL5)						
		OFFICE ACCOUNT			CLIENT ACCOUNT	
		DR	CR	Balance	DR	CR	Balance
	Cash. You Cheque indorsed to Hare Cash. You Cash. Cheque dishonoured				8,000 – 200 –	8,000 – 200 –	200 – —

Cash						
		OFFICE ACCOUNT			CLIENT ACCOUNT	
		DR	CR	Balance	DR	CR	Balance
	Griffiths. Cheque indorsed to Hare Griffiths Griffiths. Cheque dishonoured				8,000 200	8,000 200	

7.(8)

Rudge (CL6)						
		OFFICE ACCOUNT			CLIENT ACCOUNT	
		DR	CR	Balance	DR	CR	Balance
May 1 May 2 May 5	Cash. You Cash Cash. Cheque dishonoured Cash. Transfer	1,000 –		1,000 –	1,000 – 5,000 –	5,000 – 1,000 –	5,000 – 4,000 – 1,000 – DR —

Cash							
		OFFICE ACCOUNT			CLIENT ACCOUNT		
		DR	CR	Balance	DR	CR	Balance
May 1	Rudge				5,000		
May 2	Rudge					1,000	
May 5	Rudge. Cheque dishonoured					5,000	
	Rudge. Transfer		1,000		1,000		

Chapter 11

Page 97

(1)

Bill (CL2)							
		OFFICE ACCOUNT			CLIENT ACCOUNT		
		DR	CR	Balance	DR	CR	Balance
	Cash					400 –	400 –
	Cash				50 –		350 –
	Petty Cash	6 –		6 –			
	Costs	70 –		76 –			
	VAT	7 –		83 –			
	Cash. Transfer		83 –		83 –		267 –

(2)   Carol   OFFICE A/C   DR 80.90.2.10.300.40.
                                    CR 522.
                          CLIENT A/C   DR —
                                      CR —

(3)   David   OFFICE A/C   DR 3.400.55.60.700.110·30.
                                    CR 1,328·30.
                          CLIENT A/C   DR —
                                      CR —

(4)   Ethel   OFFICE A/C   DR 88.9.125.20.3.42.17.
                                    CR 304.
                          CLIENT A/C   DR —
                                      CR —

(5)

		OFFICE ACCOUNT			CLIENT ACCOUNT		
	George (CL7)						
		DR	CR	Balance	DR	CR	Balance
	Cash. You					70 –	70 –
	Cash				8 –		62 –
	Cash				9·90		52·10
	Cash. VAT	10 – ⁵		10 –			
	Costs	20 –		30 –			
	VAT	3 –		33 –			
	Cash. Transfer		33 –	—	33 –		19·10

(6)

		OFFICE ACCOUNT			CLIENT ACCOUNT		
	Henry (CL8)						
		DR	CR	Balance	DR	CR	Balance
	Cash. You					80 –	80 –
	Cash. VAT	20 – ⁵		20 –			
	Petty Cash	1 – ³		21 –			
	Cash				11 – ⁵		69 –
	Costs	30 –		51 –			
	VAT	5 –		56 –			
	Cash. Transfer		56 –	—	56 –		13 –

(7)

		OFFICE ACCOUNT			CLIENT ACCOUNT		
	Kate (CL10)						
		DR	CR	Balance	DR	CR	Balance
	Cash	80 –		80 –			
	Cash. VAT	90 –		170 –			
	Costs	100 –		270 –			
	VAT	21 – *		291 –			
	Cash. You					311 –	311 –
	Cash. VAT	20 – ⁵		311 –			
	Cash. Transfer		311 –	—	311 –		—

* See page 87: £100 + £90 + £20 = £210 @ 10%.

(8)

Phantom Co Ltd (CL12)							
		OFFICE ACCOUNT			CLIENT ACCOUNT		
		DR	CR	Balance	DR	CR	Balance
Apr. 4	Cash. Documents VAT	10* [4]		10			
Apr. 9	Cash. You					200	200
May 8	Cash. Accountant. Witness fee				88**		112
May 26	Cash. Jakes Transcripts				44**		68
May 31	Costs VAT	500 51***		510 561			
Jun. 21	Cash. You Cash. Transfer		493[6] 68	68 —	68		—

* Principal Method. If it had been an input of Phantom Co Ltd, the Agency Method would have been used.

** Agency Method. Payments made using the Principal Method cannot be paid out of clients' money, whereas Agency Method payments can.

*** Taxable supplies by Carambas to Phantom Co Ltd are costs £500 (*exclusive* of VAT) plus the £10 payment for documents, *i.e.* £510 @ 10% = £51 VAT.

(9)

Cashe, deceased (CL13)							
		OFFICE ACCOUNT			CLIENT ACCOUNT		
		DR	CR	Balance	DR	CR	Balance
Nov. 1	Balance					84	84
Nov. 3	Cash. Disbursements	126*		126			
Nov. 20	Cash. Completion					31,710	31,794
Nov. 27	Tree. Transfer				200		31,594

* The £84 could now be transferred from CLIENT ACCOUNT to OFFICE ACCOUNT. Another way of dealing with this would be to draw two cheques: £84 on CLIENT ACCOUNT, £42 on OFFICE ACCOUNT.

Guy Forkes (CL14)							
		OFFICE ACCOUNT			CLIENT ACCOUNT		
		DR	CR	Balance	DR	CR	Balance
Nov. 1	Balance					100	100
Nov. 5	Cash. Disbursement				22		78
Nov. 6	Costs	80		80			
	VAT	8		88			
	Cash. Transfer		78	10	78		—
Nov. 28	Cash. You		10⁶	—			

Fred (CL15)							
		OFFICE ACCOUNT			CLIENT ACCOUNT		
		DR	CR	Balance	DR	CR	Balance
Nov. 8	Cash. You					450	450
	Cash. Surveyor				100		350
Nov. 17	Cash. Cheque dishonoured				450		100ᴰᴿ
	Cash. Transfer	100		100		100	—

Brown (CL16)							
Date	Details	OFFICE ACCOUNT			CLIENT ACCOUNT		
		DR	CR	Balance	DR	CR	Balance
Oct. 1	Costs. Agreed fee	60		60			
	VAT	6		66			
	Cash. You		66	—			
Nov. 23	Abatement		20	20ᶜᴿ			
	VAT		2	22ᶜᴿ			
	Cash. You	22		—			

The balance on the account at the start of November is nil. When the fee was agreed with Brown, the client ledger should have been debited with the fee plus VAT and when the money due was received from Brown, the client ledger should have been credited.

No entries are needed to record the cheque for £1,243, as this was payable direct to Brown (see page 93).

The amount sent to Brown is the £22 owing to Brown on OFFICE ACCOUNT as a result of the abatement.

		OFFICE ACCOUNT			CLIENT ACCOUNT		
	Tree (CL17)						
		DR	CR	Balance	DR	CR	Balance
Nov. 27	Cash	1,200		1,200			
	Cash. You		$1,000^6$	200			
	Cashe, decd						
	Transfer					200*	200
	Cash. Transfer		200	—	200		—

* Step 1. A Ledger Transfer from Cashe, deceased, to Tree.
Step 2. A Cash Transfer of the money due from CLIENT ACCOUNT to OFFICE ACCOUNT.

		OFFICE ACCOUNT			CLIENT ACCOUNT		
	Cash Account						
		DR	CR	Balance	DR	CR	Balance
Nov. 3	Cashe, decd. Disbursements		126				
Nov. 5	Forkes. Disbursements					22	
Nov. 6	Forkes Transfer	78				78	
Nov. 8	Fred				450		
Nov. 16	Fred. Surveyor					100	
Nov. 17	Fred. Cheque dishonoured					450	
	Fred. Transfer		100		100		
Nov. 20	Cashe, decd. Completion				31,710		
Nov. 23	Brown		22				
Nov. 27	Tree		1,200				
	Tree	1,000					
	Tree. Transfer	200				200	
Nov. 28	Forkes	10					

Chapter 13

Page 106

7.(1)

Laurence (CL2): On deposit Jan. 3, removed Sept. 3							
		OFFICE ACCOUNT			CLIENT ACCOUNT		
		DR	CR	Balance	DR	CR	Balance
Jan. 2	Cash. You					5,000 −	5,000 −
Sept. 1	Deposit Cash						
	Interest					30 −	5,030 −
Sept. 4	Cash. You				5,030 −		—

Cash							
		OFFICE ACCOUNT			CLIENT ACCOUNT		
		DR	CR	Balance	DR	CR	Balance
Jan. 2	Laurence				5,000		
Jan. 3	Deposit Cash.						
	Re Laurence					5,000	
Sept. 3	Deposit Cash.						
	Re Laurence				5,030		
Sept. 4	Laurence					5,030	

Deposit Cash. Re Laurence							
		OFFICE ACCOUNT			CLIENT ACCOUNT		
		DR	CR	Balance	DR	CR	Balance
Jan. 3	Cash				5,000		5,000
Sept. 1	Laurence.						
	Interest				30		5,030
Sept. 3	Cash					5,030	—

7.(2)

Barnaby (CL3). On deposit Feb. 1. Removed Oct. 2							
		OFFICE ACCOUNT			CLIENT ACCOUNT		
		DR	CR	Balance	DR	CR	Balance
Feb. 1	Cash. You					2,000	2,000 –
Aug. 1	Deposit Cash. Interest					42 –	2,042 –
Oct. 2	Cash. Jacob				2,000 –		42 –
Oct. 3	Cash. Interest					18 –	60 –
Oct. 4	Cash. You				60 –		—

Cash							
		OFFICE ACCOUNT			CLIENT ACCOUNT		
		DR	CR	Balance	DR	CR	Balance
Feb. 1	Barnaby				2,000*		
	Deposit Cash. Re Barnaby					2,000	
Oct. 2	Deposit Cash. Barnaby				2,042		
	Barnaby. Cheque to Jacob					2,000	
Oct. 3	Barnaby. Interest				18		
Oct. 4	Barnaby					60	

* Note: This was paid into the current account and then put on deposit. It could have been paid directly into the deposit account with no need for the transfer.

Deposit Cash. Barnaby							
		OFFICE ACCOUNT			CLIENT ACCOUNT		
		DR	CR	Balance	DR	CR	Balance
Feb. 1	Cash				2,000		2,000
Aug. 1	Barnaby. Interest				42		2,042
Oct. 2	Cash					2,042	

7.(3)

Violet (CL4). On deposit Mar. 1. Removed April 3							
		OFFICE ACCOUNT			CLIENT ACCOUNT		
		DR	CR	Balance	DR	CR	Balance
Mar. 1	Cash. You					4,500 –	4,500 –
Apr. 1	Deposit Cash.						
	Interest					14 –	4,514 –
Apr. 2	Costs	20 –					
	VAT	2 –		22 –			
Apr. 4	Cash. You				4,492 –		
	Cash. Transfer		22 –	—	22 –		—

Cash							
		OFFICE ACCOUNT			CLIENT ACCOUNT		
		DR	CR	Balance	DR	CR	Balance
Mar. 1	Violet				4,500		
	Deposit Cash.						
	Re Violet					4,500	
Apr. 3	Deposit Cash.						
	Re Violet				4,514		
Apr. 4	Violet					4,492	
	Violet. Transfer	22				22	

Deposit Cash. Violet							
		OFFICE ACCOUNT			CLIENT ACCOUNT		
		DR	CR	Balance	DR	CR	Balance
Mar. 1	Cash				4,500		4,500
Apr. 1	Violet. Interest				14		4,514
Apr. 3	Cash					4,514	—

Page 110

15.(1)

Laurence (CL2)							
		OFFICE ACCOUNT			CLIENT ACCOUNT		
		DR	CR	Balance	DR	CR	Balance
	Cash. You					5,000 –	5,000 –
	Cash. You.						
	Refund						
	(plus Interest						
	£30)				5,000 –		—

Cash						
		OFFICE ACCOUNT			CLIENT ACCOUNT		
		DR	CR	Balance	DR	CR	Balance
Laurence Laurence. Refund Deposit Interest Payable. Laurence			30		5,000	5,000	

15.(2)

Barnaby (CL3)						
		OFFICE ACCOUNT			CLIENT ACCOUNT		
		DR	CR	Balance	DR	CR	Balance
Cash. You Cash. X (Interest £60 sent to Client)					7,000 –	7,000 –	7,000 – —

Cash						
		OFFICE ACCOUNT			CLIENT ACCOUNT		
		DR	CR	Balance	DR	CR	Balance
Barnaby Barnaby. Cheque to X Deposit Interest Payable. Re Barnaby			60		7,000	7,000	

15.(3)

Sue (CL3)						
		OFFICE ACCOUNT			CLIENT ACCOUNT		
		DR	CR	Balance	DR	CR	Balance
Cash. You Cash. Interest Cash					5,030 –	5,000 – 30 –	5,000 – 5,030 – —

Cash						
		OFFICE ACCOUNT			CLIENT ACCOUNT		
		DR	CR	Balance	DR	CR	Balance
Sue.				5,000		
Interest						
Payable. Sue		30				
Sue. Interest				30		
Sue					5,030	

15.(4)

Violet (CL4)						
		OFFICE ACCOUNT			CLIENT ACCOUNT		
		DR	CR	Balance	DR	CR	Balance
Cash. You						4,500 –	4,500 –
Cash					4,400 –		100 –
Costs		120 –					
VAT		12 –		132 –			
Cash. Interest						43 –	143 –
Cash. Transfer			132 –	—	132 –		
Cash. You					11 –		—

Page 113
22.(1)

Cash						
		OFFICE ACCOUNT			CLIENT ACCOUNT		
		DR	CR	Balance	DR	CR	Balance
Balance					20,000		20,000
Deposit Cash							
General Deposit						15,000	5,000
Interest							
Received		52					
Deposit Cash.							
General Deposit					2,500		7,500
Interest							
Received		34					

Deposit Cash. General Deposit							
		OFFICE ACCOUNT			CLIENT ACCOUNT		
		DR	CR	Balance	DR	CR	Balance
Cash					15,000		15,000
Cash						2,500	12,500

Deposit Interest Receivable (PL6)				
		DR	CR	Balance
Cash			52 –	52 –
Cash			34 –	86 –

22.(2)

Cash							
		OFFICE ACCOUNT			CLIENT ACCOUNT		
		DR	CR	Balance	DR	CR	Balance
Balance					18,000		18,000
Deposit Cash							
General.						14,000	4,000
A					8,300		12,300
A. Refund						8,300	4,000
Deposit Interest							
Payable. Re A			58				
Deposit Interest							
Received		108					

22.(3)

Adams (CL1). (a) On deposit. (d) Withdrawn							
		OFFICE ACCOUNT			CLIENT ACCOUNT		
		DR	CR	Balance	DR	CR	Balance
(a)	Cash. You					4,500 –	4,500 –
(d)	Deposit Cash.						
	Interest					100 –	4,600 –
(d)	Cash. You				4,600 –		—

Cash							
		OFFICE ACCOUNT			CLIENT ACCOUNT		
		DR	CR	Balance	DR	CR	Balance
(a)	Adams				4,500		
	Deposit Cash.						
	Re Adams					4,500	
(b)	Deposit Interest						
	Received	70					
(c)	Brown.					500	
	Interest Paid.						
	Re Brown		25				
(d)	Deposit Cash.						
	Re Adams				4,600		
	Adams						4,600

Brown (CL2)							
		OFFICE ACCOUNT			CLIENT ACCOUNT		
		DR	CR	Balance	DR	CR	Balance
	Balance					500 –	500 –
(c)	Cash. You (plus						
	interest £25)				500 –		—

22.(4)

Cash							
Date	Details	OFFICE ACCOUNT			CLIENT ACCOUNT		
		DR	CR	Balance	DR	CR	Balance
Mar. 1	Deposit Cash.						
	General					30,000	
May 2	Simon				10,000		
	Deposit Cash.						
	Simon					10,000	
May 3	Andrew				20,000		
Sept. 1	Deposit Interest						
	Received	35					
Sept. 2	Deposit Cash.						
	Re Simon				10,025		
	Simon. Refund					10,025	
Sept. 3	Interest Paid.						
	Re Andrew		15				
	Andrew.						
	Interest				15		
	Andrew					20,015	

Chapter 14

Page 117

5.(1)   Simon   OFFICE A/C DR 300.400.70.
                                    CR 770^6.
                              CLIENT A/C DR —
                                      CR —

5.(2)   Andrew   OFFICE A/C DR 108*.10·80.
                                    CR 118·80.
                              CLIENT A/C DR —
                                      CR —

Note: The £3 fares is debited to the Fares Account.
* Costs £100 + Sundries £8 = £108.

Page 118

10.(1)   James   OFFICE A/C DR 50.70.7.
                                    CR 127 (Mick).
                              CLIENT A/C DR —
                                      CR —

10.(2)   Matthew OFFICE A/C DR 10.40.4.
                                    CR 39·60 (Paul). 14·40 (You).
                              CLIENT A/C DR —
                                      CR —

10.(3)   John   OFFICE A/C DR 30.80.8.
                                    CR 110 (Luke). 8 (You).
                              CLIENT A/C DR —
                                      CR —

Page 120

12.(1)   Philip   OFFICE A/C DR 50.70.7.
                                    CR (Bartholomew) 127.
                              CLIENT A/C DR —
                                      CR —

          Bar-   OFFICE A/C DR (Philip) 127.
          tholomew   CR 127.
                              CLIENT A/C DR —
                                      CR —

12.(2)   Thomas   OFFICE A/C DR 10.40.4.
                                    CR (Jude) 54.
                              CLIENT A/C DR —
                                      CR —

          Jude   OFFICE A/C DR 20.50.5. (Thomas) 54.
                                    CR 129.
                              CLIENT A/C DR —
                                      CR —

Page 123

16.(1)   Peter &   OFFICE A/C   DR 19.1·90.
          Co   CR 20·90.
                     CLIENT A/C   DR —
                                   CR —

16.(2)   Benjamin   OFFICE A/C   DR 6.28·50.2·85.
          & Co   CR 37·35.
                     CLIENT A/C   DR —
                                   CR —

16.(3)   Jeremy   OFFICE A/C   DR 10.33.60.6.
                                   CR 109.
                     CLIENT A/C   DR —
                                   CR —

          Note: The £19 VAT exclusive, paid to the agents, is debited on the Agency Expenses Account.

16.(4)   Jackson   OFFICE A/C   DR 50.6.80.13.
                                   CR 149.
                     CLIENT A/C   DR —
                                   CR —
          Agency   OFFICE A/C   DR 28·50.
          Expenses   CR —

16.(5)   Tom   OFFICE A/C   DR 7.9.40.4.
                                   CR 60.
                     CLIENT A/C   DR —
                                   CR —

          Agency   OFFICE A/C   DR 17·10.
          Expenses   CR —

16.(6)(a)

Thomasina (CL16)							
		OFFICE ACCOUNT			CLIENT ACCOUNT		
		DR	CR	Balance	DR	CR	Balance
Jan. 2	Cash. You. On account					75 –	75 –
Jan. 4	Cash					900 –	975 –
Jan. 9	Cash. Bland & Co., Counsel VAT	15 – *		15 –			
Jan. 10	Costs	95 – **		110 –			
	VAT	11 –		121 –			
	Cash. Transfer		121 –	—	121 –		854
	Cash. You				854 –		—

    * The Principal Method was used because the tax invoice was addressed to you. The VAT is debited to Customs & Excise account.
    ** Our costs £40 + Agents' Costs £55 = £95.

Appendix

Customs & Excise				
		DR	CR	Balance
Jan. 9	Cash. Bland & Co	6·50*		
Jan. 10	Thomasina		11 –	

* Costs £50 + Counsel £15 = £65 × 10% = £6.50.

Agency Expenses (NL20)				
		DR	CR	Balance
Jan. 9	Cash. Bland & Co. Re Thomasina	50 –		

16.(6)(b)

A Solicitor (CL100)							
		OFFICE ACCOUNT			CLIENT ACCOUNT		
		DR	CR	Balance	DR	CR	Balance
Jan. 5	Cash. Counsel	16·50*		16·50			
Jan. 8	Costs	50 –		66·50			
	VAT	5 –		71·50			
Jan. 11	Cash. You		71·50	—			

* Agency Method. The tax invoice is NOT addressed to Bland & Co.

Page 127
21.(1)

Gamma Insurance Co (CL20)							
		OFFICE ACCOUNT			CLIENT ACCOUNT		
		DR	CR	Balance	DR	CR	Balance
	Cash					34 –	34 –
	Commission	5 –		5 –			
	Cash. Transfer		5 –	—	5 –		
	Cash. You				29 –		—

21.(2)

Zeta Insurance Co (CL21)							
		OFFICE ACCOUNT			CLIENT ACCOUNT		
		DR	CR	Balance	DR	CR	Balance
	Delta. Transfer					41 –	41 –
	Commission	16 –		16 –			
	Cash. Transfer		16 –	—	16 –		25 –
	Cash. You				25 –		—

21.(3)

Sigma Insurance Co (CL12)							
		OFFICE ACCOUNT			CLIENT ACCOUNT		
		DR	CR	Balance	DR	CR	Balance
	Commission	7 –		7 –			
	Cash. Premium					28 –	28 –
	Commission	5 –		12 –			
	Cash. You				16 –		12 –
	Cash. Transfer		12 –	—	12 –		—

21.(4)

Nonpay Insurance Co Ltd (CL34)							
Date	Details	OFFICE ACCOUNT			CLIENT ACCOUNT		
		DR	CR	Balance	DR	CR	Balance
Jan. 2	Balance	43		43			
	Cash. Brown					104	104
Jan. 17	Commission	15		58			
	Cash. Transfer		58	—	58		46
	Cash. You				46		—

Black (CL25)							
Date	Details	OFFICE ACCOUNT			CLIENT ACCOUNT		
		DR	CR	Balance	DR	CR	Balance
Jan. 7	Savall B.S. Transfer	22		22			

Savall Building Society (CL26)							
Date	Details	OFFICE ACCOUNT			CLIENT ACCOUNT		
		DR	CR	Balance	DR	CR	Balance
Jan. 7	Costs	20		20			
	VAT	2		22			
	Black. Transfer		22	—			

White (CL28)							
Date	Details	OFFICE ACCOUNT			CLIENT ACCOUNT		
		DR	CR	Balance	DR	CR	Balance
Jan. 10	Cash					1,250	1,250
	Costs	40		40			
	VAT	4		44			

Yellow (CL27)							
Date	Details	OFFICE ACCOUNT			CLIENT ACCOUNT		
		DR	CR	Balance	DR	CR	Balance
	Cash.						
	Counsel. VAT	100		100			
Jan. 14	Costs	220*		320			
	VAT	32		352			
Jan. 18	Cash. You					364	364
	Cash. Agents						
	Court fee	12		364			
	Cash. Transfer		364	—	364		—

* Our Work £100 + Agents' Work £120 = £220.

Cash							
Date	Details	OFFICE ACCOUNT			CLIENT ACCOUNT		
		DR	CR	Balance	DR	CR	Balance
Jan. 2	Nonpay.				104		
Jan. 10	White				1,250		
Jan. 17	Nonpay.						
	Transfer	58				58	
	Nonpay					46	
Jan. 18	Yellow				364		
	Agency						
	Expenses		100*				
	VAT		10				
	Yellow.						
	Court fee		12				
	Yellow. Transfer	364				364	

* £120 − £20 = £100.

Chapter 15

Page 139
17.(1)

Statement

Oliver. Sale of "Whiteacre"

	£		£
Discharge of mortgage	20,000	Deposit	6,000
Mortgagee's costs	33	Sale	54,000
Costs	140		
VAT	14		
BALANCE DUE	39,813		
	60,000		60,000

17.(2)

Statement

Robert. Purchase of . . .

	£		£
Search	15	You	7,000
Deposit	7,000	Mortgage advance	30,000
Completion	63,000	BALANCE DUE	33,535
Mortgagee's costs	66		
Costs	340		
VAT	34		
L.R. Fees	80		
	70,535		70,535

17.(3).

Statement

Sarah. Sale of "Greenacre" and Purchase of "Blueacre"

PURCHASE of Blueacre	£	£	£
Payments			
Search	10		
Deposit	11,000		
Completion	99,000		
Search	8		
Costs	450		
VAT	45		
Stamp duty	550		
Mortgage costs	99*		
		111,162	
Receipts			
On account	11,000		
Mortgage advance	20,000		
		31,000	
			80,162
SALE of Greenacre			
Receipts			
Deposit	8,000		
Completion	72,000		
		80,000	
Payments			
Mortgage redemption	9,230		
Costs	350		
VAT	35	9,615	
			70,385
BALANCE DUE from you			9,777

* Any price quoted is deemed to include VAT unless the contrary is made clear.

Page 140

18.(1)

Albert (CL1)							
Date	Details	OFFICE ACCOUNT			CLIENT ACCOUNT		
		DR	CR	Balance	DR	CR	Balance
Jan. 2	Cash. Deposit					2,000 –	2,000 –
Feb. 1	Cash. Completion					18,000 –	20,000 –
Feb. 2	Costs	300 –					
	VAT	30 –		330 –			
	Cash. Transfer		330 –	—	330 –		
	Cash. You				19,670		—

18.(2)

		OFFICE ACCOUNT			CLIENT ACCOUNT		
		Brian (CL2)					
Date	Details	DR	CR	Balance	DR	CR	Balance
Sept. 1	Cash. Search	1·85		1·85			
Oct. 14	Petty Cash. Search	1·50		3·35			
Oct. 15	Costs	200 –					
	VAT	20 –		223·35			
Oct. 29	Cash. You		223·35²	—		9,000 – ²	9,000 –
Nov. 1	Cash. Completion				9,000 –		—

18.(3)

		OFFICE ACCOUNT			CLIENT ACCOUNT		
		Charles (CL3)					
Date	Details	DR	CR	Balance	DR	CR	Balance
May 1	Petty Cash. Search	1·85		1·85			
May 16	Cash. You. Deposit					1,800 –	1,800 –
	Cash. You. Deposit				1,800 –		—
Jun. 9	Costs	135 –		136·85			
	VAT	13·50		150·35			
Jun. 19	Cash. You		150·35*	—		16,240²	16,240 –
Jun. 24	Cash. Completion				16,200 –	—	40 –
Jun. 25	Cash. L.R. fees				40 –		—

   * Of the £16,390.35, only £150.35 is office money. The £40 in respect of the land registry fees is clients' money, since payment has not yet been made.

18.(4)

William (CL4)							
Date	Details	OFFICE ACCOUNT			CLIENT ACCOUNT		
		DR	CR	Balance	DR	CR	Balance
Jan. 13	Cash. Search	4 –		4 –			
Jan. 19	Cash. You					3,000 –	3,000 –
Jan. 22	Cash. Survey fee	165 – **		169 –			
Jan. 27	Cash. Deposit				3,000 –		—
Feb. 12	Cash. Search	2 –		171 –			
Feb. 13	Costs	200 –		371 –			
	VAT	20 –		391 –			
Feb. 15	Cash. You		391 – [2]	—		27,072 – *	27,072 –
Feb. 17	Cash. Completion				27,000 –		172 –
	Cash. Stamp duty				72 –		—

* This includes the stamp duty to be paid later.
** The £3,000 in CLIENT ACCOUNT is to be used for paying the deposit and the solicitor is not authorised to use it to pay for another item.

18.(5)

Edward (CL5)							
Date	Details	OFFICE ACCOUNT			CLIENT ACCOUNT		
		DR	CR	Balance	DR	CR	Balance
Jan. 2	Petty Cash. Search	6 –		6 –			
Jan. 10	Petty Cash. Search	4 –		10 –			
Jan. 20	Costs	150 –		160 –			
	VAT	15 –		175 –			
Jan. 30	Cash. You		175 – [2]	—		1,055 – [2]	1,055 –
Feb. 10	Cash. Vendors' Solicitors Completion				1,055 – *		—

* Note:

Completion Moneys		9,000.00
Mortgage Advance	8,000.00	
Less	55.00	7,945.00
		1,055.00

18.(6)

Fishy Building Society (CL6)							
Date	Details	OFFICE ACCOUNT			CLIENT ACCOUNT		
		DR	CR	Balance	DR	CR	Balance
Feb. 8	Costs	50 –		50 –			
	VAT	5 –		55 –			
Feb. 9	Cash. You					8,000 –[2]	8,000 –
Feb. 10	Cash.						
	Completion				7,945 –		55
	Cash. Transfer		55 –	–	55 –		–

18.(7)

George (CL7)							
Date	Details	OFFICE ACCOUNT			CLIENT ACCOUNT		
		DR	CR	Balance	DR	CR	Balance
Apr. 1	Cash. Search	7 –		7 –			
May 8	Costs	400 –		407 –			
	VAT	40 –		447 –			
May 17	Cash. You		447 –	–		8,077 –[2]	8,077 –
May 19	Cash. Vendors'						
	Solicitors.						
	Completion				8,077 –*		–

* Note:

Completion		23,000.00
Mortgage	15,000.00	
Less	77.00	14,923.00
	———	———
		8,077.00

Grim Building Society (CL8)							
Date	Details	OFFICE ACCOUNT			CLIENT ACCOUNT		
		DR	CR	Balance	DR	CR	Balance
May 8	Costs	70 –		70 –			
	VAT	7 –		77 –			
May 18	Cash. You					15,000 –[2]	15,000 –
May 19	Cash. Vendor's						
	Solicitors.*						
	Completion				14,923 –		77 –
	Cash. Transfer		77 –	–	77 –		–

* The £14,923 could be transferred to George's account, which would then be debited with the total purchase money of £23,000.

18.(8)

Henry (CL8)							
Date	Details	OFFICE ACCOUNT			CLIENT ACCOUNT		
		DR	CR	Balance	DR	CR	Balance
Jun. 1	Petty Cash. Search	3 –		3 –			
Jun. 20	Cash. You. Deposit indorsed to Vendor's Solicitors				5,000 –	5,000 –	
Jun. 30	Petty Cash. Search	4 –		7 –			
Jul. 1	Costs	200 –		207 –			
	VAT	20 –		227 –			
	Ink BS	33 –		260 –			
Jul 15	Cash. You		260 –²	—		35,120 –²	35,120 –
Jul. 16	Cash. Completion				35,000*		120 –
Jul. 17	Cash. Stamp duty				100 –		20 –
Jul. 18	Cash. L.R. fees				20 –		—

Ink Building Society (CL10)							
Date	Details	OFFICE ACCOUNT			CLIENT ACCOUNT		
		DR	CR	Balance	DR	CR	Balance
Jul. 1	Costs	30 –		30 –			
	VAT	3 –		33 –			
	Henry		33	—			
Jul. 15	Cash. You					10,000 –	10,000 –
Jul. 16	Cash. Vendor's Solicitors.* Completion				10,000 –		

* The £10,000 could be transferred to Henry's account, which would be debited with the total purchase money of £45,000.

18.(9)

John (CL12)							
Date	Details	OFFICE ACCOUNT			CLIENT ACCOUNT		
		DR	CR	Balance	DR	CR	Balance
Jun. 1	Cash. Completion					9,000 –	
	Stakeholder. Transfer					1,000 –	10,000 –
	Kate. Transfer				5,000 –		5,000 –
Jun. 2	Costs	50 –		50 –			
	VAT	5 –		55 –			
	Kate. Transfer	22 –		77 –			
	Cash. Transfer		77 –	—	77 –		4,923
	Cash. You				4,923		—

Kate (CL13)							
Date	Details	OFFICE ACCOUNT			CLIENT ACCOUNT		
		DR	CR	Balance	DR	CR	Balance
Jun. 1	John. Transfer					5,000 –	5,000 –
Jun. 2	Costs	20 –		20 –			
	VAT	2 –		22 –			
	John. Transfer		22 –	—			
	Cash. You				5,000 –		—

Stakeholder (CL11)							
Date	Details	OFFICE ACCOUNT			CLIENT ACCOUNT		
		DR	CR	Balance	DR	CR	Balance
May 1	Cash. Purchaser's Solicitors. Re John					1,000 –	1,000 –
Jun. 1	John. Transfer				1,000 –		—

18.(10)

Mary (CL14)							
Date	Details	OFFICE ACCOUNT			CLIENT ACCOUNT		
		DR	CR	Balance	DR	CR	Balance
Jan. 2	Cash. Search	4 –		4 –			
Feb. 2	Cash. Deposit	2,000 –		2,004 –			
Feb. 15	Cash. You.						
	On Account					5,500 – *	5,500 –
Mar. 1	Cash. Sale.					13,500 –	19,000 –
	Cash. Purchase				18,000 –		1,000 –
Mar. 2	Cash.						
	Stamp Duty				180 –		820
	Cash.						
	L.R. Fees				70 –		750 –
Mar. 3	Cash. Noddy &						
	Co. Deposit					1,100 –	1,850 –
Mar. 8	Costs	150 –		2,154 –			
	VAT	15 –		2,169 –			
	Cash. Transfer		1,850 –	319 –	1,850 –		—

* This could have been split. If so, it would have meant that there was insufficient clients' money on March 1 to pay £18,000, so that office money would have had to be used.

18.(11)

Statement

Dick. Sale of "The Habendum". Purchase of "The Testatum"

PURCHASE of The Testatum	£	£	£
Payments			
Search	10		
Completion	52,200		
Costs	400		
VAT	40		
Mortgage costs	115		
L.R. fees	440		
		53,205	
Receipts			
Mortgage advance		15,000	
			38,205
SALE of The Habendum			
Receipts			
Completion		36,000	
Payments			
Mortgage redemption	3,000		
Mortgage costs	22		
Costs	200		
VAT	20		
		3,242	
			32,758
			5,447
less: Received on account			5,000
BALANCE DUE from you			447

Mrs Dick (CL17)							
Date	Details	OFFICE ACCOUNT			CLIENT ACCOUNT		
		DR	CR	Balance	DR	CR	Balance
Mar. 1	Petty Cash. Search	10 –		10 –			
May 1	Cash. You					5,000 –	5,000 –
May 5	Cash. Completion of sale					36,000 –	41,000 –
	Gibson BS Transfer. Mortgage redemption				3,000 –		38,000 –
	Cash. Completion of purchase				37,755 – *		245 –
May 8	Costs**	600 –					
	VAT	60 –					
	Gibson BS. Transfer. Mortgage costs	22 –		692 –			
	Cash. Transfer		245 –	447 –	245 –		—

```
* Note:
Completion Money                                    52,200
Mortgage                          15,000
Less Costs          115
     L.R. Fees      440            555           14,445
                                                 37,755
```

```
**Purchase    400
   Sale       200        600
```

Gibson BS (CL18)							
Date	Details	OFFICE ACCOUNT			CLIENT ACCOUNT		
		DR	CR	Balance	DR	CR	Balance
May 5	Mrs Dick. Transfer. Mortgage redemption					3,000 –	3,000 –
	Cash. You				3,000 –		—
May 8	Costs	20 –					
	VAT	2 –		22 –			
	Mrs Dick. Transfer		22 –	—			

18.(12)

Statement

Hotspur. Sale of "Blackwater". Purchase of "Greenmead"

PURCHASE of Greenmead	£	£	£
Payments			
Searches	4		
Deposit	6,500		
Costs	74		
VAT	7.40		
Mortgage costs	17.60		
Search	1		
Completion	58,500		
Stamp Duty	325		
L.R. fees	20		
		65,449	
Receipts			
Mortgage advance	25,000		
less: deductions	160		
		24,840	
			40,609
SALE of Blackwater			
Receipts			
Deposit	4,000		
Completion	36,000		
		40,000	
Payments			
Costs	60		
VAT	6		
		66	
			39,934
BALANCE DUE from you			675

Hotspur: Sale of "Blackwater". Purchase of "Greenmead"							
Date	Details	OFFICE ACCOUNT			CLIENT ACCOUNT		
		DR	CR	Balance	DR	CR	Balance
Aug. 31	Cash. Search	3		3			
	Cash. Search	1		4			
Sept. 17	Cash. Deposit Sale					4,000	4,000
	Cash. Transfer. Loan to Hotspur	2,500*		2,504		2,500	6,500
	Cash. Deposit. Purchase				6,500		—
Sept. 30	Costs	134		2,638			
	VAT	13·40		2,651·40			
	Whinshire B.S. Transfer. Mortgage costs	17·60		2,669			
Oct. 12	Cash.		675	1,994			
Oct. 16	Petty Cash. Search	1		1,995			
Oct. 18	Cash. Completion. Sale					36,000	36,000
	Whinshire B.S. Transfer.					24,840	60,840
	Cash. Completion Purchase				58,500		2,340
Oct. 19	Cash. Stamp duty				325		2,015
	Cash. L.R. fees				20		1,995
Oct. 30	Cash. Transfer		1,995	—	1,995		—

* Alternatively (a) two cheques could have been drawn: one on OFFICE ACCOUNT for £2,500, one on CLIENT ACCOUNT for £4,000; or

(b) £6,000 could have been drawn on OFFICE ACCOUNT and then the £4,000 transferred from CLIENT to OFFICE ACCOUNT.

Whinshire Building Society							
Date	Details	OFFICE ACCOUNT			CLIENT ACCOUNT		
		DR	CR	Balance	DR	CR	Balance
Sept. 30	Costs	16		16			
	VAT	1·60		17·60			
	Hotspur. Transfer		17·60	—			
Oct. 17	Cash. You					24,840	24,840
Oct. 18	Hotspur. Transfer				24,840		—

Black Bobb & Co

Smith. Purchase of "The Padd". Sale of "Coslot"

18.(13)

Date	Details	OFFICE ACCOUNT			CLIENT ACCOUNT		
		DR	CR	Balance	DR	CR	Balance
Nov. 3	Petty Cash. Search	2		2			
Nov. 9	Cash. Survey fee	165		167			
Nov. 16	Cash. Nonsuch Bank					2,500	2,500
Nov. 20	Cash. Deposit. The Padd				2,500		—
Dec. 8	Costs	230		397			
	VAT	23		420			
Dec. 11	Cash. You					3,150	3,150
Dec. 14	Cash. Completion. Sale					14,400	17,550
	Stakeholder. Transfer					1,600	19,150
	High Rate B.S. Transfer					6,956	26,106
	Cash. Completion Purchase				22,500		3,606
	Cash. Nonsuch Bank				2,500		1,106
	Cash. Stamp duty				250		856
	Cash. L.R. fees				51		805
Dec. 15	Cash. Estate agents' fees				385		420
Dec. 31	Cash. Transfer		420	—	420 —		—

Statement

Purchase of "The Padd". Sale of "Coslot"

PURCHASE of The Padd	£	£	£
Payments			
Search	2		
Survey fee	165		
Deposit	2,500		
Completion	22,500		
Mortgage costs	44		
Stamp duty	250		
L.R. fees	51		
Costs	140		
VAT	14		
		25,666	
Receipts			
Mortgage advance		7,000	
			18,666
SALE of Coslot			
Receipts			
Deposit	1,600		
Completion	14,400	16,000	
Payments			
Costs	90		
VAT	9		
Estate agents' commission	385		
		484	15,516
			3,150
Bridging Loan			
Loan		2,500	
less: Repaid		2,500	—
BALANCE DUE from you			3,150

Brown's Solicitors							
Date	Details	OFFICE ACCOUNT			CLIENT ACCOUNT		
		DR	CR	Balance	DR	CR	Balance
Nov. 3	Cash	11		11			
Nov. 15	Cash. Bungo					2,400	2,400
Nov. 18	Costs	130		141			
	VAT	13		154			
	Cash. You				2,246		154
Dec. 31	Cash. Transfer		154	—	154		—

Chapter 17

Page 149
(1)

Date	Details	OFFICE ACCOUNT			CLIENT ACCOUNT		
		DR	CR	Balance	DR	CR	Balance
	Cash. IRC Capital duty	300 –		300 –			
	Cash. Registration fee	50 –		350 –			
	Costs	200 –		550 –			
	VAT	20 –		570 –			
	Cash. You		570 – [2]	—		40 – [2]	40 –
	Cash. Stationers				40 –		—

NU Ltd Company formation (CL1)

(2)

Date	Details	OFFICE ACCOUNT			CLIENT ACCOUNT		
		DR	CR	Balance	DR	CR	Balance
	Cash. Police Report	7 –		7 –			
	Cash. Medical Report	30 –		37 –			
	Cash. Defendant					1,500 –	1,500 –
	Costs	75 –		112 –			
	VAT	7·50		119·50			
	Cash. You				1,380·50		119·50
	Cash. Transfer		119·50	—	119·50		—

Albert Hill (CL2)

(3)

Bill (CL3)							
		OFFICE ACCOUNT			CLIENT ACCOUNT		
		DR	CR	Balance	DR	CR	Balance
	Cash. Court Fees	20 –		20 –			
	Cash. Counsel VAT	30 – [4]		50 –			
	Petty Cash. Witness fee	5 –		55 –			
	Costs	50 –		105 –			
	VAT	8 –		113 –			
	Cash. Charles' Solicitor					2,094.50	2,094.50
	Cash. Transfer		113 –	—	113 –		1,981.50
	Cash. You				1,981.50		—

(4)

Romeo (CL4)							
Date	Details	OFFICE ACCOUNT			CLIENT ACCOUNT		
		DR	CR	Balance	DR	CR	Balance
May 1	Cash. You					40 –	40 –
May 4	Cash. Enquiry agent				30 –		10 –
May 10	Cash. Court fees	20 –		20 –			
Jun. 10	Cash. Witness fee	22 –		42 –			
	Cash. VAT Counsel	50 –		92 –			
July 1	Costs	75 –		167 –			
	VAT	12.50		179.50			
Jul. 20	Cash. Juliet's Solicitors		124.50*	55 –			
Jul. 26	Cash. Transfer		10 –	45 –	10 –		—
Aug. 1	Cash. You		45 – [6]	—			

Note: Fred & Co's fees, on payment, are debited to Agency Expenses Account.
 * Costs £55 + Counsel £40 = £95; VAT on total = £9.50; Court fees = £20; Total = £124.50.

(5)

Desmond (CL5)							
Date	Details	OFFICE ACCOUNT			CLIENT ACCOUNT		
		DR	CR	Balance	DR	CR	Balance
Jan. 2	Cash. You					400 –	400 –
Jan. 3	Petty Cash. Court fee	10 –		10 –			
Feb. 3	Cash. Enquiry Agent. VAT	30 – [5]		40 –			
Feb. 4	Cash. Witness fee				22 –		378 –
Feb. 5	Cash. Witness fee				9 –		369 –
Apr. 18	Costs	200 –		240 –			
	VAT	29 –		269 –			
	Interest Payable Account		31**	238 –			
Apr. 29	Cash. You					1,356.20 [2]	1,725.20
May 1	Cash. Percy's Solicitors				1,427.20*		298 –
May 2	Cash. Counsel VAT	60 – [5]		298 –			
May 3	Cash. Transfer		298 –	—	298 –		—

Note: April 18. The VAT includes the tax on Counsel's fees paid on May 2.

* The invoice of Percy's solicitor is addressed to Percy, not you. Thus, you could not use the Principal Method.

** In this case, no Cash Account entries are made, merely DEBIT Interest Payable Account.

(6)

George (CL6)

Date	Details	OFFICE ACCOUNT			CLIENT ACCOUNT		
		DR	CR	Balance	DR	CR	Balance
May 30	Cash. X & Co Valuation. VAT	200 –		200 –			
Jun. 1	Cash. Newspaper Adverts	7 –		207 –			
Jun. 2	Cash. George's Bank Loan					1,200 –	1,200 –
Jun. 3	Cash. Probate Fees	10 –		217 –			
	Cash. IRC. IHT				1,200 –		–
Jul. 20	Cash. Building Society					3,400 –	3,400 –
Jul. 21	Cash. George's Bank					800 –	4,200 –
Jul. 22	Cash. Life Policy					4,200 –	8,400 –
Jul. 24	Cash. IRC Tax Arrears				600 –		7,800 –
	Cash. George's Bank				1,200 –		6,600 –
Aug. 2	Cash. Legacy. Ethel				1,000 –		5,600 –
	Frank				1,000 –		4,600 –
Aug. 31	Costs*	330 –		547 –			
	VAT	53 –		600 –			
	Cash. Transfer		600 –		600 –		4,000 –
	Cash. George's Son				2,000 –		2,000 –
	Cash. George's Daughter				2,000 –		–

* Costs £300 – + General disbursements £30 – = £330 –.

(7)

Cash							
		OFFICE ACCOUNT			CLIENT ACCOUNT		
Date	Details	DR	CR	Balance	DR	CR	Balance
Apr. 11	Tempest & Flood Insurance. Premium				40		
Apr. 15	Tempest & Flood Insurance	2	20			38	
	Tempest & Flood Insurance. Transfer		2			2	
May 8	Dodds & Co. Enquiry agent	66					
	VAT						
May 15	Dodds & Co				5,000		
May 16	Margaret						
May 18	Margaret	154				4,846	
	Margaret. Transfer					154	
May 20	Margaret. Transfer		11		11		

[WORKINGS]

Margaret

Date	Details	OFFICE ACCOUNT			CLIENT ACCOUNT		
		DR	CR	Balance	DR	CR	Balance
May 16	Cash. You	140		140		5,000	5,000
May 18	Costs	14		154			
	VAT						
	Cash. You		154	—	4,846		
	Cash. Transfer				154		154
May 20	Abatement		10	10CR			
	VAT		1	11CR			
	Cash. Transfer	11		—		11	11

On May 20 the entries were made to record the abatement which resulted in the ledger account of Margaret having a credit balance in the OFFICE ACCOUNT. Normally such a balance would indicate a breach of Solicitors' Accounts Rules (see page 56). In this case, I do not think you have broken the Rules. However, you do now hold OFFICE ACCOUNT £11 which belongs to Margaret. (In retrospect what you did was to transfer £11 too much to OFFICE ACCOUNT on May 18.) I think you should immediately either send an OFFICE ACCOUNT cheque for £11 to Margaret or transfer £11 from OFFICE ACCOUNT to CLIENT ACCOUNT. This would mean that you are now holding £11 in CLIENT ACCOUNT on Margaret's behalf for return to her or for any other use on her behalf. This is what I have shown in the answer.

(8)

Date	Details	OFFICE ACCOUNT			CLIENT ACCOUNT		
		DR	CR	Balance	DR	CR	Balance
Sept. 5	Tom. On account				800		
Sept. 6	Tom				4,270	63	
Sept. 7	Jones Family Trust						
Sept. 8	Simon	57[6]					
Sept. 9	Michael. House Purchase	12,340				800	
Sept. 12	Tom. Cheque dishonoured				63		
	Tom. Rectification of breach		63				
Sept. 13	Jones Family Trust					2,500	
	Jones Family Trust. Transfer to Trust Bank Account					1,770	
Sept. 14	Nancy. Cheque indorsed				8,000 – *	*8,000 – *	

Cash

* See pages 93 and 94.

(9)

Cash

Date	Details	OFFICE ACCOUNT			CLIENT ACCOUNT		
		DR	CR	Balance	DR	CR	Balance
May 3	Bill. Interest	40					
	Bill. Transfer		40				
May 4	Deposit Cash. General deposit				500		
May 5	Interest Payable. Re Christine		42				
	Christine. Interest Payable				42		
	Christine					6,042	
May 8	Peter. On account				200		
May 9	Robert. On account				14,000	14,000	
	Deposit Cash. Specially designated Re Robert					8,000	
May 15	Stephen						
	Interest Payable. Re Stephen		50		200		
May 16	Ethel. On account		30				
May 17	Ethel. Stationers' fees		3				
	VAT						
May 19	Frances. Agreed fee	20					
May 20	Peter		120			200	
May 22	Peter	40					
May 30	Interest Receivable	85			85		
	Interest Receivable. Transfer					85	

Notes:

May 1 & 2. No entries in the firm's books.

May 3. Clients' money wrongly paid into office bank account, and transferred under Rule 7 SAR, to the specially designated bank account if so desired.

May 19: The £20 includes the VAT because unless it is otherwise stated any price quoted is deemed to include the VAT.

(10)

Cash

Date	Details	OFFICE ACCOUNT			CLIENT ACCOUNT		
		DR	CR	Balance	DR	CR	Balance
(a)	Stakeholder. Lucy & King. Re Quentin	75*			710		
(b)	Ian. Current Account. Marshire CC Salary						
(c)	Ian & Jane Ltd. Litigation				18		
(d)	Zebedee. L.R. fees		20·75				
(e)	Oliver Trust. Violet					800	
(f)	Susan. Agreed fee	30					
(g)	Pauline. Re Fish Hall	62·85			550²		
	Pauline. Completion of Fish Hall						
	S Building Society. Completion of Fish Hall					550	
						4,400	
(hi)	Rotten Insurance Co. Re Nancy		47·50				
	Nancy. Transfer	45					
(hii)	Marshire RDC. Rates		82·80				
	Ian. Current Account		44·50			45**	

* Whether the credit is on Ian's current account or the firm's Costs Account depends on the partnership agreement.

** There was insufficient clients' money. The full amount was drawn on OFFICE ACCOUNT, which was then partially reimbursed by a transfer from CLIENT ACCOUNT. As an alternative, two cheques could have been drawn (see the answer to question 9 on page 232—May 20).

(11)

Date	Details	OFFICE ACCOUNT			CLIENT ACCOUNT		
		DR	CR	Balance	DR	CR	Balance
Feb. 1	Cash. Bank. Re IHT				4,000 –		4,000 –
Feb. 3	Cash. IRC. IHT					4,000 –	—
Feb. 20	Cash. Probate Fees	38 –		38 –			
	Agreed Fee	90·91		128·91			
	VAT	9·09		138 –			
Mar. 22	Cash. Deposit					4,800 –	4,800 –
Mar. 25	Cash. Investments					700 –	5,500 –
Mar. 26	Cash. Funeral expenses				125 –		5,375
	Cash. Debts				3,100 –		2,275 –
Apr. 22	Cash. Completion of Sale					43,200 –	45,475 –
	Cash. You				3,800 –		41,675 –
May 3	Costs	400 –					
	VAT	40 –		578 –			
	Cash. Timothy Legacy				5,000 –		36,675
	Cash. Transfer		578 –	—	578 –		36,097
	Cash. William				36,097 –		—

(12)

Statement

Sale of "The Count House". Purchase of "Tangerine Cottage"

PURCHASE of Tangerine Cottage	£	£	£
Payments			
Deposit	3,000		
Completion	27,000		
L.R. fees	80		
Costs	300		
VAT	32		
General disbursements	20		
Mortgage costs	33		
		30,465	
Receipts			
Mortgage advance		25,000	
			5,465
SALE of The Count House			
Receipts			
Deposit	1,580		
Completion	14,220		
		15,800	
Payments			
Mortgage redemption	10,187		
Costs	200		
VAT	20		
		10,407	
			5,393
BALANCE DUE from you			72

Mr Hare. Sale of the Count House. Purchase of Tangerine Cottage (CL9)

Date	Details	OFFICE ACCOUNT			CLIENT ACCOUNT		
		DR	CR	Balance	DR	CR	Balance
Jun. 2	Cash. Deposit. Tangerine Cottage	3,000 –		3,000 –			
Jun. 29	Plenty B.S. Transfer. Mortgage Advance					25,000 –	25,000 –
Jun. 30	Cash. Completion. Tangerine Cottage	2,000 –		5,000 –	25,000 –		—
	Cash. Completion. The Count House					4,033 –	4,033 –
	Stakeholder. Transfer					1,580 –	5,613 –
Jul. 1	Cash. Transfer		5,000 –	—	5,000 –		613 –
Jul. 18	Cash. L.R. fees				80 –		533 –
Jul. 28	Costs	520		520			
	VAT	52 –		572 –			
	Plenty B.S.	33 –		605 –			
Aug. 1	Cash. Transfer		533 –	72 –	533 –		—

(13)

Statement

Simpson. Sale of "Bolt House". Purchase of "Dyer Hall"

PURCHASE of Dyer Hall	£	£	£
Payments			
Deposit	5,000		
Searches	5		
Completion	45,000		
Costs	250		
VAT	25		
Mortgage costs	35		
		50,335	
Receipts			
On account	5,000		
Mortgage advance	40,000		
		45,000	
			5,335
SALE of Bolt House			
Receipts			
Deposit	4,000		
Completion	36,000		
		40,000	
Payments			
Mortgage redemption	35,000		
Costs	150		
VAT	15		
		35,165	
			4,835
			500
less: Received on account generally			300
BALANCE DUE from you			200

Simpson. Sale of Bolt House. Purchase of Dyer Hall (CL10)

Date	Details	OFFICE ACCOUNT DR	OFFICE ACCOUNT CR	OFFICE ACCOUNT Balance	CLIENT ACCOUNT DR	CLIENT ACCOUNT CR	CLIENT ACCOUNT Balance
Mar. 1	Cash. You. Deposit Dyer Hall				5,000 –	5,000 –	5,000 –
Mar. 2	Cash. Vendor's Solicitors: Deposit					5,000 –	—
Mar. 3	Cash. Search	2 –		2 –			
May 25	Petty Cash. Search	3 –		5 –			
Jun. 1	Cash. You. On account					300 –	300 –
Jun. 3	Cash. Purchaser's Solicitors. Completion Bolt House					1,000 – *	1,300 –
	Stakeholder. Transfer					4,000 –	5,300 –
	Cash. Vendor's Solicitors. Completion Dyer Hall				5,000 –		300 –
Jun. 6	Costs	400 –		405 –			
	VAT	40 –		445 –			
	Mercer B.S. Transfer. Costs	55 –		500 –			
	Cash. Transfer		300 –	200 –	300 –		—

* The purchaser's solicitor brought two drafts to completion as follows:

Mortgage redemption (payable to mortgagee's solicitors)	35,000
Balance payable to you	1,000
TOTAL	36,000

The Mercer Building Society (CL12)

Date	Details	OFFICE ACCOUNT DR	CR	Balance	CLIENT ACCOUNT DR	CR	Balance
Jun. 1	Cash. You					40,000 –	40,000 –
Jun. 3	Cash. Vendor's Solicitors. Completion						
	Costs	50 –		50 –			
	VAT	5 –		55 –			
Jun. 6	Simpson. Transfer		55 –	—	40,000 –		—

Stakeholder (CL11)

Date	Details	OFFICE ACCOUNT DR	CR	Balance	CLIENT ACCOUNT DR	CR	Balance
Apr. 1	Cash. Re Dyer Hall					4,000 –	4,000 –
Jun. 3	Simpson. Transfer				4,000 –		—

(14)

Statement

Jack. Sale of "The Manor House". Purchase of "Half Moon Street"

	£	£	£
PURCHASE of Half Moon Street			
Payments			
Search	10		
Costs. Sale	140		
VAT	14		
Costs. Mortgage	66		
Completion	27,000		
		27,230	
Receipts			
Mortgage advance		18,000	
			9,230
SALE of The Manor House			
Receipts			
Deposit	2,000		
Completion	18,000		
		20,000	
Payments			
Mortgage redemption	13,000		
Costs	100		
VAT	10		
		13,110	
			6,890
BALANCE DUE from you			2,340

Jack. Sale of The Manor House. Purchase of Half Moon Street (CL13)

Date	Details	OFFICE ACCOUNT			CLIENT ACCOUNT		
		DR	CR	Balance	DR	CR	Balance
Mar. 3	Cash. Search	10 –		10 –			
Apr. 1	Costs	240 –		250 –			
	VAT	24 –		274 –			
	Ernest B.S.	66 –		340 –			
Apr. 11	Cash. You		340 –	—		2,000 – [2]	2,000 –
Apr. 12	Cash. Purchaser's Solicitors. Completion. The Manor House					5,000 –	7,000 –
	Stakeholder. Transfer					2,000 –	9,000 –
	Cash. Vendor's Solicitors. Completion Half Moon Street				9,000 –		—

Ernest Building Society (CL14)

Date	Details	OFFICE ACCOUNT			CLIENT ACCOUNT		
		DR	CR	Balance	DR	CR	Balance
Apr. 1	Costs	60 –		60 –			
	VAT	6 –		66 –			
	Jack		66 –	—			
Apr. 11	Cash. You					18,000 –	18,000 –
Apr. 12	Cash. Purchaser's Solicitors. Completion The Manor House					13,000 –	31,000 –
	Cash. Vendor's Solicitors. Completion Half Moon Street				18,000 –		13,000
	Cash. You				13,000 –		—

Stakeholder (CL11)

Date	Details	OFFICE ACCOUNT			CLIENT ACCOUNT		
		DR	CR	Balance	DR	CR	Balance
Mar. 1	Cash. Re The Manor House					2,000 –	2,000 –
Apr. 12	Jack. Transfer				2,000 –		—

(15)

		Jan. 12 £23,400 on deposit Jan. 22 £13,000 removed			Jan. 28 £80,000 on deposit Feb. 4 £90,400 removed		
	Executors of Chasm, deceased (CL1)	OFFICE ACCOUNT			CLIENT ACCOUNT		
Date	Details	DR	CR	Balance	DR	CR	Balance
Dec. 10	Cash.** Transfer to Insurance Co	245		245			
Dec. 11	Cash. Probate fees	100		345			
Jan. 5	Cash. Adverts VAT	40		385			
	Petty Cash. Adverts VAT	20		405			
Jan. 7	Cash. You					4,876	4,876
Jan. 11	Chasm. Transfer*					507	5,383
Jan. 12	Deposit Cash. Life assurance policy					23,400	28,783
Jan. 14	Cash. Debts				2,424		26,359
	Cash. Funeral expenses				775		25,584
Jan. 20	Cash. House contents					1,297	26,881
Jan. 22	Cash. Legacy. Secretary				5,000		21,881
	Cash. Legacy. Charity				1,000		20,881
	Fissure. Transfer				10,000		10,881
Jan. 27	Cash. Completion					87,494	98,375
	Stakeholder. Transfer					12,000	110,375
	Cash. Estate agents'. Commission				2,761		107,614
Jan. 29	Costs (Sale) 600 (Admin.) 900	1,500		1,905			
	VAT	156		2,061			
Feb. 1	Cash. Transfer		2,061	—	2,061		105,553
Feb. 4	Cash. Interest					108	105,661
Feb. 5	Cash. Interest					194	105,855
	Fissure. Transfer				105,855		—

N.B. No double entries needed for December 11 £22,923
January 4 £12,420.

** The "Cash" entry is essential, since money is being transferred from OFFICE ACCOUNT (executors) to CLIENT ACCOUNT (Insurance Co).

* The question says that "the net amount" is transferred. It has been assumed that the amount due to OFFICE ACCOUNT (£482) is transferred from CLIENT ACCOUNT to OFFICE ACCOUNT and the balance of £507 transferred to the Executors' Account. See the entries on the Cash Account dated January 11.

Fissure: Purchase of "Epicentre" (CL2)

Date	Details	OFFICE ACCOUNT			CLIENT ACCOUNT		
		DR	CR	Balance	DR	CR	Balance
Dec. 1	Balance			104			
Jan. 21	Cash. Survey fee	276		380			
	Petty Cash. Search	24		404			
Jan. 22	Executors of Chasm. Transfer					10,000	10,000
	Cash. Deposit				10,000		—
Feb. 5	Executors of Chasm. Transfer					105,855	105,855

Cash

Date	Details	OFFICE ACCOUNT			CLIENT ACCOUNT		
		DR	CR	Balance	DR	CR	Balance
Jan. 5	Executors of Chasm. Adverts		40				
	VAT		4				
Jan. 7	Executors of Chasm. You	482			4,876		
Jan. 11	Chasm. Transfer*					482	
Jan. 13	Stakeholder. Re Goodinvest				12,000		
Jan. 14	Executors of Chasm. Debts					2,424	
	Executors of Chasm. Funeral expenses					775	
Jan. 20	Executors of Chasm. House contents				1,297		
Jan. 21	Fissure. Survey fee		276				
Jan. 22	Deposit Cash. Executors of Chasm. Transfer				13,000		
	Executors of Chasm. Legacy. Secretary					5,000	
	Executors of Chasm. Legacy. Charity					1,000	
	Fissure. Deposit					10,000	
Jan. 27	Executors of Chasm. Completion				87,494		
	Executors of Chasm. Commission					2,761	
Jan. 28	Deposit Cash. Executors of Chasm. Transfer					80,000	

* See note on page 243.

(16)

Aspen

Apr. 1 £20,000 on deposit; removed Apr. 28

Date	Details	OFFICE ACCOUNT			CLIENT ACCOUNT		
		DR	CR	Balance	DR	CR	Balance
Apr. 1	Balance						20,232
Apr. 11	Petty Cash	14		43			
Apr. 27	Cash. Horse Chestnuts. Completion					49,500	69,732
	Stakeholder			57		5,500	75,232
	Cash. Estate agents				770		74,462
Apr. 28	Costs	400		457			
	VAT	40		497			
	Deposit Cash. Interest					83	74,545
	Cash. Transfer. Interest					106	74,651
	Cash. Transfer		497	—	497		74,154
	Cash. You				74,154		—

Larch

Date	Details	OFFICE ACCOUNT			CLIENT ACCOUNT		
		DR	CR	Balance	DR	CR	Balance
Apr. 1	Balance						600
Apr. 7	Maple Insurance. Premium					250	350
May 3	Cash. Transfer*	650		650		650	1,000
	Cash. Rowan*				1,000		
	Cash. You		400	250			
	Cash. You. Indorsed cheque		250	—			
May 9	Cash. Cheque dishonoured	250		250			—

* Another way of dealing with this would have been: (1) Pay £1,000 to Rowan out of office account; (2) Transfer the £350 from CLIENT ACCOUNT to OFFICE ACCOUNT.

Maple Insurance Ltd							
Date	Details	OFFICE ACCOUNT			CLIENT ACCOUNT		
		DR	CR	Balance	DR	CR	Balance
Apr. 7	Larch. Premium					250	250
Apr. 29	Commission.	37		37			
	Cash. Transfer		37	—	37		213
	Cash. You				213		—

Mr and Mrs Poplar							
Date	Details	OFFICE ACCOUNT			CLIENT ACCOUNT		
		DR	CR	Balance	DR	CR	Balance
Apr. 12	Petty Cash. Search	14		14			
Apr. 18	Cash. You					4,000	4,000
Apr. 25	Cash. V's Solicitors. Deposit				4,000		—

Stakeholder							
Date	Details	OFFICE ACCOUNT			CLIENT ACCOUNT		
		DR	CR	Balance	DR	CR	Balance
Apr. 11	Cash					5,500	5,500
Apr. 27	Aspen. Transfer				5,500		—

Willow							
Date	Details	OFFICE ACCOUNT			CLIENT ACCOUNT		
		DR	CR	Balance	DR	CR	Balance
Apr. 1	Balance						1,500
Apr. 15	Cash. Willow & Co.						
	Disbursements	100		100			
	Costs	1,200		1,300			
	VAT	120		1,420			
Apr. 20	Cash. Transfer		1,420	—	1,420		80
	Cash. Transfer						
	Interest					42	122
	Cash. You				122		—

Appendix

Statement

Milk. Sale of "Churn". Purchase of "The Dairy"

SALE of Churn

	£	£	£
Receipts			
Deposit	24,000		
Completion	216,000		
		240,000	
Payments			
Estate agents	3,960		
Costs	500		
VAT	50		
Mortgage redemption	50,462		
Mortgage redemption costs	44		
		55,016	
			184,984
PURCHASE of The Dairy			
Payments			
Search	26		
Survey fee	330		
Deposit	12,000		
Completion	108,000		
Costs	600		
VAT	60		
Repaid loan interest	12,170		
Stamp duty	1,200		
L.R. fees	160		
		134,546	
Receipts			
Bridging loan		12,000	
			122,546
			62,438
Interest			794
			63,232
To Mr and Mrs Butter			4,000
			59,232

Milk

Date	Details	OFFICE ACCOUNT DR	OFFICE ACCOUNT CR	OFFICE ACCOUNT Balance	CLIENT ACCOUNT DR	CLIENT ACCOUNT CR	CLIENT ACCOUNT Balance
Mar. 6	Petty Cash. Search	26		26			
Mar. 9	Cash. Survey fee. VAT	300		326			
Mar. 15	Cash. Round Stilton Loan					12,000	12,000
Mar. 16	Cash. Deposit. Churn				12,000		—
Apr. 10	Costs*	1,100		1,426			
	VAT**	140		1,566			
		44		1,610			
Apr. 12	Cheese B.S. Transfer					216,000	216,000
	Cash. Completion Sale					24,000	240,000
	Stakeholder. Transfer				50,462		189,538
	Cheese B.S. Transfer redemption				108,000		81,538
	Cash. Completion. Purchase				12,170		69,368
	Cash. Loan redemption				1,200		68,168
	Cash. Stamp duty				3,960		64,208
Apr. 18	Cash. Estate agent				160		64,048
Apr. 20	Cash. L.R. fees				1,610		62,438
	Cash. Transfer		1,610	—			
Apr. 25	Mr and Mrs Butter. Transfer				4,000		58,438
May 16	Cash. Interest					794	59,232
	Cash. You				59,232		—

* Purchase £600 + Sale £500 = £1,100.
** VAT: £1,100 + £300 = £1,400 × 10%.

Cheese Building Society

Date	Details	OFFICE ACCOUNT			CLIENT ACCOUNT		
		DR	CR	Balance	DR	CR	Balance
Apr. 10	Costs	40		40			
	VAT	4		44			
	Milk. Transfer		44	—		50,462	50,462
	Milk. Transfer						
Apr. 12	Cash. You				50,462		—

Mr and Mrs Butter

Date	Details	OFFICE ACCOUNT			CLIENT ACCOUNT		
		DR	CR	Balance	DR	CR	Balance
Apr. 11	Petty Cash. Search	26		26			
Apr. 24	Cash. You					6,000	6,000
	Milk. Transfer					4,000	10,000
Apr. 25	Cash. Deposit				10,000		—

(18)

Statement

Bream. Sale of "Pike View". Purchase of "Perch Cottage"

SALE of Pike View	£	£	£
Receipts			
Deposit	10,000		
Completion	90,000		
		100,000	
Payments			
Estate agents	2,200		
Costs	150		
VAT	15		
Mortgage redemption	12,465		
Mortgage redemption costs	44		
		14,874	
			85,126
PURCHASE of Perch Cottage			
Payments			
Search	30		
Survey fee	330		
Deposit	8,000		
Completion	72,000		
Costs	350		
VAT	35		
Stamp duty	800		
L.R. fees	160		
		81,705	
Receipts			
On account		1,000	
			80,705
			4,421
Interest			326
BALANCE DUE to you			4,747

Bream

Date	Details	OFFICE ACCOUNT			CLIENT ACCOUNT		
		DR	CR	Balance	DR	CR	Balance
Nov. 4	Cash. You					1,000	1,000
Nov. 6	Petty Cash. Search	30		30			
Nov. 8	Cash. Survey fee VAT	300		330			
Nov. 17	Cash. Transfer	7,000		7,330		7,000	8,000
	Cash. Deposit				8,000		—
Dec. 10	Costs*	500		7,830			
	VAT**	80		7,910			
	Roach B.S. Transfer costs	44		7,954			
Dec. 16	Cash. Sale					90,000	90,000
	Stakeholder. Transfer					10,000	100,000
	Roach B.S. Mortgage. Transfer				12,465		87,535
	Cash. Purchase				72,000		15,535
	Cash. Stamp duty				800		14,735
Dec. 18	Cash. Estate agents				2,200		12,535
Dec. 20	Cash. L.R. fees				160		12,375
	Cash. Transfer		7,954	—	7,954		4,421
Jan. 16	Cash. Interest					326	4,747
	Cash. You				4,747		—

* Purchase £350 + Sale £150 = £500.
** VAT: £350 + £150 + £300 = £800 × 10%.

Roach Building Society

Date	Details	OFFICE ACCOUNT			CLIENT ACCOUNT		
		DR	CR	Balance	DR	CR	Balance
Dec. 10	Costs VAT Bream. Transfer	40 4	44	40 44 —			
Dec. 16	Bream. Transfer Cash. You				12,465	12,465	12,465 —

(19)

Statement

Brass. Sale of "Goldmine". Purchase of "Cobalt Lodge"

SALE of Goldmine	£	£	£
Receipts			
Deposit	14,000		
Completion	126,000		
		140,000	
Payments			
Estate agents' fee	2,640		
Costs	400		
VAT	40		
		3,080	
			136,920
PURCHASE of Cobalt Lodge			
Payments			
Search	36		
Survey fee	440		
Deposit	10,000		
Completion	90,000		
Costs	600		
VAT	60		
Stamp duty	1,000		
L.R. fees	160		
			102,296
			34,624
Interim distribution from estate of Nickel, deceased			10,000
Final distribution from estate of Nickel, deceased			116,875
Interest distribution from estate of Nickel, deceased			534
BALANCE DUE to you			162,033

Brass

Date	Details	OFFICE ACCOUNT			CLIENT ACCOUNT		
		DR	CR	Balance	DR	CR	Balance
Apr. 1	Balances			—			—
Apr. 6	Petty Cash. Search	36		36			
Apr. 8	Cash. Survey fee. VAT	400		436			
Apr. 15	Executors of Nickel. Transfer					10,000	10,000
Apr. 16	Cash. Deposit. Cobalt Lodge				10,000		—
	Costs	1,000		1,436			
	VAT*	140		1,576			
May 14	Executors of Nickel. Transfer					116,875	116,875
May 18	Cash. Sale. Goldmine					126,000	242,875
	Stakeholder. Transfer					14,000	256,875
	Cash. Purchase. Cobalt Lodge				90,000		166,875
	Cash. Stamp duty				1,000		165,875
May 19	Cash. Estate agents				2,640		163,235
May 20	Cash. L.R. fees				160		163,075
	Cash. Transfer		1,576	—	1,576		161,499
Jun. 1	Cash. Interest					534	162,033
	Cash. You					162,033	—

* VAT: £1,000 + £400 = £1,400 × 10%.

Executors of Nickel, deceased							
Date	Details	OFFICE ACCOUNT			CLIENT ACCOUNT		
		DR	CR	Balance	DR	CR	Balance
Apr. 1	Balances			—			125,000*
Apr. 15	Brass Transfer				10,000**		115,000
May 14	Deposit Cash.						
	Interest					1,875	116,875
	Brass Transfer				116,875***		—

* On deposit.
** £10,000 removed on April 15.
*** Removed May 14.

Antimony							
Date	Details	OFFICE ACCOUNT			CLIENT ACCOUNT		
		DR	CR	Balance	DR	CR	Balance
Apr. 1	Balance			560			—
Apr. 2	Cash. You		560	—		190	190
Apr. 21	Costs	1,200		1,200			
	VAT	120		1,320			
[May 4	No entries needed]						
May 7	Cash. You		1,130	190			
May 12	Cash. Dishonoured cheque	1,130		1,320			
May 19	Cash. Tin Lid Insurance					4,000	4,190
May 25	Cash. Consultant	1,100		2,420			
	Cash. Transfer		2,420	—	2,420		1,770
	Cash. You				1,770		—

(20)

Chestnut							
Date	Details	OFFICE ACCOUNT			CLIENT ACCOUNT		
		DR	CR	Balance	DR	CR	Balance
Oct. 1	Balances			735			1,020
Dec. 2	Cash. Transfer		735	—	735		285
	Executors of Chestnut. Transfer				285		—

Executors of Chestnut, deceased							
Date	Details	OFFICE ACCOUNT			CLIENT ACCOUNT		
		DR	CR	Balance	DR	CR	Balance
Oct. 15	Cash. Probate fees	140		140			
Nov. 2	Cash. Bank: Dcd's current account					2,910	2,910
Nov. 3	Cash. Advert	44		184			
	Petty Cash. Advert	44		228			
Nov. 10	Cash. Life policy					30,000	32,910
	Cash. Loan account				8,600		24,310
Nov. 15	Cash. Deposit. The Stables					14,000	38,310
Nov. 22	Cash. Auctioneer. House contents					16,476	54,786
Dec. 1	Cash. Debts				2,315		52,471
	Cash. Funeral expenses				980		51,491
Dec. 2	Chestnut. Transfer					285	51,776
Dec. 3	Cash. Last Fence B.S.					21,046	72,822
Dec. 13	Cash. Sale of The Stables					95,537	168,359
	Cash. Estate agents' commission				3,080		165,279
Dec. 16	Costs: Sale	400		628			
	Administration	1,800		2,428			
	VAT	220		2,648			
	Cash. Transfer		2,648	—	2,648		162,631
Dec. 17	Palomino. Transfer				2,000		160,631
Dec. 20	Cash. Skewbald				120,000		40,631
	Cash. Interest					220	40,851
	Skewbald. Transfer				40,851		—

Palomino							
Date	Details	OFFICE ACCOUNT			CLIENT ACCOUNT		
		DR	CR	Balance	DR	CR	Balance
Dec. 8	Cash. Bookmaker	1,800		1,800			
	Cash. You		1,000	800			
Dec. 13	Cash. Cheque dishonoured	1,000		1,800			
Dec. 17	Executors of Chestnut. Transfer					2,000	2,000
	Costs	80		1,880			
	VAT	8		1,888			
	Cash. Transfer		1,888	—	1,888		112
	Cash. You					112	—

Skewbald							
Date	Details	OFFICE ACCOUNT			CLIENT ACCOUNT		
		DR	CR	Balance	DR	CR	Balance
Oct. 1	Balances			340			—
Dec. 20	Executors of Chestnut. Transfer					40,851	40,851*

* On deposit: £10,000.

INDEX

Abatements, 89–90
Account, 13
   definition, 13
   layout, 22–24
   nominal, 25–26
   personal, 24–25
   real, 25
Agency, 120–123
Assets, 8–9
   classification, 8–9
   current, 8–9
   fixed, 8–9

Bad Debts, 35, 36, 90–91
Balancing an Account, 21–22
Balances,
   client account, 55–56
   office account, 56–58
Balance Sheet, 7–10
Bank,
   overdraft, 32
   transfers, 63–67
Bill, Delivery of, 59–60. *See also* Costs.
Bills of Costs, 100–101
Bills Delivered Book, 34–35
Book-keeping, 7–11

Capital Account, 8
Carbon System, 44
Cash, 14–15, 17–19, 45–47
Cash Book, 31–32, 41
Cheques, 92–95
   indorsed, 93–94
   returned, 94–95
   split, 92–93
   third person, 93
Client Account, 39–41
   balance, 55–56
Client's Ledger, 33, 41, 46–47
Client's Money, 51, 53–54
   interest, 103–112
Computer Accounts, 44
Conveyancing, 129
   deposits, 129–130
   mortgages, 130–133
   simultaneous sale and purchase, 134
   stakeholder, 129–130
   statements, 135–137
   vendor, agent for, 129

Costs, 23, 26, 34–35, 58–59, 99–102
   bills of costs, 100–101
   conveyancing, 133–134
   disbursements, 101–102
   fees, 100
   losing party paying, 117
   relevant law, 99
   Solicitors' Accounts Rules, 99
Credit, 13–14
Creditor, 25
Current Assets, 8–9
Current Liabilities, 9–10

Debit, 13–14
Deposit Interest, 103–112
   general deposit, 111–112
   interest received, 112
   interest due where money not specifically
      designated, 107–110
   specially designated deposit accounts,
      103–107
Deposits, 129–130
Dishonour of Cheques, 32, 94–95
Double-Entry, 13–14

Errors,
   correction of, 35, 36
   trial balance, not revealed by, 27–28
Examination Preparation, 1–6
Expenses, 26, 34–35

Fees, 100
Fixed Assets,
   credit, purchase on, 35, 37
   definition, 8
Folio, 13
   column, 22–23

Income Accounts, 26
Indorsed Cheques, 93–94
Insurance Commission, 124–127
Interest, 103–112
   deposit interest,
     paid, 107–110
     received, 112

Journal, 35–36

Ledger, 13–14
  clients', 33
  nominal, 34
  private, 34
  transfers, 65–67
Liabilities, 9–11
  current, 9–11

Manual Card Systems, 43–44
Miscellaneous Sundry Transfers, 115–128
Mortgages, 130–134

Nominal,
  accounts, 26
  ledger, 34, 39, 41, 47–49

Office Account, 39–41, 47–48, 56–59
Office Money, 39–41
Overdraft, 32

Payments, 45–46
  cheque, 45, 52–54
  petty cash, 33, 46, 54–55
Personal Accounts, 24–25
Petty Cash, 33, 41, 46–47, 54–55
Private Ledger, 34, 48–49
Professional Disbursements, 101–102
Profit and Loss Account, 7–8
Purchases, 17–18

Real Accounts, 25
Receipts, 14–15, 45, 51–52
Returned Cheques, 94–96

Sales, 17–18
Solicitors' Accounts Rules, 99
Stakeholder, 129–130
Split Cheques, 92–93
Statements, 135–138
Stock, 15–17
Sundry Disbursements, 115–127

Trading Stock, 15–17
Transaction, 13
Transfer, 35, 61–67
  book, 37
  client to office account, 61–63
  ledger, 65–67
  office to client account, 63–65
Trial Balance, 21, 27–28
Trusts, 147–148

Value Added Tax, 69–88
  agency method, 78–81
  double entries, basic, 75–77
  input tax, 71–72
  invoices, 73
  law, 69–75
  non-taxable payments, 79–80, 84
  offices, 71
  output entries, 84–85
  partial exemption, 72–73
  principal method, 78–84, 86–88
  records, 74–75
  tax point, 86–87
  taxable payments, 82–83
  taxable person, 69
  taxable supply, 70–71